F

The BUSINESS of LIVING

Stephen M. Pollan and Mark Levine

A Fireside Book
Published by Simon & Schuster
New York   London   Toronto   Sydney   Tokyo   Singapore

SIMON & SCHUSTER/FIRESIDE
Simon & Schuster Building
Rockefeller Center
1230 Avenue of the Americas
New York, New York 10020

SIMON & SCHUSTER, FIRESIDE, and colophon
are registered trademarks of Simon & Schuster Inc.

DESIGNED BY BARBARA MARKS
Manufactured in the United States of America

10 9 8 7 6 5 4 3 2 1
10 9 8 7 6 5 4 3 2 1 PBK

Library of Congress Cataloging in Publication Data
Pollan, Stephen M.
    The business of living / Stephen M. Pollan and
    Mark Levine.
            p.   cm.
    "A Fireside book."
    Includes bibliographical references.
    1. Finance, Personal.   2. Consumer education.
    I. Levine, Mark. 1958– . II. Title.
    HG179.P55543   1991
    332.024—dc20   91-22578
                                                  CIP

ISBN 0-671-74922-6
        0-671-68273-3 PBK

Acknowledgments

The authors would like to thank Corky Pollan and Deirdre Levine for their unflinching support and encouragement. A special note of thanks is due the late Tim McGinnis for inspiring this project. Also thanks to John Duffy for his invaluable assistance. We would especially like to thank our parents for everything they taught us.

Contents

CONTENTS

Introduction

Our parents probably were, and continue to be, loving, nurturing, and supportive people. Like most parents everywhere, they want only the best for their children. Almost universally, parents instinctively do everything in their power to protect their young, to shield them from danger, and to prepare them to stand on their own two feet as fully functioning adults. Or so they think.

While their motives are generally pure, parents, and our society in general, don't really do an adequate job of preparing us for the real world. From an early age we are insulated from the nitty-gritty details of daily life. The only discussions of money that most children hear are whispered asides from one parent to another, which may occasionally erupt into louder arguments usually held behind closed doors. The same holds true for discussions of sex, relationships, or death. Though they believe they are protecting us from harsh realities and allowing us to develop without the burden of such worries, our parents are actually stunting our growth. We grow up unprepared for the day-to-day details of life.

Rather than educating us about the mundane, our parents and our educational system teach us on the grand scale. We are taught the workings of the human digestive system, but never taught how much to tip a waiter. We are taught the economic forces that caused the Great Depression, but never taught how to establish our own credit. We are taught how to interpret great works of literature, but never taught how to read an apartment lease.

Understanding these larger issues is obviously valuable. It is the pursuit and grasping of these loftier topics that to a certain extent separate us from the animals. We human beings, particularly we Americans, free from having to struggle for the necessities of life, are able to concentrate on higher callings. Unfortunately, we are building castles in the air, castles that often come crashing down when we cannot master the rudimentary basics of getting through life.

A mother bird teaches her hatchlings carefully. She teaches her young how to find food, how to protect themselves, and how to spot and avoid trouble. Finally, she helps them learn to fly. Then, and only then, with the basics for survival in place, do the young birds leave the nest.

Contrast this with the way our parents taught us. Our education centered on the theoretical, rather than the practical. It is as though our parents provided us with a thorough grounding in aeronautical theory and expected us to teach ourselves how to fly. Is it any wonder that so many of us leave the nest and then come crashing back to earth?

Our parents rationalize their failure to teach us the basic techniques for making it in the world by saying that the only way to learn is through "the school of hard knocks." Since no one ever taught our parents these basic techniques, and since they picked them up only through trial and error, they assume that's the only way survival skills can be learned, or is at least the best way they can be learned. Our parents think that the myriad problems and obstacles we face in the operation of our lives are distinct and unique; that there is no unifying theory or group of rules that covers all situations. They are wrong.

There is a surprising commonality to almost all the problems and obstacles we face in the pursuit of our lives, and therefore, a discipline—almost a science—that can be applied to solve and overcome them. I call this discipline "the business of living." Reduced to its essential element, this approach is based on my belief that we should operate our personal financial life as if it were a business. That may sound cold and calculating, but the business of living isn't just the application of logic to our daily lives. It is also the acceptance and application of five simple rules and truisms:

- *Take charge and be decisive*—It is always better to take an action, any action, than to remain stagnant. Procrastination is the "eighth deadly sin." Don't wait for things to happen, make them happen yourself.
- *Traditional values work*—Ideas and beliefs that have persisted for years and years have generally done so because they have continued to work for years and years. The Ten Commandments have lasted for more than 3,500 years because they have remained valid.
- *Look forward to the future*—Things get better each and every day. As we get older, we get wiser and smarter and become better at

whatever it is we do. Sometimes success is just a matter of putting in enough time.

- *Start early and stop late*—The more time you spend doing something, the more you prepare for something, the harder you work at something, the more you will be successful. Genius is often just the result of persistence.
- *Get out of your own way*—We do things to ourselves that we would never let others do to us. The world does not revolve around you. You are not responsible for everything that happens. Your insecurities and uncertainties will vanish once you stop judging yourself against standards that don't exist except in your head.

I didn't learn the business of living when I was young, nor did it come to me fully developed in a burst of inspiration. For more than thirty-five years I have been counseling and advising people about their money and their lives. In that time I have had to help people from all walks of life—from movie stars to masons—with the topics, problems, and situations covered in this book. The "business of living" philosophy, and the attitudes and techniques offered in this book, are the sum of these thirty-five years of experience. None of it is conjecture or groundless theory. Each and every chapter offers advice and step-by-step guidelines that have worked, and continue to work, for my clients and myself. Don't be intimidated by the size or scope of this book—it wasn't meant to be read in one sitting. Use it as a reference, a refresher course, or a source of inspiration.

The only thing I cannot do for you is get you started. I can't take the place of your parents and spoon-feed you the things they never taught you. You'll have to take the first step by turning these pages and seeking out the advice that lies within.

STEPHEN M. POLLAN

ACCOUNTANTS

Finding and Selecting Your Tax Advisor

Far too many Americans turn to the wrong sources for advice on preparing their taxes, opting to listen to their uncle Max, a storefront tax preparer, or Internal Revenue Service (IRS) employees, instead of a certified public accountant (CPA). And many of those people who do use CPAs make the mistake of seeing them only once a year. Your personal CPA can be the source of invaluable advice in planning and maintaining a year-round financial strategy that maximizes your income while minimizing your taxes, and should therefore be someone you speak with on a regular basis.

The advantage of using CPAs is that they are professionally accountable for their actions while other accountants are not. CPAs are licensed by the states and must pass a rigorous three-day exam given by the American Institute of Certified Public Accountants. CPAs are required to maintain professional standards and ethics or else they risk losing their licenses and right to practice.

Accountability is no small matter when it comes to tax preparation. In 1987 *Money* asked fifty different tax experts—including CPAs, franchised tax preparers, and licensed enrolled agents—to prepare a return for the same hypothetical consumer. No two came up with the same results. *Money* repeated the test in 1988, and again no two answers were the same. In fact, in the 1988 test, only ten of the experts came within $500 of what *Money* and the IRS determined was the right answer. All the more reason to have someone on your team whose reputation and license are on the line along with your finances.

In addition, a CPA—whether he or she works for him or herself or for a large accounting firm—is a year-round financial professional. Many tax preparers rent a storefront or office for three months—from January 15 through April 15—and then vanish, going back to their full-time professions as travel agents, teachers, or carpenters. A CPA will be there if you have questions about what to do during the year to minimize your taxes, or if the

IRS has any questions about your return. While they may charge more than a tax preparer, their accountability and year-round availability more than make up for the difference . . . especially since, as a savvy taxpayer, you will be seeing your accountant at least twice during the year.

In addition to meeting with your accountant at the end of the year in order to prepare your tax returns, you should also schedule a meeting during the beginning of the year. Sit down with him or her, estimate what your income and expenses will be during the coming year, and plan your tax-avoidance strategies. That doesn't mean that your accountant should be your chief financial advisor. An accountant is an expert tax consultant, not a financial planner, and should not be used for investment advice.

The best way to find a CPA is through recommendations from financially savvy individuals. Ask your attorney and banker for their recommendations. Speak to friends whose incomes parallel your own about their accountants. Be on the lookout for young, small firms. While large, established firms can offer you a host of specialists and clout, they charge substantially higher fees and provide much less personalized service. A young, small accounting firm will be eager to take on new clients and more often than not will go out of its way to be responsive to your needs.

Once you have a list of candidates, schedule an appointment with each. Bring your tax returns and financial statements from at least the previous year along with you and be prepared to have a frank discussion of your finances. In addition to making the standard inquiries of any potential professional (which are covered in the chapter "Interviewing Professionals"), make sure to ask about their experience in dealing with clients similar to you. Ask if they are members of the American Institute of Certified Public Accountants (AICPA). Find out if they will be handling your taxes personally, or if a staffer will be assigned to the task, and inquire about their postgraduate and continuing education. Surprisingly, accountants learn little about taxes in their undergraduate years, making further education a must. And with the tax laws changing so frequently, a good CPA will be taking classes and seminars on a regular basis.

Make sure that they will be available all year long for questions and advice. Ask how the CPA would characterize his or her philosophy toward taxes—aggressive or conservative?—and decide whether that complements your own philosophy. Try to make a judgment on whether or not the CPA enjoys challenges or prefers to massage every return until it fits into a standard pattern. Beware of accountants who claim to have pull with bankers—they are trying to con you into hiring them with false promises of easy borrowing.

Don't hesitate to discuss fees with each candidate—they are entirely negotiable. While fees vary by region, experience, and the size of the accountant's firm, they average between $75 and $150 per hour. As with any other professional you hire, the terms of your agreement should be spelled out in an engagement letter. (See the chapter "Interviewing Professionals" for information on preparing engagement letters.)

While your chances of ever being audited are only one in fifty, tax laws and regulations change yearly, becoming more and more complex. That's why it is more important than ever before to have a savvy, knowledgeable, accountable professional to help with your tax return and your year-round finances. You owe it to yourself to get the best tax advice possible.

BE WARY OF TAX PREPARERS' ADVERTISEMENTS

Many tax preparers must use advertising to pull in customers since they are in business only a short period of time each year, often in out-of-the-way locations. While there is nothing wrong with advertising per se, some tax preparers make false or misleading claims. For example:
- Quoted fees of "thirty dollars and up" are simply come-ons—explain what type of help you need and ask for a written estimate of complete costs.
- Sometimes the fine print of an ad will explain that you are paying only for advice, not the actual preparation of the return.
- Claims of a low flat fee per return usually refer to only the simplest of forms and returns.
- Electronic filing may speed up refunds, but the added preparation charges are often exorbitant. If you need the money right away, take a cash advance on your credit card instead; it will end up costing you less.

WARNING SIGNS OF CROOKED TAX PREPARERS

Most tax preparers are honest businesspeople looking to make some money out of the consumers' feeling inadequate in the face of tax returns. However there are some con artists out there. Here are some of their tricks, which no legitimate accountant or tax preparer would ever use:

- Having you sign a blank form or a return filled out in pencil;
- Getting you to agree to have the refund sent directly to the preparer;
- Telling you they know how to "get away with" paying little or no tax;
- Promising or guaranteeing you a refund without even having seen your financial information; and
- Taking as their fee a percentage of what they "saved you" through their preparing your return.

NATIONAL AND REGIONAL TAX PREPARING COMPANIES

I'm against using a national or regional tax preparing company to help fill out and file your returns for three reasons. First, very often the individual who prepared your return will not be able to accompany or represent you in case of an audit. Second, rather than developing a relationship with a person, you are developing one with a company. There is no way that a company—no matter how efficient or caring—can provide the same year-to-year personal service as an individual. Third, while the individuals who work for most of the better firms are trained tax preparers, they are not accountants. They cannot help you plan for next year's taxes and that's just as important as preparing a return.

AFFORDABILITY

Calculating How Much You Can Spend on a Home

The purchase of a home is the single most important long-term financial move you can make. Not only will it be your most valuable investment, but it can also serve as the primary source of funds for a child's college education and your own retirement. While the earlier in life you buy a home, the better off you are, many people wait due to fear and ignorance: fear of not being able to afford the monthly payments and ignorance of how to raise a down payment or get a mortgage. Fears can be eased through understanding, and ignorance can be overcome through education.

Few people really understand how to gauge home affordability . . . but this hasn't kept them from voicing opinions.

Real estate brokers, concerned only with closing deals quickly, simply double yearly income and say that's all you can afford. There's absolutely no logic to this approach.

Bankers, concerned only with getting their loan paid back, apply a mathematical formula based on national averages for successful loans. They take your weekly pay stub and multiply it by 4.33 to come up with your monthly income. They then add in any other provable income. Next they reach into their bag of tricks and pull out a percentage—generally between twenty-eight and thirty—multiply it by your total monthly income, and decree that you can spend this much each month on housing. Finally, they add in your down payment—which they look on as proof of your moral fiber—and make a judgment on how much you can afford.

Parents, concerned that you don't get wiped out financially and may have to return to the nest, throw cold water on your dreams. They look at what they paid for their homes and can't fathom why anyone should pay more—if they spent one week's salary per month on shelter, so should you. Often they refuse to acknowledge that both spouses have an income, thinking that when (not if) you have children, only the husband will be bringing in money. They don't realize that in today's world the lion's share of your monthly income should go toward shelter, and that most couples will remain two-income families whether or not they have children. (Interestingly, all these outdated beliefs vanish when they want to sell their home.)

Rather than relying on others to gauge how much you can afford, it is up to you to do the analysis. All you'll need is a sheet of paper, a sharp pencil, a calculator, and a mortgage chart, which is available at any bookstore. The secret is to look upon affordability as a function of monthly payments, not the gross purchase price.

Write down how much you are now spending each month on shelter. (If your current rent is pathetically cheap, start with a reasonable estimate of what you could be paying.) In another column total up all the things you are willing to give up in favor of owning your own home. Can you buy only one new outfit per year? Could you give up membership in your health club? Can you go without a vacation for two years? Is it possible to carpool or walk to work? Will family and friends be annoyed if you stop giving expensive gifts or entertaining them lavishly? It is acceptable, even appropriate, to include payments to retirement and pension plans in your list of give-ups. Your home will become the main source of retirement funds, and any tax savings will continue since mortgage interest payments are deductible. Once you go over carefully how much you are actually spending each month, you'll be surprised at the possible savings. I've found that most people have no idea where 15 to 25 percent of their cash goes.

Add the total of your monthly "give-ups" to what you are now paying monthly for shelter. Remember to consider your next probable raise in salary and allow for that as well. The next step is to translate this monthly "available for rent" figure into a mortgage payment.

Mortgage payments are, and in all likelihood will remain, tax deductible, while rent payments are not. If you are paying $1,000 a month on a mortgage rather than rent, you will receive back a portion of it. What portion, of course, depends on your tax bracket. Go back to your most recent federal tax return and figure out your marginal tax bracket. Let's assume that you fell in the 28 percent bracket. This means that if your $1,000 rent was a mortgage payment, you would not have to pay taxes on it, so you would pay $280 less in taxes. Of course, when making this calculation you have to consider your state and local taxes as well. For example, if you live in New York City, your total tax bracket could be 42 percent.

Remember, you don't have to wait for the end of the year to realize this savings. By increasing the number of dependents you claim, after consultation with your accountant, you can drastically reduce your withholding. For your information, there is no limit on the number of dependents you can claim, and the IRS won't even look twice unless the number is over ten. Rather than taking that money and putting it in your pocket, you can apply it directly to your monthly shelter payments. Take the monthly "available for rent" total you determined earlier and multiply it by your marginal tax bracket. Add this amount to your total.

Using this new total as an indication of how much you can afford for your monthly mortgage payment, take a look at the mortgage chart. Look for a thirty-year fixed-rate mortgage. See exactly how much of a gross mortgage your monthly payment translates into. Next, add to this mortgage amount whatever down payment you can raise.

RAISING DOWN PAYMENTS

Once you realize that home affordability is actually a measure of your ability to meet a monthly mortgage payment, you'll soon see that the only stumbling block to buying a home is having the down payment. Down payments are actually just your way of proving to the bank that you are a solid citizen—all they are looking for is a sign that you have the wherewithal to come up with some cash. Generally, banks today want down payments of between 10 and 20 percent of the purchase price of a home.

The simple answer to the question "Where do I get the down payment money?" is anywhere you can. In our current economy it is difficult for young people to save enough money on their own to come up with a $10,000 to $20,000 down payment. The first thing to do is return to the nest. In the 1990s the nest stays open for a long time—if not forever. Your parents were able to buy their home in better economic conditions and have seen their real estate appreciate in value dramatically. There is no reason why they should not, if able, provide help—either as a loan or a gift—with their child's down payment. If your grandparents or other relatives have put money aside for you, ask for it now as opposed to when they die. Not only will they be helping you when you need it, but they will get the joy of seeing you enjoy their generosity and will be able to receive your thanks.

If going back to the nest doesn't provide you with enough money, take a close look at your financial holdings. Any IRAs or Keoghs that you have set up should be cashed in and used for down-payment money. Your first home, not your actual monetary savings, is your safety net for old age. In addition, money well invested in a home will grow quicker and more than money in retirement accounts. Take out cash advances on your credit cards. Sell personal property. Cash in old savings bonds. Anything short of stealing is justified in coming up with your down-payment money.

HOME AFFORDABILITY WORKSHEET

Amount you are currently spending on shelter each month	$_____
Plus additional money you could divert to shelter	+_____
Equals your maximum monthly rent	$_____
Multiplied by your marginal tax bracket (i.e.: 28%)	x 28%
Equals total tax deductibility benefit	$_____
Plus maximum monthly rent	+_____
Equals maximum monthly mortgage payment	$_____
Size of mortgage that maximum monthly mortgage payment will allow you to borrow. (Based on consulting a mortgage chart)	$_____
Multiplied by 20 percent	× 20%
Equals size of down payment required	$_____
Plus size of mortgage	+_____
Equals total you can afford to spend on a home	$_____

FOR MORE INFORMATION . . .

You can learn more about home affordability from the following books:
- *The Field Guide to Home Buying in America* by Stephen M. Pollan and Mark Levine
- *The New Real Estate Game* by Hollis Norton
- *Tips and Traps on Buying a Home* by Robert Irwin

ALLOWANCES

Turning Lollipop Money Into an Educational Tool

A mericans generally have misguided attitudes toward money. Money has no intrinsic value of its own. It is simply a tool. And while it is indeed a powerful device, it is not a panacea. It cannot buy love, happiness, freedom, power, self-esteem, respect, or security. Most of these incorrect, or even neurotic, attitudes toward money are developed early in our lives through the well-meaning, but ill-conceived, messages our parents pass on to us. And while clearing up your own misconceptions about money is important, it is perhaps more important that you break the chain and make a conscious effort to help your children develop healthy attitudes toward money and finance.

The single most effective method for correctly teaching your children about money is to provide them with a regular allowance. The regular pocket money you give them to use or misuse can not only answer their need for some independence, but can also instill in them a financial discipline sorely lacking in most Americans. After thirty-five years as a financial consultant, it was only this year that I realized the value of the allowance as a learning tool, after analyzing where my clients' financial problems really began.

It's essential that an allowance be treated as a regular stipend rather than an occasional bonus or gift. If you simply give your child money when they ask for it or need it, you, rather than they, become the one judging and weighing the merits of each purchase. By giving them money for things you approve of, and withholding it when you don't approve of their choices, you are teaching your children that money equals control and freedom.

Similarly, don't tie the allowance to a list of chores or link it to good behavior or grades. That distorts family relationships and teaches children that money can be acquired through manipulation. And paying a child for good grades is really just a form of bribery.

Allowances should be given on the same day each week so the children can have a basis on which to make some rudimentary budgeting decisions. Don't be too hard on your children if they make mistakes with their money. Making mistakes is probably the best way to learn. But along with this freedom, make a hard-and-fast rule that you will not bail them out or advance them money. If they spend their money foolishly or forget to save for a special occasion or event, and you rescue them, you will just be reinforcing their bad judgment. On the other hand, you should feel free to arrange a special bonus for them as long as it is tied to doing a special chore or job around the house.

It's best to begin providing your children with pocket money when they reach the age of five or six. Even if you don't give them an allowance per se, let them pay for small items when they accompany you to the store so they begin to get a grasp of the money-exchange process. Don't be too hard on them if they fail to grasp the concept of saving for a rainy day. Up until the age of eight or nine they will have a hard time understanding that saving for an unforeseen need or want is important. Instead, try to teach saving habits by targeting their savings to the purchase of a particular toy that they want.

Obviously, the size of an allowance must vary according to your family's income, the socioeconomic level of your community, the age and maturity of the child, what purchases it is designed to cover, and how frequently it is given. It shouldn't be so small as to become a constant source of frustration, or so large as to keep the child from having to make any choices. It also shouldn't be completely allocated to the purchase of necessities so that they never have to choose between two things they want. Let the children get involved in deciding how big their allowance should be, but bear in mind youthful tendencies toward exaggeration.

Don't be afraid of discussing your own finances with your children. While it is probably better that your exact income remain a mystery to them until they are old enough to put things in perspective, there is nothing wrong with telling them what percentage of your income goes toward various items, such as food or clothing. Show them your credit card bills, pointing out purchases that they saw you make, and explain that you now have to write a check and actually pay for the items. This way they will learn that credit card buying is not painless. If and when they begin to save up some money, help them open a bank account and explain the added bonus of receiving interest on their savings. When they are old enough, encourage them to get a part-time job.

As they grow older and become accustomed to receiving a regular allowance, pay out the money less frequently and increase the amount to cover more than just their personal entertainment. Move from a weekly to a monthly allowance. Include money for their lunches, for example. By the time they reach their early teens, supplement their monthly allowance with a seasonal clothing allowance. This will help them develop long-range budgeting and decision-making skills. By the time they are ready for college they should be able to handle lump-sum amounts calculated to last for an entire semester.

But even as you practice all of these sound allowance principles, don't forget that the main way children learn about money is by watching their parents. If your children see you buy everything you want, or buy things based on their status rather than their practicality, they will learn to do the same.

ANNUAL REPORTS AND PROSPECTUSES
Cutting Through the Propaganda and Puffery

Annual reports and prospectuses are the only financial documents that you should read from back to front. The single most important part of an annual report or prospectus is the auditor's statement. But since it has no flowery language and does little to inspire sales, it is often relegated to the last page.

This boring and brief little statement consists of the opinion of an outside auditor—invariably a certified public accountant from a large accounting firm—on the validity of the company's financial statements. It indicates how much care went into checking the company's claims. An in-depth audit requires the accountant to check and verify independently every claim made by the company. If the financial statements list accounts payable of $50,000 and accounts receivable of $75,000, an accountant doing a thorough audit will write to debtors and customers to verify the numbers. The auditor will physically verify that all inventory claims are accurate, even if it involves going to the warehouse and counting crates. The more in-depth the audit, and the more prestigious the firm conducting it, the more you can rely on the company's financial claims.

Other important parts of an annual report are also hidden—in fine print. They are the footnotes explaining and expanding on the information that appears in the financial statement. These are the places that companies note their contingent liabilities—debts that may come due—and point out exceptions to their assumptions and statements. The footnotes in annual reports and prospectuses are time bombs—if something bad is looming on the horizon, accept it as a given that it will be hidden in a footnote.

It's not accidental that the most important information in an annual report or prospectus is hidden in fine print or buried in the back. Annual reports and prospectuses are selling documents. The mission of these documents is to put the best possible light on a company, making it appear to be the most innovative, successful, dynamic, and simultaneously stable player in its industry. Ignore all the glossy photos, impassioned prose, and optimistic projections included in these reports. They are indicative only of management's tendency toward self-promotion.

You should never make investment decisions based solely on annual reports or prospectuses. Study the useful information and ignore the rest. The real place to look for information on the financial health of a potential investment is a 10K or 10Q form. The Securities and Exchange Commission requires that these forms be filed with them periodically. They are objective, factual documents, not marketing propaganda.

TEN THINGS TO LOOK FOR WHEN READING A PROSPECTUS

- The company's or fund's policies and objectives
- The experience of key officers and their succession plan
- Any potential litigation
- Any possible conflicts of interest
- The size and stability of the company's or fund's customer/ supplier base
- The net income per share
- The company's or fund's cash position
- The track record of current management
- How proceeds are, or will be, used
- What fees are charged and when

HOW TO OBTAIN FINANCIAL STATEMENTS

The best source for current corporate financial statements is the Securities and Exchange Commission. For information on obtaining a corporation's annual 10–K statement, call (202) 523–5506. For help in getting quarterly 10–Q statements, registration statements, proxy material, and other reports, call (202) 523–5360. For information on copies of 6–K statements filed by foreign companies selling stock in this country, call (202) 272–3246.

FOR MORE INFORMATION . . .

You can learn more about reading financial statements from the following books:
- *How to Read a Financial Report* by John A. Tracy
- *Understanding Financial Information* by Michael M. Coltman

APARTMENT AND HOUSE RENTAL AGREEMENTS

Protecting Your Rights as a Tenant

Forty percent of American families rent the homes in which they live, paying a landlord from 25 to 40 percent of their monthly income. Not only are they losing the myriad advantages of home ownership, but they are often victims of the most one-sided, heinous document in America—the apartment or house rental agreement, commonly called the lease.

In no other business relationship is there such an imbalance of power. The roots of this situation stretch back to the days of feudalism when the landlord was truly a lord who owned the property, and the tenant was a supplicant serf who worked and lived on the land. To the serfs the feudal landlord was an almost divine being with the power of life and death over them. Unfortunately, things haven't changed all that much.

The lease is the heart of the relationship between tenant and landlord, stating the key terms of your occupancy. It is virtually your only form of legal protection, yet most leases allow landlords to keep all their rights and call for you to give up most of yours. Leases are almost always prepared by the landlord's attorney or an organization representing landlords.

Except for municipalities that have rent control or rent stabilization laws, leases can say or not say anything the landlord wishes. No matter what the landlord orally promises about renewals, options to buy, rent increases, repairs, and services, nothing is binding unless written into the lease. That's why it is vital to read leases completely, using a magnifying glass if necessary to decipher the fine print. Don't accept claims that "this is the standard form" or "we never make changes." Everything in a lease is negotiable. The growing trend in courts is to make landlords as responsible for their rental units as manufacturers are for their products—this can add strength to your negotiating stance. In fact, in urban areas, the judges of landlord/tenant courts traditionally go out of their way to be fair to tenants and come down hard on landlords in an effort to even out the inequity of the relationship.

Pay attention to any clauses that limit the alterations you can make to the apartment or stipulate that improvements become the landlord's property. Try to have this clause struck out or changed to allow you to make modifications with permission. Stipulate that any alterations or improvements that are not permanent remain your property.

Look for explicit information on your right to renew. Check if there are any fees or rent escalations stipulated. If renewal isn't mentioned, you might try to insert a paragraph that gives you the right of first refusal on subsequent leases.

Investigate what the lease says about repairs and maintenance. Who is required to make them? Who pays the bills? Does the landlord pay for the exterminator? Have a clause added that requires the landlord to make repairs in a timely manner. Insert language requiring the landlord to paint the apartment every two years or as needed.

See what rights to cancel and sublet the lease gives you. The lease is made a more valuable asset if you retain the right to assign or sublet. The more control you have over how, to whom, and when it can be turned over to another party, the more powerful you are. Remember that one of the most powerful and valuable rights to real estate is the right to possession, and to the extent that you can renew, extend, or transfer your right of possession, you increase the lease's value to you.

Make sure the lease allows you to conduct a home occupation from the premises. If expressly forbidden, negotiate a modification allowing you to operate a business that does not violate the character of the neighborhood or building. A landlord can reasonably object to your operating a wholesale business from his building, but should have no qualms about your free-lance writing.

Check for any restrictions on who or how many people can occupy the apartment. Leases can bar you from having children, pets, or live-in lovers. Modify the language of this provision to allow for overnight guests regardless of age or sex, and to differentiate between Great Danes and goldfish.

If no mention is made of the landlord's responsibility to provide insurance, add a clause of your own requiring that coverage be adequate.

Modify and weaken as many of the landlord's powers as you can. When the number of days is mentioned in the lease, change the phrase to "business" days. If the lease calls for actions against you to take place in seven days, change it to ten business days. Stretch a week's notification into a month's. Change thirty days to sixty days, and sixty to ninety.

Finally, there a series of traps that many landlords try to slip through in their leases: the right to show the apartment at any time; a waiver of your right to trial by jury; a waiver of your right to notice for insignificant defaults; an automatic confession of judgment; a clause canceling the lease if the building is sold; stipulations on the condition of the apartment must be left in; cash penalties for time spent in the premises after the expiration of the lease; the right to change the locks on default; a waiver of your right to counterclaim; and the right to pass along other charges, such as tax increases, to you.

Finding any of these, point them out to the landlord and state that their removal is a prerequisite to your signing the lease. If you can't get them removed or modified, find another apartment.

Make your rent payment codependent with the landlord's obligations. Most leases state that even though the landlord does something wrong, you have no right to retain your rent. Try to get an option to buy or a right of first refusal. This is often easy to obtain and may make your lease an even more valuable asset.

THE TENANT'S OMNIBUS RIDER

Here's an excellent omnibus rider that makes the standard apartment or house rental agreement a bit less one-sided. Before signing the lease, write the following on the final page: "Whenever the landlord's consent is required, such consent shall not be unreasonably withheld." While not a suit of armor, this language should protect you from any potential Simon Legrees.

LEARNING ABOUT YOUR RIGHTS AS A TENANT

Since landlord/tenant laws vary from state to state and even from city to city, there is no single national source for tenants' rights information. The best way to find out about your rights is to call the noncriminal division of the local legal aid society. They may even be able to put you in touch with a tenants' rights coalition or association in your area.

AUCTIONS

Realizing There Is More to Them Than Meets the Eye

Everyone loves a bargain. And in recessionary times this love is often replaced by need. That's why auctions have suddenly become all the rage. Not only are antiques, collectibles, rugs, and works of art being sold in auction houses, but now every imaginable seller has latched onto the auction as a way of maximizing their profits. Real estate developers who have a glut of apartments or homes have taken to auctioning them off. Even agencies of the government now offer confiscated or unclaimed goods at auctions.

The reason we all associate auctions with bargains is that we see them as the purest form of capitalism. All the potential buyers gather in one place and compete for items openly. The item is right there, available for inspection. The person who is willing to pay the most for an object gets it. But auctions are really the icebergs of capitalism. What you see on the surface is just a small part of the story.

It is possible that you aren't aware of all the bidding that is actually taking place. While you may show up at an auction, register, receive a paddle or card with a number on it, and actually bid on items you want, there are other people bidding less openly.

If a buyer cannot be present at an auction, he or she may place an "order bid" with the auction house. They fill out a form that states the maximum amount they will pay for an item and leave the actual bidding up to a staffer of the auction house, who, in honest auction houses, will try to get the item for the absent bidder at the lowest price possible.

Bids may be submitted over the telephone to other staff people, who are relaying information to another absent bidder. Some of the people bidding may be agents—friends or more likely, paid consultants—who are representing someone who cannot or chooses not to be present. Bids can also be submitted through prearranged signals with the auctioneer, making it difficult to tell exactly whom you are bidding against.

Even the seller of the item may bid on it by confidentially agreeing with the auction house that an item will not be sold for under a certain amount. That means that even if you are the only person bidding on an item, you may not be able to buy it unless you top the "reserved price." An auctioneer may announce that the item has been "bought in," meaning that you didn't meet the minimum price. Dishonest auction houses may even place shills in the audience. These individuals are instructed to create competition and push the prices up if there isn't enough actual competition. An unscrupulous auctioneer can even cite nonexisting "phantom bids" just to get the price higher.

Finally, it is possible a "ring" is at work at the auction. A ring is an informal group of dealers who usually work together to keep prices down. Before the auction begins, they select what items they want and agree that only one of them will bid, thus keeping the prices down. After the auction they will all get together privately and hold their own auction for the items.

And if reading about these devices isn't enough to get you to think twice about the economics of an auction, there are other nonbidding devices that sellers or auction houses can use to take advantage of unsuspecting bidders.

Auction houses often tack on added charges to either the seller or buyer to cover their overhead and bring in a profit. These may be called insurance, commission, shipping charges, or photography costs. While sometimes legitimate, don't be surprised if you have to pay up to another 15 percent on top of what you bid to actually purchase the item, or if you receive 15 percent less of what was bid on an item you put up for auction.

While it is important to study an auction catalog before the actual bidding takes place, remember to take everything you read with a grain of salt. So-called house experts are generally responsible for describing the item and estimating its value. They may be actual experts, but they are also employees of the auction house, which is trying to get the most money for each item, so it is in their best interest to make the item sound as good as possible. There may even be fine print in the catalog, stating that the item up for bid is damaged, nonworking, or is available for "export only." It is even possible that a "chameleon" might be included in the catalog. These otherwise ordinary objects take on the value of antiques since they are being sold along with actual antiques.

It is a good idea to beware of all auction house claims. To inflate the value of a set of impressionist paintings it has up for auction, a house may claim that it has already sold four of the ten to a well-known collector when actually it has only sold one. A house may claim that a piece is being sold on consignment when actually it is owned by the house. That's because people assume, sometimes wrongly, that items owned by the auction house are fakes that had to be brought back from duped buyers. It has become fairly common practice to mix items from a number of sellers together under one banner as an estate sale, since estate-owned items are presumed to be better buys.

All of this may lead you to swear off auctions entirely. You need not go that far, however. But since auction houses are in the business of representing both buyer and seller and only make money when items are actually sold, you must be a cautious consumer on the lookout for the hidden side of the auction:

- Be aware of the rules of the game. Attend a number of auctions as an observer before actually taking part.
- Always examine an item before bidding on it. These objects are often sold "as is," so there may be no opportunity to get your money back.
- Never assume something is a legitimate antique, a priceless work of art, or a valuable collectible unless you have first hired an independent expert to verify it for you. And don't go by your own opinion unless you are actually an expert.
- Remember that in many cases the bulk of the people attending the auction are dealers. If they aren't bidding on something, there is probably something wrong with it.
- On the other hand, don't let the fact that other people are bidding on an item convince you that it is more valuable that you originally thought.
- Always have a maximum price you are willing to pay for each item, and a total budget in mind, before the auction begins. And never go over either, no matter how exciting the competition gets.
- Remember that just because an auctioneer is wearing overalls, or because the auction is being held in the country or in an old mansion, it doesn't mean the auction offers any more opportunity for bargains.
- In order to get the truly best buys, search for true estate auctions where you can find objects that have not yet entered the antique or collectibles market.

FOR MORE INFORMATION . . .

You can learn more about auctions from the following book:
- *How to Profit from Public Auctions* by Bill Adler, Jr.

AUDITS

Surviving Them With Your Nerves and Assets Intact

There is nothing more chilling, more intimidating, more terrifying, than an audit notice. These form letters from the IRS reduce even the most self-possessed recipient to jelly. The aura of fear that surrounds the audit process is encouraged by the IRS, which views it as a deterrent. It's no coincidence that you hear more about audit cases, sentencings, and indictments in the early spring.

And don't think you're immune. While tax reform has done some good, it has also increased your chances of being audited. With the removal of many flashy tax shelters, the IRS doesn't have many easy targets, so its attention has shifted to the ordinary taxpayer. If you are self-employed, work at home, or do a great deal of traveling for business, the odds are high that you will be audited at least once.

That's because returns from these individuals contain high Discriminant Functions (DIF)—a score that is assigned to your return. The IRS computers are programmed to look at a variety of different numbers and ratios. For example: a high ratio of expenses to income; unusual items, such as air travel expenses for a plumber; and any evidence of an intent to mislead, such as missing numbers. The computer calculates each return's DIF, and those above a certain score are singled out for auditing.

These returns land on the desk of an examiner. In addition to verifying the computer's suspicions, the examiner looks for documentary information attached, such as a police report to back up a casualty claim. Unless the examiner can easily discern the answer to the computer's question, he sends out an audit notice.

But even if your DIF is low, it's possible you'll receive an audit notice. Every three years as part of its Taxpayer Compliance Measurement Program (TCMP), and in an effort to update its scoring system, the IRS randomly selects fifty thousand returns for a line-by-line audit. The last TCMP year was 1988.

While it is impossible to avoid TCMP audits, there are ways to make sure your DIF is low and therefore your chances of being hit with an audit are minimized. Remember, the IRS is auditing your return, not you.

Prepare a neat, typed return. If possible, have a CPA with tax experience prepare the return for you. Avoid fly-by-night tax preparers—you need someone who is accountable.

Whether you or someone else prepares your return, triple-check the math. Make sure that you and your preparer both sign and date the return.

There are some areas that the IRS pays particular attention to: home offices; foreign bank accounts; omissions or mistakes in reporting income; travel and entertainment deductions; charitable contributions; casualty losses; individuals who are self-employed but not incorporated; Individual Retirement Account deductions; passive income losses; depreciation; losses resulting from hobbies that were never intended to be serious money-making businesses; and vacation-home deductions.

IRS computers and examiners see if the amounts you have reported as deductions exceed the averages for your income level. For example, do you contribute more to charities than others with similar incomes? The average deductions taken in various tax brackets are available at your local library (in a book titled *The Master Tax Guide*), so you can easily check whether or not your numbers fall outside the safety zone. If one or more of your deductions is out of line, attach an explanation, such as a receipt for a donation or a police report for a casualty loss.

If all your efforts at lowering your DIF fail—or you have the bad luck to be selected for TCMP audit—and you receive an audit notice, don't panic. You are not powerless in the audit process.

Recently passed federal legislation created a taxpayer's bill of rights. The laws states that audits must be held at a convenient place and time; that you can have someone represent you; you can adjourn a meeting and call in expert assistance; you can appeal; and you can sue the IRS for reckless disregard of your rights.

The first thing to do is to check what type of audit the IRS wants to conduct. Aside from the line-by-line TCMP procedure, the IRS conducts three types of audits: correspondence audits in which the IRS wants you to send them documentation for a particular claim you have made; office audits in which the IRS wants you to come to them for a face-to-face meeting about one or more items on the return; and field audits in which the IRS wants to visit you and go over your return.

Next, bring the audit letter to your accountant and have him or her explain what the IRS is looking for. Show your accountant your documentation and ask about possible penalties. If you have made an honest effort to comply with tax laws and have kept decent records, you'll have a good defense.

There are pros and cons to having your accountant accompany you on an audit. Accountants know IRS procedures and the tax codes inside and out, but having them present could turn your meeting into a battle of egos. Rather than its being the IRS against a simple, poor taxpayer, it could become a gladiatorial battle of one-upmanship. You may not know as much as your accountant, but sitting there by yourself generates sympathy and demonstrates confidence in your return. If you feel comfortable with your return and your ability to answer questions about it, I advise that initially you attend the audit without professional representation. If at any point you feel as if you are getting in over your head, assert your right to an adjournment and bring professional assistance to the next meeting.

While at an audit, remain calm. Don't show your anger about the IRS or taxes in general. Even though this is an adversarial procedure, don't get hostile. No matter how dumb the auditor is, don't question his or her intelligence. It's generally to your advantage to settle the matter with the auditor directly. Since most supervisors will back up their employees, calling them in on a case may result in your "paying" for their time and trouble.

Never volunteer information. Say as little as possible and respond to questions with a simple yes or no. Auditors are trained to spot slips in conversation that may mean you owe additional taxes. Auditors actually have quite a bit of latitude. The IRS permits them to accept oral evidence and allows them to ask personal questions if they doubt the accuracy of your stated income. Don't give in too easily. An audit can be a two-way street: You may also be able to point out justified deductions not included in your return and get *more* money back.

Steer the audit to your strong points. Good documentation for one item leads the IRS to believe that you have good documentation for the balance of the return. Bear in mind that the auditor may be more concerned with the accuracy of a number than its validity as a deduction. Defend yourself first with facts and documentation proving the amount, and hold back with your defense of its validity.

Don't try to play mind games with the auditor. You're lucky if the audit is scheduled for a Friday rather than a Monday, or an afternoon rather than a morning (an examiner eager to get home for the day or weekend may be less picky), but don't try to out-maneuver the IRS—leave that to your CPA. Finally, remember that your strongest defense is simply to tell the truth.

FOR MORE INFORMATION . . .

You can learn more about surviving tax audits from the following books:
- *Barron's Keys to Surviving a Tax Audit* by D. Lawrence Crumbley and Jack P. Friedman
- *Sprouse's How to Survive a Tax Audit* by Mary L. Sprouse

BANKRUPTCY

The Tool of Last Resort

B ankruptcy used to be a dirty word, a last-ditch tool used only when every other means available had failed. But today, otherwise savvy Americans are treating bankruptcy as just another weapon in their financial arsenal. They couldn't be more wrong.

For the benefit of consumers, the federal government has reformed bankruptcy laws—placing limits on the number of years such an action can appear on your credit bureau report. And the much publicized cases of large corporations opting to enter Chapter 11 in the face of potentially large liabilities have even lent a perverse glamour to bankruptcy. But that doesn't mean you should look at bankruptcy as an effective tool, or that it's any easier to rehabilitate or recover from.

Lenders and your future creditors have long memories. I guarantee you that bankers and future creditors can learn about and react to any past bankruptcy. And there is no banker or lender progressive enough to overlook personal bankruptcy. It is still considered an admission of your inability to pay your bills, your failure to manage your life.

The only times a bankruptcy may be forgiven by sophisticated creditors is if it was business related or necessary for your mental health. If you can convince a lender that your business dragged your personal finances down, or that your sanity was at stake, then you may be able to rehabilitate yourself in his or her eyes— but only if they are among the most enlightened and aggressive of lenders.

The best option is still refinancing your debt over a longer period of time, with nominal interest one hopes. Almost every lender or creditor would rather you pay something, sometime, than nothing, forever. They will work with you. Compromises are not difficult to work out—particularly if you can move up the ladder in the creditor's organization and deal with someone having real authority.

Never go to a bankruptcy attorney for advice on whether or

not to declare bankruptcy. Since they only sell one thing, they tend to suggest it to everyone who walks in their door. Instead, speak with your financial advisor, accountant, and personal attorney. If *they* advise declaring bankruptcy, you can then seek out a specialist. The only times I advocate bankruptcy are when your sanity or ability to get on with your life are at risk. A young lawyer I know of was in trouble with the IRS. Unlike other creditors, the IRS almost never makes compromises and never gives up—it is a government agency that places no value on its time. It refused to negotiate a repayment plan that he could afford, and it became impossible for him to start his financial life over again. Because certain tax obligations are discharged through bankruptcy, I recommended that he choose that option in an effort to save his sanity and be able to start fresh.

But that is one of the few instances when I have ever advised a client of mine to declare bankruptcy. Not being able to pay your bills is still an American stigma. No matter how many attempts are made to conceal that scar through protective legislation and good press notices, lenders and creditors continue to treat bankruptcy like the mark of Cain.

BANKS

Choosing One That's Responsive to Your Needs

Before the 1970s boom in banking, when it was time for a young person to choose a bank, they generally walked to the nearest neighborhood branch—often a monumental marble structure—passed through its ornate lobby, stepped up to a distinguished-looking gentleman in a three-piece suit, extended their hand, and *asked* to open an account or *begged* for a mortgage loan.

Today, with three or four different financial institutions in even the smallest of towns, and literally hundreds in our major cities, and with the airwaves filled with pitches from "hungry," "understanding," and "friendly" bankers, it's a great deal more difficult choosing a bank, even if just for rudimentary banking needs, such as checking and passbook-savings accounts.

The best way to cut through all the noise and confusion is to start paying attention to all those advertisements. Don't worry about keeping track of which bank offers the highest or lowest rates—in the final analysis, after taking into account all the variables and fine print, rates are nearly identical. Instead, try to determine to whom the bank is aiming its advertising. Is it targeting small businesses, or is it going after young couples, or perhaps senior citizens? Look for a bank that wants *your* business: not only will they be more responsive to your needs and wants, but they are apt to offer services and conveniences that fit in well with your lifestyle. For example, a bank targeting younger people will tout its mortgage loans and credit cards and will have plenty of twenty-four-hour automated teller machine locations.

Don't be skittish about foreign, specialty, or ethnic banks. In their efforts to carve out a niche in the crowded American banking market, these institutions are using the average citizen as a "foot in the door." Often these smaller banks will be more accommodating than the well-known monolith on the opposite corner. And these institutions won't reject your business if you aren't from the same country, ethnic group, or special-interest group mentioned in the name above the door. As long as the bank is

FDIC-insured and hands out green money with the right faces in the center, don't worry about its solvency. Just make sure you keep no more than $100,000 in any one bank—that's the limit to FDIC insurance.

Also, don't let the physical appearance or size of a bank influence your decisions. Marble, ornate lobbies and antique desks do not make a bank any more solvent, dependable, or generous— in fact, a small bank may be a great deal more helpful. As a banking customer it is always better to be a big fish in a little pond.

I opened my first law office in a small suburban community that was just beginning to be developed. Walking to my office for the first time, I passed by the local bank. Even though it was only seven forty-five A.M. there were lights on inside. Through the blinds I saw the president of the local bank sitting at his desk, personally reading the day's mail. Later that day he stopped by my office to welcome me to the community and offer his services. I took him up on his offer and never regretted placing my accounts in his hands. Whenever I had a problem or a question, I knew that there was someone in my bank who knew me as an individual, not just as an account number and a balance.

That is the final key in selecting a bank: realizing that you are actually selecting a banker. You are looking for an individual who will deal with your problems him or herself, not delegate them to tellers. After you have narrowed down the field of candidate banks, set up an interview with an officer of the bank. Tell them that you are interested in establishing a banking relationship with them and would like to sit down and discuss what they have to offer. You want a banker who is caring and concerned, as well as educated and erudite.

If they are taken aback by the idea of being interviewed, find another banker in another bank who is willing to deal with you as a discriminating individual. Don't worry—there are banks and bankers like that out there. In fact, there is a trend in the banking industry toward what is called "core" banking or having a "personal" banker—having one individual at the bank deal with all your financial needs, from checking to mortgage or business loans.

Don't limit yourself to the local branches. If you cannot find a bank/banker combination you like locally, go out of town. In fact, if your banker moves from one bank to another, you might want to consider moving along with him or her. A cooperative, savvy

banker can be an invaluable aid in your financial life, helping to
cut through red tape and steer you in the right direction. While
most banking decisions these days are made by committee, it's
wonderful to have an advocate—your personal banker—sitting
on that committee. In selecting a bank and a banker you are
starting an important, lifelong relationship—just make sure the
bank sees it that way as well.

Buying vs. Leasing a Car

Financing Your New Automobile

Ever wonder why you see so many BMWs and Mercedeses on the road these days? No, those drivers aren't making that much more money than you, they simply have chosen to lease, rather than buy, their cars, choosing ego rather than equity.

In the major metropolitan areas on the east and west coasts, about 22 percent of all new BMWs and 35 percent of all new Mercedeses are leased. Once the province of businesses, leasing has become a popular alternative to private ownership of automobiles. The number of cars leased for personal use each year has grown from 500,000 to 900,000.

The mechanics of leasing are fairly straightforward. A bank estimates what an individual car will be worth at the end of the lease term. This is called the residual value. The bank then subtracts the residual value from the sticker price of the car. Overhead, capital costs, and a profit are added to the result. This total is then divided by the number of months in the lease—the result is the monthly payment.

There are four basic types of auto leases. In an open-end or finance lease a price is established for the residual value of the car. When the lease concludes, you must pay the agreed-upon sum regardless of the actual market value of the car. If you sell it for more, *you* keep the profit. If you sell if for less, *you* must make up the difference. Closed-end leases are those in which the lessor takes back the car at the end of the lease period and assumes profit or loss from its subsequent sale. Full-maintenance leases require the lessor to provide complete service for the vehicle as insurance against the lessee's getting stuck with a lemon. The opposite is the nonmaintenance lease in which you assume all responsibilities for service and repairs.

What accounts for the boom in auto leasing? Many leases require no down payment, so those funds can be put to other, interest-earning, uses. Monthly lease payments are often lower than monthly auto-loan payments. Changes in the tax laws have made buying less attractive since interest on car loans is no longer deductible. Businesses, however, can deduct the full cost of leasing—subject to certain limitations—while tax reform has slowed their ability to depreciate cars they own. Finally, auto dealers have discovered that leasing allows them to, in effect, sell their cars twice: first to the lessee, and then to the long-time user.

Before you run out and lease a new car, it is important to consider the negatives:

Car leasing is a form of voodoo economics. The deals are so complex and different—involving deposits, service charges, and fees—that it is next to impossible to comparison shop.

Lessees may actually need a better credit rating than buyers, since lessors must cover their greater risk.

By leasing you are simply paying for the use of the vehicle. Even after months and months of payments you will have nothing to show for it. If you want to own the car, you still have to buy it.

The mileage requirements written into many leases can result in astronomical fees—sometimes as high as eight to ten cents per mile for every mile over the maximum.

If you are leasing from anyone other than an auto dealer, you may have serious trouble getting your car serviced—with or without warranties.

I know of no insurance policy that covers the lease payment as well as the value of the car. It's possible that the insurance company could pay the lessor for the car, and you could still end up owing monthly payments on it.

The lease contracts themselves are minefields filled with one-sided clauses.

Finally, if your auto is leased through a business, as a commercial vehicle it doesn't fall under consumer protection regulations. Even "lemon laws" won't protect you since most specifically exclude leased cars.

After weighing the pros and cons, I've found that leasing is a good choice in only three situations:
1. If you are an independent business owner—you'll be able to write off a large amount of the lease cost;
2. If you trade in cars every four years or less—new cars depreciate so fast that if you sell them within four years of purchase, you may not get enough to pay the balance of your loan; and
3. If you must have a car but cannot afford to buy one.

Everyone else should find a car they can afford, take out as short a loan as possible, and drive it until it dies. Leasing a fancy car that you could not afford—opting for ego rather than equity—is the height of stupidity.

If leasing is a viable option for you, pay careful attention to the terms, clauses, and provisions of the agreement. Regardless of what the lessor says, the contract and all its provisions are open to negotiation. Have your attorney examine the document before you sign it.

Most leases provide that payments must continue regardless of whether the car is damaged, stolen, or inoperable. One client of mine learned about this the hard way.

He leased a beautiful new Lincoln Town Car for himself. One day it was stolen from the parking lot outside his office. After calling the police, he contacted the leasing company, who stiffly informed him that he was responsible for making his monthly payments regardless of whether he actually had the car or not. The car was recovered three months later, but was in such bad shape that it had to spend another two months in the repair shop. My client had to continue to make lease payments on the car throughout this entire period.

So be forewarned: if your lease has such a provision, cross it out and insert a clause which states that if there is a problem with the vehicle, payments may be stopped.

Many leases also stipulate that the lessee is responsible for all repairs. If you choose to sign such a nonmaintenance lease, make sure it is with a dealership, not a separate company. That way you will be able to make them somewhat responsible for its condition by having them do necessary repairs. In addition, insert language that assigns all warranties to you and suspends your obligations if the warranties are breached.

Some leases allow the lessor to refinance, which may cause problems in obtaining title. Try to strike this provision out, or failing that, insert language which says that refinancing agreements must end at the same time as the original lease.

Check carefully for large balloon payments or exorbitant service fees hidden behind the low monthly charges. Study the mileage section of the lease and negotiate the limitations up or the costs down.

Look for any penalties for giving up the lease before its due date—sometimes they can cost you as much as holding on to the lease. Remove these penalty clauses or plan on keeping the car for the full length of the lease. Forget about subleasing. The majority of leases won't allow it, and in some states it is even illegal.

If you plan on purchasing the car from the lessor when the lease period ends, make sure the contract specifies the residual value. Don't accept vague language such as "fair market value."

BUYING VS. RENTING A HOME

Timing the Leap Into Home Ownership

The time to buy a home is now. The question shouldn't be "when should you buy," but "when shouldn't you buy," for in almost every situation the benefits of home ownership far outweigh the costs . . . and that goes for single men and women and unmarried couples, as well as for married couples. Regardless of market aberrations or short-term trends, over the long haul, the purchase of a home is still the single best long-term investment you can make and remains the foundation of personal wealth.

The primary reasons to buy a home are actually emotional in nature. It will offer security, satisfaction, and immense pleasure. You will be amazed at the personal gratification that comes from owning and living in your own wonderful space. After you've made the jump into ownership, you'll wonder what took you so long and how you could have lived any other way. Suddenly you can control your surroundings, dictating how they should look and feel, and all the while you are improving your investment. How could you have gotten by without all the storage space . . . or the spare bedroom . . . or the home office . . . or the eat-in kitchen . . . or the formal dining room . . . or the garage . . . or the deck . . . or the view.

Owning a home will accelerate the maturation process. It seasons you and prepares you for life, making you better at your career, more confident of your abilities, and a better manager of both time and money. It will not make you feel old or tie you down. Just the opposite is true. It will rejuvenate you and make you feel freer than you ever have before. While buying a home, like having a child, is not a panacea for troubled relationships, it can bring a relationship to a new level—the joint goals and struggles leading to a more solid union.

There are still more reasons to buy rather than rent. Home ownership isn't only a spiritual blessing—it's the ultimate retirement asset, the source of children's college tuition, the foundation for starting your own business, and the asset that can be borrowed against in emergencies. The stock market can go through booms and busts, interest rates can rise and fall, yet through it all your real estate—if purchased wisely—will continue to increase in value, historically growing, over the long term, at a higher rate than the cost of living. God no longer makes land, yet continues to make people, and as a consequence, real estate continues to rise in value.

All other investments that you make throughout your life are actually controlled by someone else. You can't control the companies in which you own stock. You can't dictate interest rates to the Federal Reserve Board. But you can control your investment in a home by constant maintenance and occasional improvement.

Home ownership is one of the few ways that average Americans can take advantage of the power of leverage. By spending $10,000 as a down payment on a $100,000 home, you not only get use and possession of it, but your $10,000 investment also grows as if it were $100,000. While this is happening, you are paying the lender back with dollars constantly shrinking in value due to inflation. By using leverage to buy a home, you can commence your career of asset acquisition, creating personal net worth and truly beginning your personal financial life.

Owning your own home is also the single best tax shelter available. A large portion of your mortgage payment is—and will continue to be—tax deductible, as opposed to rent, which is basically money thrown down the drain. While the initial costs of owning a home are greater than renting, over the long haul ownership is more affordable. And when it comes time to sell your home, taxes on the profit you make can be deferred, providing you reinvest the money in another home within two years. If you wait until you reach the age of fifty-five to sell your home, the first $125,000 in profit is completely tax free.

Home ownership isn't painless or worry free, however. A mortgage is indeed a large financial obligation that stretches over a long period of time. Increases in taxes and utility rates will now affect you directly and immediately, rather than being filtered into rent increases. Your personal mobility will be limited to some degree. You will be responsible for the upkeep and repair of your dwelling—there is no superintendent or landlord to call when the toilet backs up or the heat doesn't come on. You will probably have a longer commute to and from the workplace. Finally, it is possible to make a mistake and buy a home either that you can't afford or that does not grow in value.

All of these burdens are real and not inconsiderable, but they are actually fears, not disadvantages—fears that can be dispelled if closely examined. A mortgage is actually a tool, not a ball and chain. You are investing your money in something that grows in value and are establishing the foundation of your financial future. Once you witness firsthand the power of leverage you will learn to regret the expiration of your mortgage and may even refinance in order to take full advantage of your personal wealth—your home.

If you are fearful of being able to handle mortgage payments, consider this: the last thing a bank wants to do is foreclose on your home. They want you to pay back the loan and will help you if you have problems. Worries about disasters striking are absurd. You cannot go through life planning for every contingency. If you dwell on all the potentially negative things that could happen to you, you will never take any action. (For more information see the chapter "Affordability.")

While taxes and utility rate increases will be felt directly, they will bring with them a deeper sense and awareness of the environment and community you live in. Once you begin to pay taxes in a community, you'll suddenly find yourself interested in the quality of its parks, police, fire department, schools, garbage collection, and library.

Loss of mobility isn't necessarily a bad thing. If you are forced at some point to relocate, you can always sell your home. And if the idea of being tied to one region frightens you, ask yourself why that is. Do you believe that your lot in life will improve simply because you are free to change your mailing address frequently? If that's the case, you have problems that buying a home can't solve. You are responsible for your own happiness or unhappiness—not the city you live in, the job you have, or the home you reside in.

It is true that it's possible to make a mistake and buy a lemon. But by being a savvy shopper you'll be able to spot the warning signs and avoid mistakes. Another way to dispel all these fears is to realize that you are not buying a home to last thirty years. This will not be the only home you ever buy and live in. This is only house number one. Down the road, when your needs change, there will probably be a house number two, and perhaps even a house number three. At some point there may even be a summer or vacation home. You aren't buying a perfect-fitting glass slipper—so don't worry if you have to squeeze or grow into it.

WHEN TO STAY A RENTER

The only people who should continue to rent are those who *know* that they will be moving, getting married, or somehow dramatically changing their life within five years; and those who have not yet established their *short-term* career goals. Anything less than five years isn't enough time for the initial costs of purchase to be outweighed by increasing market value. In addition, the purchase of a home should not interfere with establishing your short-term career goals. In the early stages of your career you want to be able to move where the job opportunities are, rather than settle for the opportunities that exist near your home.

FOR MORE INFORMATION . . .

You can learn more about buying real estate from the following books:
- *The Field Guide to Home Buying in America* by Stephen M. Pollan and Mark Levine
- *The New Real Estate Game* by Hollis Norton
- *Tips and Traps on Buying a Home* by Robert Irwin

Car Buying
Making Your Second-Largest Purchase a Sound One

Buying a new car is one of the most important purchases we
ever make, second in size only to the purchase of a home.
Prices continue to climb to the point where we are spending
on a car what our parents spent on a home. But unlike real estate,
automobiles are not designed to last forever. That's why it is
essential that you approach the purchase of a car with all the
ammunition and expertise you can muster.

As with any major purchase, your first job is to get your
priorities straight. There is no such thing as an "in" car. An automobile is a means of transportation—no more and no less. It
is not a reflection of your wealth, status, or personal worth.
And it certainly is not an investment. You must put your ego
aside and carefully decide exactly what your needs are, forgetting your wants and dreams. The more effort you put into evaluating your needs, the less time you will have to put into
visiting auto dealers.

Ask yourself some insightful questions. When and how often
will you be using the car? Will you be driving it every day all year
long, or will you be using it primarily on weekends during the
summer, for example. How many people, on average, will be
riding in the car? Will you usually be driving alone or with one
other person, or will most of your trips involve the entire family?
What types of trips will you be using the car for? Will it serve to
take you on frequent short trips around town, or will you be
using it for long highway drives?

Next, give careful though to how much you can afford to
spend on a new car. Rather than thinking of this purchase as a
large, onetime expense, consider it a monthly outlay for transportation. It really makes the most sense to finance the purchase
of a new car, so as with any credit buy, the number that really
matters is your monthly payment. Once you have a rough idea of
what you can afford to spend monthly on the car itself, add in
estimates of what you will be spending on fuel, repairs, and insurance. These estimates should be based on your present costs,

but be adjusted to include higher prices and your projected use of the vehicle.

Once you have determined your basic needs, try to figure out which class of cars is right for you. If you will generally use the car for frequent, short solo trips around town, it makes sense to look for a fuel-efficient subcompact car, for example. On the other hand, if you will be using the car primarily for one long drive each week with the whole family, it may make sense to buy a midsized sedan or a compact wagon. I advise you steer clear of large, luxury vehicles. The cost of auto opulence in price, fuel, and routine repairs and maintenance far outweighs the added benefits of comfort. The only time I believe you should consider purchasing a luxury car is when you are using someone else's money.

With a class of car in mind, pick up a copy of the most recent *Consumer Reports* car-buying issue or the magazine's annual *Buying Guide*. Find the listing of cars in the class you have selected and carefully look over the test reports and data. Because cars cost so much money to buy, insure, operate, and repair, it is important that you place your highest priority on durability and fuel efficiency. After economy, place your next priority on safety. Only then consider comfort and convenience. It is justifiable to spend more for a car that has a better repair and safety record, but it is plain foolish to pay more for luxury, styling, or speed. Match your resources with the list of cars and select the one or two most reliable and efficient vehicles you can afford.

Take out the telephone directory and find the nearest dealers selling the cars you have selected. Make a trip to the showroom and, ignoring the price sticker, look over the car. Sit in the driver's, passenger, and rear seats. How much leg, head, and shoulder room do you have? Is there sufficient support for your lower back? Look over the dashboard and instrumentation. Check out the trunk space. If a salesperson tries to involve you in a discussion, simply tell them you are just looking and are not interested in talking price.

When you return from your scouting trip, find the section of *Consumer Reports* that describes the magazine's auto-pricing service. The secret to getting the best buy from an auto dealer is to base your price negotiations on his or her cost, not on the list or sticker price of the car. By ordering and purchasing *Consumer Reports* auto-price printouts for each model of car you are interested in, you can determine exactly what the car, and various options, cost the auto dealer.

When you receive your printouts, follow the directions carefully and select exactly which options you would like included in the car. Once again, remember you want durability and safety, not style and luxury, and keep in mind that options and extras are where the dealer makes his profit. Using the formulas provided on the printout, total up the dealer's price for the car and the options you want, then add in acceptable profits and fees ($200 to $500 above dealer cost is a fair price for both parties). With your numbers complete, type or print a description of the car you want, with the options you would like, and the price you are willing to pay for it.

Rather than traveling around from showroom to showroom, take out your telephone directory once again and compile a list of every auto dealer in your area that sells the car you are interested in. Proceeding alphabetically, call every dealer on your list and ask to speak to a salesperson. Explain that you are a serious buyer and that you have done considerable research. Read your description to the salesperson and state what you believe the dealer's cost to be. Make it clear to the salesperson that you will be comparison shopping and that you are willing to pay a fair markup. State that you are not looking to engage in an extensive price negotiation but are interested in getting their best price for the car.

Be prepared for some shrewd salesmanship on the part of the auto dealer. He or she may use any number of devices to try to complicate the transaction or sway you from your course:

- If they say, "Shop the other dealers first and then come back to us with your best price," respond by saying, "While I do intend to shop around, I want a firm price from you now, otherwise I will not be calling you back."
- If the sales person says, "This is my best price, but you have to buy it today," explain that "a legitimate offer that is good today should also be good tomorrow, and I do not intend to be pressured into making an immediate decision."
- If the dealer questions your numbers and says, "I don't know where you got those figures from, but they are all wrong," say that "I will be happy to look at your invoice for the car in question, but if it matches the numbers I have quoted, I will not be doing business with you, and in any event I will only discuss a price based on your cost, not on the sticker price."
- If the salesperson indignantly says, "We don't think the customer should dictate how much profit we make," explain that "I

am not dictating anything, I am simply asking for your best
price."
- Beware of salespeople who quickly respond with what you
  know to be a lowball price. Ask them to check the price with
  their sales manager, and to verify that there will be no other
  "extras" added to the bottom line of the sales contract.
- Ignore all attempts to discuss color or styling. Remember, you
  are buying transportation, not prestige. If a salesperson asks,
  "What color would you like," tell them, "I'd like whatever color
  is cheapest."

Don't complicate the deal with other issues. Discussions of
financing and loans should be separate from price negotiations.
Generally, regardless of claims to low rates and special deals, you
will be better off getting a loan from a bank than through an auto
dealer. Only bring up the issue of a trade-in after you have finalized your price negotiations. A liberal trade-in allowance does not
turn a bad deal into a good one. Once again, you will probably do
better selling your car privately than trading it in to a dealer.

If a salesperson says that they don't have the exact car you are
looking for on the lot, ask them to swap with another nearby
dealership. Ordering a car direct from a manufacturer complicates
the purchase even further, requiring you to make provisions for
timely delivery. It makes more sense to go to another dealer, or
ask them to quote you a price on a comparable car they do have
in stock.

Service contracts and extended warranties are big money-
makers for auto dealers. Sometimes they have one salesperson
who specializes in pushing these profitable products. Don't fall
for their pitches. Auto service contracts are almost never worth
what they cost.

Ask that any rebates in effect be taken as an up-front discount
off the price of the car. It is better to save the sales tax on the
purchase of the car and to get the saving right away than to wait
a month to receive a check from the manufacturer.

You must remain vigilant at every step in the transaction.
Often, car dealers will initially agree to a low selling price and
then when it comes time to close the deal and sign the contract,
will add in any number of superfluous charges for unnecessary
items such as undercoating, protective finishes, floor mats, fabric
finishes, mud flaps, pinstripes, and rust-proofing. Watch out for
special "advertising charges." National advertising costs are already figured into the cost of the car, and local or regional adver-

tising expenses should already have been factored into the dealer's markup.

If you find any of these charges added to your sales contract, express your anger and walk out of the showroom immediately. You must keep your objectivity until you actually own the car. Never allow yourself to become emotionally committed to a car. You must be prepared to walk away from the deal at every step in the negotiation. Don't worry: invariably the salesperson will call you back and strike out the extra charges.

FOR MORE INFORMATION . . .

You can learn more about buying cars from the following books:
- *Don't Get Taken Every Time* by Remar Sutton
- *The Car Buyer's Art* by Darrell Parish

CHARITABLE CONTRIBUTIONS

Donating Money Where It Does the Most Good

Giving money to those less fortunate than ourselves, or helping someone in need, is a wonderful thing to do. Most of us would be thrilled to be able to donate large sums of money to deserving charities if we could afford it. And I truly believe that what goes around comes around: if you are generous to others and are a caring person, others will be generous toward you and care about your well-being. Unfortunately, some people have learned that it is easy to take advantage of our generous natures.

In a study of $9 million raised for charities through telephone fund-raising, only twenty-six cents out of each dollar actually reached the intended groups. The remaining seventy-four cents was kept by the fund-raising groups. In addition, many charities have grown into swollen bureaucracies that spend the lion's share of the money they receive on administrative costs and salaries. While there is nothing wrong with applying a percentage of donations received toward costs and overhead, the majority of the money contributed should go directly to those in need.

As government has, rightly or wrongly, cut back on social spending, more and more emphasis has been placed on volunteerism and charitable contributions as a way of taking care of the less fortunate among us. But along with this increased emphasis has come a complementary increase in the number of fraudulent charities. In 1988 the Federal Trade Commission received 110 complaints and inquiries about charities, as compared to the 49 they received in the previous four years combined. The burden of separating the cons from the legitimate causes, therefore, is firmly on the shoulders of the contributor.

There are some telltale signs of fraudulent charities that you should be aware of:

- Watch out for charities whose names are only slightly familiar. Many scams involve charities that play off the names of respected organizations. For example, there are twenty different fund-raising groups that have the word *cancer* in their names, and not all of them are as reputable as the American Cancer Society.

- Be wary of mail order appeals tied to sweepstakes, or telemarketing campaigns. Many of these are run by fund-raising organizations that take the bulk of monies for themselves.
- Don't let yourself be swayed by guilt into contributing if you receive an unsolicited gift. Anything you receive without request through the mail is yours to keep with no strings attached, according to federal regulations.
- Avoid requests to have your donation immediately charged to a major credit card. This may well be a device to latch onto your account number and milk you of funds.

The best way to approach charitable contributions is to initiate them yourself and avoid all requests for donations no matter how valid. Giving to charity should be proactive, not reactive. It should be a conscious, deliberative process, rather than an impulsive or reflexive gesture generated by guilt. Spend some time researching charities or causes you are interested in. Contact a representative of the charity and request information on how much of every dollar received goes directly to those in need. Some organizations manage to pass along as much as 95 percent of their donations. Ask about what they do and whom they serve. Inquire about how large their staff is.

Once you find a charity that you are interested in, and that is truly dedicated to helping others, give and give generously. When you are contacted by other organizations simply say that you concentrate all your charitable efforts on this one organization. There is no need to feel guilty. It is impossible for you, or anyone, to give money to every good cause. As long as you are giving something—whether it is time or money—and know that it is actually helping people, you are doing your part in making the world a better place.

CHECKING UP ON CHARITIES

To find out what percentage of each dollar donated to national charities actually goes to those in need, contact the National Charities Information Bureau (212) 929-6300. It publishes the *Wise Giving Guide*, which contains this and other useful information, three times a year. Your initial copy of the booklet is free. In order to uncover similar information about local charities, ask a representative for an audited financial statement. If the numbers meet with your approval, follow up by speaking with someone at the nearest chapter of the Better Business Bureau. Only after you're sure the charity is both legitimate and efficient should you make a donation.

DONATING TIME OR GOODS

Donating your time to a charity, even if you are self-employed or a professional, is not tax deductible. Donating goods to a charity of the goods donated is $500 or more you will need to have it appraised.

Climbing the Ladder

Advancing in the Corporate Environment

The climb up the corporate or organizational ladder isn't automatic—there is no elevator from the lobby to the board-room. The passage of time has no magical qualities to speed you on your way to the top. Waiting for superiors to retire, or die, just means you will have to climb over their bodies. Periodic reviews and evaluations won't hasten your advance. In today's world, excellence and hard work are the rule, rather than the exception. If you simply wait for something to happen, it won't. The climb up the ladder has to be a conscious, overt process. To move ahead you will have to take control of your career and develop a plan of action that makes career advancement your priority.

Communicate your willingness to be a doer. Ask questions. Contribute ideas. Bypass the suggestion box on your superior's door and present your proposals in person. Remember, the ideas that will gain you the most glory are those that save money.

Make sure you are noticed. Become a social animal. Be caring, courteous, and friendly. Smile. Look vibrant, alive, and awake. Cultivate a reputation of honesty, truthfulness, and integrity. Congratulate your peers and superiors on their excellence. If you are at a desk in the rear of the office, circulate up front as well. Never speak about anyone unless you have something good to say.

Despite all the common analogies, the climb up the ladder is not a war. You do not want to be labeled a killer or make too many enemies. Your superiors will be unlikely to promote you if they suspect that you are capable of attacking them as you did others.

Don't take appearances for granted. Dress appropriately, but not ostentatiously. Show up early and stay late. Don't abuse privileges. Make sure you are noticed for only the right reasons. Your exterior has to match your interior.

Become a student of your company. To get ahead in an organization you will have to truly commit to it. Study annual reports and product literature. Scour the newspapers and trade journals for mentions of your company. Analyze the competition. Know your company and industry inside and out. Further your education, and let your superiors know about it. The greater your knowledge, the more your ideas and suggestions will come from a position of strength.

Stress that you're a company person—loyalty is always appreciated. But that doesn't mean you can't show ambition. Volunteer to take on added responsibilities. Look for vacuums you can fill. Personally, I have always been most impressed by employees of mine who looked to broaden their job descriptions on their own, who automatically stepped into breaches in the organization.

One excellent means of moving ahead is to offer to help peers in a different but complementary department. Their praise will help boost you in the eyes of your superiors, and it won't come at the expense of any of your coworkers. Enlarging your importance to the company in a nonthreatening manner is a surefire way to move up the rungs of the organizational ladder.

Greater financial reward is the long-term, not short-term goal. Opt for promotions in lieu of pay increases. The raise you receive after being promoted will more than compensate for the one you passed up.

The climb to the top is neither automatic nor easy. But if you take charge and get the message across that you are valuable, you'll reach the summit.

FOR MORE INFORMATION . . .

You can learn more about climbing the corporate or organizational ladder from the following books:

- *Blow Your Own Horn—How to Get Noticed and Get Ahead* by Jeffrey P. Davidson
- *Further up the Organization* by Robert Townsend
- *Swim With the Sharks Without Being Eaten Alive* by Harvey Mackay
- *What They Still Don't Teach You at the Harvard Business School* by Mark H. McCormack

COLLEGE EDUCATIONS

Realizing They Are Not for Everyone

The value of a college education has become diluted in America. While the idea that everyone should be able to get a higher education if they choose to is a noble one, the resulting proliferation of colleges and universities has led to a lowering of admission standards. As a result, having a college degree is no longer the sign of intellectual excellence it once was.

Today, a college degree is an admission ticket to the job market. As the educational value of a college degree has diminished, the social aspect of the experience has taken on more importance. Some people even look on college attendance as a necessary stage in the maturation process. I am continually amazed by the number of young people who pursue a course of study for four years, then totally abandon the field when it comes time to enter the job market. I'm also shocked by how many people view their four years at college as a "pit stop" on their journey through life—a forty-eight-month respite from the real world.

Even though its value may have shrunk, a college education is still a valuable experience. However, it may not be right for everyone. With the costs of higher education rocketing upward year after year, the time has come to give serious thought to whether or not you, or your children, truly need to attend college right after graduating from high school. A career can be launched prior to age twenty-one, and a college education can be pursued at any age.

I believe that someone should go to college only if they are going to get out of it value comparable to what they are spending. I don't think someone should pay $40,000 or more to mature or to meet a mate or to have a good time for four years. There is nothing wrong with presenting your child with the option of going to college, buying a home, or starting their own business. For many people, attending college full-time might just be a waste of time. They may be better suited to entering the job market, or launching their own business and, if they wish to, taking college classes during the evening. And I also believe that the money you have saved for a child's education would be equally well spent helping them establish a business or buy their first home.

If you or your child do choose to go to college, it is important to be pragmatic in the selection of a school. Pick one where attending and graduating will clearly make an addition to your life. College is not summer camp. It is primarily an educational experience—any social benefits that come with it are an added bonus. A college degree is a credential, but it is not irreplaceable. A diploma helps in getting a first job, but from there on career advancement is based on job skills and experience, not on a sheepskin.

PAYING FOR A CHILD'S COLLEGE EDUCATION

The time to begin saving for your child's college education is as soon as you learn you are going to have a child. Make a rough estimate as to what a college education will cost seventeen years from now. Obviously this is going to be a guess. One way to lend some credence to your guesswork is to find out how much a four-year course of study at a state university costs today. Then increase that figure 6 percent for each of the next seventeen years. Your goal here is to provide for *a* college education, not *the best* college education. If, when the time comes, your child wants to attend a private school, he or she can take out student loans to make up the difference between what you have saved and what it will cost.

My advice is to buy zero coupon bonds as the basis of your child's college fund. Let me explain. Normal bonds pay out interest as well as being worth their face value upon maturity. For example, a ten-year, $100 bond may generate 10 percent interest each year over the ten-year period. So in addition to being worth $100 upon maturity, the bond would pay out a further $10 for each year remaining until maturity. Since the potential yield from the bond is up to $200, it will be sold for more than its face value of $100. A zero coupon bond, on the other hand, is one that has been stripped of its interest coupons and therefore is sold at a discount. For example, the same ten-year, $100 bond, stripped of its interest coupons (these are either retained or sold separately), would still be worth $100 upon maturity, but would generate no interest income to the bondholder. That means it would be sold for much less than its face value. The buyer, however, knows that he will receive the face value at the maturity date. If you know you'll need $50,000 in fifteen years to pay for a child's college education, by purchasing $50,000 worth of fifteen-year zero coupon bonds for perhaps $5,000, you guarantee there will be enough money to pay the tuition bill.

FUTURE COSTS OF A FOUR-YEAR COLLEGE EDUCATION*

Year	Public	Private
1991	$21,000	$57,000
1995	$27,000	$72,000
2000	$36,000	$96,000
2005	$48,000	$128,000
2010	$64,000	$172,000

* Based on the current average annual tuition cost according to the College Board, and assuming a 6 percent annual increase. Numbers are rounded to the nearest thousand.

FOR MORE INFORMATION . . .

You can learn more about whether college is right for your child, selecting colleges, and financing college tuition from the following books:
- Choosing a College: A Guide for Parents and Students by Thomas Sowell
- Financing a College Education: The Essential Guide for the 1900's by Judith B. Margolin
- The Question Is College by H. Kohl

COMPLAINTS

Resolving Them to Your Satisfaction

Americans are so used to being victimized by purveyors of products and services that they generally don't complain when things go wrong. Assuming that mistakes are a part of everyday life and are too time-consuming to correct is foolish. If you have a complaint and it involves a significant amount of money, make your feelings known.

The first secret to effective complaining is to choose your language carefully. Simply using the word *complaint* creates an adversarial situation implying criticism of the other party. American businesses and their employees don't respond well to criticism. However, most companies and people will respond to problems. Taken out of the corporate mentality, they react like most Americans—eager to help another person with a problem. Treat your situation as a problem that needs to be solved and describe it as such.

Next, choose your battles carefully. Effective complaining is hard work and will take time. Even though you may be right, it's foolish and a waste of time to complain about small sums of money or matters of principle. Make sure your goal is money, not justice. That being the case, press the issue.

Never get angry and don't make threats—they will get you nowhere. Some large companies have managers whose sole job is to deal with "cranks." Your criticism of individuals, procedures, or policies only puts the other party on the defensive and will get you little. You want to come across as an eloquent and sophisticated complainer, not a nag. Anger can be an effective tool, but only if it is used in a calculated manner. True anger is ineffective.

If at all possible, make your complaint face-to-face rather than over the phone or through the mail. Begin your dialogue by complimenting the company or individual about previous positive experiences you have had dealing with them. Then tell them that you "have a problem" and "would like help in solving it." Try to enlist the other party as an ally. Ask them, "What would you do in my situation?" Don't be sidetracked by someone who continually responds, "We never do that." Pretend you didn't hear them and keep on presenting your case.

Small companies are easier to complain to than large ones, since their procedures are less bureaucratic. If the company is local, visit its headquarters and ask to see the owner or the owner's secretary. If the company is far away, telephone or write the chief executive directly. A brief phone call can elicit the person's name.

Complaining to large organizations requires more steps. Work through the hierarchy—don't try to go right to the top. For example, problems with teachers should be directed first to the teacher, then to the department chairperson, next to the dean of faculty, and finally to the school principal or college president.

Telephone to get the name of your primary contact. Get their name, title, and a description of their authority. After each conversation send a letter confirming the discussion. Invariably, large companies prefer at least some written communications. Make sure you type all your letters. Keep copies of this correspondence.

If you have difficulty resolving your problem, don't hesitate to "push the up button" and ask to speak to the person's immediate superior. As you wend your way up through the bureaucracy, avoid criticizing lower echelons. Go all the way to the chief executive officer if necessary.

There are options open if your first round of complaints doesn't lead to satisfaction. Product-related complaints can be directed to the manufacturer if you fail to get satisfaction from a retailer. Make sure to mention the name of the retailer and your previous failure to get results. For unresolved complaints about companies in regulated industries—banks, insurance companies, and utilities, for example—contact the revelant state or federal agency. If you have a problem with a federal, state, or local agency, go directly to your local representative, whether city councilman, state legislator, or congressional representative. You pay their salaries and keep them in office—you'll be surprised how quickly they'll apply some pressure.

The appeals process can be long. If you don't have the time, go directly to a small claims court.

Also, don't forget the media's enormous clout. Many newspapers, radio stations, and local television stations have reporters interested in consumer complaints. If your situation is newsworthy, they may become your advocate. They may also have problem-resolution specialists on staff who may be willing to help.

Your biggest strength is persistence and a sense of urgency. The bureaucrats in American businesses yield to persistence. Pursue your complaints diligently and you'll get satisfaction.

COMPLAINING TO A GOVERNMENTAL AGENCY

The secret to solving problems you may have with a governmental agency is to do some name-dropping. Before writing a complaint letter, call the office of your local congressional representative and ask their advice on where to send your letter. Then begin your letter with the following: "On the advice of Congressman John Doe, I am writing to you regarding a problem I have." Governmental agencies need congressional support for their continued existence, and any letter that is tied to a specific representative will get immediate attention.

COMPLAINING TO A CEO

If you have had difficulty resolving your problem with lower-level people in a large company, writing directly to the chief executive officer can yield results. It is important to stress, early on, that you are not a crank but rather a longtime customer who has had difficulty in this one particular instance. For example, begin your letter like this: "As a longtime satisfied customer, I have always had a great deal of respect for the management of your company. In the past, whenever some difficulty arose, it was handled promptly and courteously. That is why I was surprised when . . ."

COMPUTERS

When You Need One and Which You Should Buy

Our society is so technology driven that quite often a new product hits the market before there is really a need for it. The manufacturers of the new technology then spend tens of millions of dollars convincing the American consumer that they really do need this new product—they just never realized it before. In fact, some people may really need the product, but others may fall for the onslaught of propaganda. That is exactly what happened with personal computers.

Few of us actually *need* a personal computer. In most cases we simply *want* one because we are attracted by the technology or have fallen for all the advertising pitches. It is just plain foolish to buy an expensive item—such as a personal computer system—based on want rather than need. There are only three instances when you truly need a personal computer in your home:

1. If you conduct a business from your home;
2. If you regularly bring work home from your office or place of business; or
3. If you have a child between the ages of ten and seventeen.

Regardless of all the claims to the contrary, you do not need a computer unless you fall into one of those three camps. Yes, you can keep track of your family finances on a personal computer. Sure, you can do your banking electronically. Airline reservations can be made from your own keyboard. Your personal diary and your recipe file and your telephone directory can be stored on disks. In fact, there are hundreds of things that can be done with a personal computer. But all of them can be done without a personal computer as well, often for much less money and sometimes much faster. A personal computer should be a labor-saving or an educational device, not a labor-creating device or a status symbol.

If you truly do need a computer, the place to begin your search is in the software section of the store. Computer purchasing decisions should be software, not hardware, driven. A computer is an incredible tool, but without software—which provides the programs and applications—it is useless. The first thing to do, therefore, is to determine what software you will be using on a regular basis. In some circumstances that may be easy. For example, if you work on Lotus 1-2-3 at the office, you'll want to work on that at home as well. Similarly, if you are looking for specialized software, such as dental office management or tax preparation and accounting, you may find that there are only one or two programs or applications to choose from. In this scenario you simply buy the computer that can run your chosen software.

However, if your needs are more generic, such as general word processing and bookkeeping, or if you are buying the computer for your child's educational needs, the selection becomes more complicated. You'll find that excellent business, educational, and entertainment software is available for every type of computer, and that there is often little advantage to one program as opposed to another. In some cases you may even find the same program available for different machines. That means you'll have to base your decision on hardware.

As the personal computer market is currently structured, that will mean choosing between two alternative operating systems: the Macintosh disk operating system (Mac) and the IBM/Microsoft disk operating system (MS/DOS). There are alternatives to these two systems—notably Commodore's Amiga—but most software is written for Mac or MS/DOS machines. The two systems, unfortunately, are not compatible. While some top-of-the-line computers have the ability to cross over between the two operating systems, they are far too expensive for home use, meaning you will have to make a choice.

The Macintosh system is easier to learn and use. That makes it especially popular with children and computer neophytes. Since it works on a graphic interface (commands and concepts are pictorial rather than numerical or alphabetical) it is a more transparent system—you don't feel as though there is anything separating you from your work. That endears it to writers, artists, and musicians. In addition, this interface is used in every piece of software available for the Macintosh, so once the system is mastered, it becomes easy to learn how to use new programs or applications. The downside is that Macintosh machines are generally much higher in price than MS/DOS machines since they are available from only one supplier—Apple Computer. Even with the recent introduction of low-cost Macs, a complete Macintosh system, including a printer, costs more than its MS/DOS equivalents.

The MS/DOS system, on the other hand, has been the industry standard for many years, meaning that there is more software—particularly business-oriented programs—available to choose from (although the gap is closing). In addition, there are many different manufacturers of MS/DOS hardware besides IBM. These clones, as they are known in the business, have brought hardware prices down dramatically. A good MS/DOS system, including a printer, can generally be bought for less than an equivalent Mac system. The one problem with MS/DOS is that it can be difficult for a child or computer novice to master. Most of the programs use difficult-to-remember keyboard commands, and there is no carryover of commands between software programs. MS/DOS users have to go through a learning process every time they buy or use a new program. There are signs, however, that the MS/DOS world is moving toward a Mac-like interface in order to make the learning process easier and shorter.

In today's market, if it comes down to a hardware-based choice, the best thing to do is to buy a Macintosh if you can afford it. The advantages of the Mac system—accessibility and ease of use—outweigh the higher prices and more limited software options. If you cannot afford or justify the added expense, opt for an MS/DOS machine.

FOR MORE INFORMATION . . .

You can learn more about buying computers from the following book:
- *Consumer Reports—Personal Computer Buying Guide* by Olen R. Pearson

CREDIT BUREAU REPORTS

Making Yours as Spotless as Possible

Credit reports have become adult report cards. More and more, employers, landlords, and business associates are joining potential lenders in scrutinizing your past credit history and using it to make a judgment on you as an individual. They view a stable credit file as an indication of good character and responsibility.

This trend has fed the credit-reporting industry, which is growing in leaps and bounds. The bureaus are getting larger and even more omniscient—if you can believe that's possible.

Yet most consumers remain unaware of the contents of their credit reports. That's inexcusable. Don't, however, fall for the credit-report cleaning services, which advertise frequently in financial magazines and newspapers. They, and the "services" sponsored by the credit bureaus themselves, are useless, money-wasting enterprises. You and only you have the ability to clean up your credit report, and you can get access to it for little money, or for free if you have been turned down for credit recently.

Credit reports are computer-printed documents that, thanks to their appearance, carry the weight of authority. The extended illness you had five years ago that caused you to be three weeks late in paying your bills looks like today's news on a credit report. You may have been a pillar of virtue since, but that brief period of slow payment will still stick out. And while lending professionals may be used to the jargon and terminology that appears on your report card, those outside the industry who are first using the report as a tool will find it confusing.

It is essential first to insure that there are no errors in your credit history. If you call the credit bureau's attention to what you feel is an error in your report, they must, by law, investigate the matter. The burden of proof is on them. If the questionable information can't be verified, it must be stricken from your report. And once removed, an amended copy must be sent to all those who had requested the report in the past six months.

Go back to your lenders and negotiate to have their judgments of you upgraded if need be. The only person who can change an accurate but negative characterization in a credit report is the person who placed it there. If you owe them money, it should be easy to negotiate a change in their characterization of you: simply tell them you will pay what you owe in exchange for their eliminating their negative opinion of you.

You are allowed to include a one-hundred-word statement in your credit file and have it sent along with the bureau's data to anyone requesting the report. It is a good idea to take advantage of this right if your file has a negative tone. This statement can be used to present your case to the average reader of the document, spelling out reasons and explanations for any less-than-spectacular performances in your past. The simple fact that you cared enough about your credit status to do something about it is viewed positively by potential creditors.

Make every effort to present as spotless a credit history as possible. The few hours of effort that go into cleaning up your credit report will pay off if but one judgment based on its contents is swayed in your direction.

SAMPLE 100-WORD STATEMENTS

Here are two examples of one-hundred-word statements that clients of mine have used to help clean up their credit bureau reports:

- "With reference to your credit report on me, I would like to explain the following items that appear to reflect negatively on my creditworthiness. The credit card judgment for $2,000 was levied after my estranged spouse purchased merchandise in a spiteful buying spree after our separation. My attorney has been trying to straighten this matter out for some time now. My slow payment record in 1980 was caused by an illness that resulted in a temporary cash shortage. Despite this shortage, all payments were eventually met. The IRS tax lien that you show on my file took me completely by surprise. I have no idea how it originated and have instructed my accountant to inquire into the matter. As soon as I learn what he discovers, I shall contact you."
- "In the past few years I have had several serious problems—an extended illness, a divorce, the death of a loved one. However,

I have now reached a point in my life when I am ready to correct all my past mistakes and move beyond my past problems. I would truly appreciate if you could begin judging my credit-worthiness from the date of this letter onward, since there is no reason why I should ever be delinquent in paying my bills ever again."

WHAT CREDIT BUREAUS DON'T KNOW ABOUT YOU

Credit bureaus only seem to be omniscient. Don't become paranoid and feel that every little slipup you have ever made is on file somewhere in their massive computers. Credit bureaus never learn about and can therefore never report on bounced checks, late utility or telephone bill payments, book or record club memberships, or newspaper or magazine subscriptions.

EXPLAINING A BANKRUPTCY IN A 100-WORD STATEMENT

While you can't obscure a personal bankruptcy in your credit history, it's possible to minimize the damage it may cause you. Add a 100-word statement to your credit file explaining that the bankruptcy "was caused by problems with your business," and is not an indication of your inability to manage your personal affairs. Stress that your previous difficulties were "interfering with your health." State that while you "explored every avenue of possible compromise," your creditors "were relentless and unwilling to compromise," even though it would have taken you 15 years to pay off your debts. Add that your debts had made you "unemployable." Explain that because you "were constantly being badgered by judgment creditors and subject to garnishment," potential employers treated you "as if you had the plague." Sum up by writing that you "simply had to declare bankruptcy to be able to go on with your life."

OBTAINING COPIES OF YOUR CREDIT BUREAU REPORTS

There are three major credit bureaus in America, each with its own clients, policies, jargon, codes, and report form. In order to check your credit thoroughly, you need to obtain copies of your file from every one of the bureaus that has a file on you since they share neither information nor corrections. Here are the addresses and telephone numbers of the main offices of the big three. If possible, telephone before writing since the bureau may require your request be directed to a branch or regional office.

TRW Credit Data
National Consumer Relations
  Center
12606 Greenville Avenue
P.O. Box 749029
Dallas, TX 75374–9029
(214) 235–1200 extension 251

Equifax (also known as CBI)
P.O. Box 4081
Atlanta, GA 30302
(404) 885–8000

Trans Union
(East)
P.O. Box 360
Philadelphia, PA 19105
(215) 569–4582

(Midwest)
Consumer Relations
222 South First Street, Suite 201
Louisville, KY 40202
(502) 584–0121

(West)
P.O. Box 3110
Fullerton, CA 92634
(714) 738–3800

CREDIT CHECKING CLUBS

Some of the major credit bureaus have established credit checking clubs which, for an annual fee, provide periodic updates and notify members of requests to review their credit file. While I'm a firm believer in keeping an eye on your credit file, I think these clubs are a waste of money. There's no reason why you need to know every time someone checks your credit. And obtaining a copy of your file once a year, or just prior to major purchases or job hunts is sufficient—especially since it costs less than membership in the club. Finally, if you are ever turned down for a loan or credit card, you can obtain a copy of your credit report free for a specified period of time after the rejection.

FOR MORE INFORMATION . . .

You can learn more about credit bureau reports from the following books:
- *How to Borrow Money* by Stephen M. Pollan and Ronald and Raymond Roel
- *Conquer Your Debt* by William Kent Brunette
- *The Credit Power Handbook* by Daniel K. Berman

CREDIT CARD USE

Staying Free of the Nasty Habit

Credit card buying is the financial equivalent of cigarette smoking—it's one of the most dangerous habits you can have. Paying for something with a piece of plastic removes the pain from the buying process. When you have to reach into your wallet and pull out actual cash, or go through the process of writing a check and retabulating your account balance, you are almost automatically forced to pause. You think to yourself, "Do I really need this?" Credit cards anesthetize the entire buying process and often lead to indiscriminate shopping and inattention to prices.

Credit card companies, not unlike tobacco companies, go out of their way to encourage the habit. They offer extensions, free months, delayed billing, and other incentive plans to suck us into their clutches. Remember, they want you to take your time in paying so that their almost usurious interest charges can compound over and over and over.

The continuing overuse of credit cards is one of the most dangerous trends in our society. I find it incomprehensible that otherwise financially savvy individuals would use a credit card for anything other than: as a credit credential; to rent a car—which you can't do any other way; or to buy an important big-ticket item—such as a much-deserved vacation, a practical appliance such as a washing machine, or a piece of needed furniture.

Many of us fail to realize that implicit in the use of a credit card is a surcharge, overt or hidden, that is tacked onto every transaction. Credit cards are actually quite painful for the vendor. Not only does he or she have to wait for funds, but quite often a charge is levied by the credit card company as well. That's why the old-fashioned bargaining technique of offering cash payment in exchange for a lower price still works today.

Back when credit card interest was deductible, a case could be made for using credit regularly. But now that the 15- to 24-percent interest rates aren't offset by tax advantages, it is preposterous to pay these exorbitant rates simply to satisfy our urge for immediate gratification.

If you can't wait three months to save the cash for that new television set you want, you should seek counseling. Save your money. Pay cash. If you don't want to carry large amounts of cash around or need to keep records of expenditures for tax purposes, use a charge card that requires you to pay your entire balance at the end of each month. Don't take your lead from Washington and continually borrow. If you do, your personal finances will be in as deep a quagmire as our government's.

AVOIDING CREDIT CARD FRAUD

Here are some tips for avoiding credit card problems and scams:

- Never give your credit card number to anyone over the telephone unless you initiated the call and the other party is well-known and reputable. If someone finds out your credit card number and its expiration date, and couples that with your name, address, and telephone number, they can go on an illegal telephone shopping spree and stick you with the tab.
- Tear up the carbon paper from credit card receipts. By scouring through trash cans and copying valid credit card numbers from these carbons, thiefs are able to charge purchases to your account.
- Keep all your credit card receipts and check them against your monthly billing statement. If you find that you are being billed for a charge you didn't make, contact the credit card company immediately and contest the charge. If the problem continues, cancel the card.
- Report the loss or theft of credit cards immediately. While theoretically your liability for charges made on lost or stolen credit cards is limited, it is important that you report the situation as quickly as possible.
- Retain a copy of any police report for your files.
- Carefully dispose of any preapproved credit card offers you receive in the mail. By simply gathering some obvious information third parties can fill in these applications and acquire fraudulent cards.
- Cut old credit cards into pieces. Very few retail clerks actually check the expiration date of credit cards. An old card in the

wrong hands can cause a great deal of trouble for the real card-holder.

- Don't fall for affinity credit cards. These are credit cards that carry the emblem of an organization or contribute a certain amount of each dollar charged to a specific charity. While there is nothing illegal about these cause-related cards, you are probably paying a premium interest rate and a high annual fee, while the charity is probably receiving little in return for your sponsorship.

- Beware of secured credit cards. These cards require you to make a minimum deposit with a bank, which then issues you a credit line equal to the amount you deposit. Not only aren't these cards credit credentials, but they rob you of interest you could earn elsewhere, and the broker offering the card often tacks on consultation charges and fees as well.

CREDIT CARD SECURITY CLUBS

Some credit card companies and a few independent organizations have established clubs that provide card holders with easy cancelation and reissuing. The clubs work this way: you pay a fee and register all your credit card numbers with the club. If your wallet or purse is ever stolen or lost, you simply make one telephone call to the club, which will then cancel all your cards and request that new ones be issued. Some clubs also offer an insurance package that will cover any charges made on stolen cards. While I don't think membership in such a club is essential, it's a good idea if you carry a lot of credit cards with you all the time. However, the insurance coverage is superfluous since most homeowner's policies offer identical coverage automatically. If your wallet is packed with plastic, shop around for the cheapest such club you can find—and don't worry if it doesn't offer insurance coverage.

HELP IN FINDING LOW-INTEREST CREDIT CARDS

For some good guides to obtaining low-interest credit cards, join the Bankcard Holders of America. This nonprofit organization provides a valuable service as well as lots of useful information.

The $18 membership fee could pay for itself with one major charged purchase. They can be reached by calling (800) 638–6497. [If you're in Washington D.C., call (703) 481–1110.]

FOR MORE INFORMATION . . .

You can learn more about credit card use from the following books:
- *How to Borrow Money* by Stephen M. Pollan and Ronald and Raymond Roel
- *Conquer Your Debt* by William Kent Brunette
- *The Credit Power Handbook* by Daniel K. Berman

CRUISES

Making Sure a Dream Trip Doesn't Become a Nightmare

Cruises have become increasingly popular vacations, combining the advantages of resort living, sea air, and exotic locations. Unfortunately, a cruise is also the riskiest vacation you can take, since once the ship leaves port you are a captive traveler.

It is important to understand that, despite common misconceptions, cruises are not all glorious excursions. Your stateroom may well be the size of your bathroom at home. Your tablemates at dinner may be obnoxious bores. The weather may turn bad, leading to seasickness and keeping you stuck below decks. And you may find that you and your roommate are the only singles on board, or that you and your spouse are the only married couple on board. There are ways to minimize the risks, however, and make sure that your dream vacation doesn't turn into a nightmare.

Begin by taking all the promotional materials offered by the cruise line with a sizable grain of salt. Many of these brochures are masterpieces of deceptive advertising. Photographic tricks may be employed to make the ship and its facilities and accommodations seem larger than they really are, and the huge stateroom suites pictured may be the exception rather than the rule. Price quotes in the brochures are usually minimum fares for the worst cabins. Stays in exotic ports, touted as features of a cruise, may actually only last a few hours. Don't rely on travel agents' advice either. Few of them are really knowledgeable about cruises, and many simply promote one or two lines.

Rather than relying on the marketing materials or agent pronouncements, consult magazines such as *Travel Weekly* and ask for specific information about such things as the size of the room you will be staying in, the size of the ship itself, and the typical passenger profile.

Cruise ships are generally measured in tonnage. For example, the famous ship on "The Love Boat" is 50,000 tons and holds 1,200 people, while the average cruise ship is 18,000 tons and carries 700 people. Keep in mind that the larger the ship the more stable it will be and the less likely your chances of getting seasick.

Cruise lines tend to go after a specific class and type of passenger. If you don't match up with their passenger profile, you could find yourself odd man out and be in for a long and uncomfortable trip. Ask everyone you can about what type of person usually takes the cruise in question. Check the photographs in brochures. Are all the passengers pictured grey-haired people dressed in suits and gowns, or are they tanned and nubile, dressed in swimsuits? Go over the facilities mentioned with an eye toward whom they are designed to appeal to. Do they place more priority on the on-board medical facilities or the disco?

If the cruise line gives you the option of choosing how many people you would like to dine with, opt for as big a table as possible—you have more opportunity to find someone you like at a table of ten than a table of four.

Avoid travel agents and booking clerks who advise you to buy a room guarantee in order to save money. This is simply a document that guarantees you a room on board the ship. It is not the same as having a cabin assigned to you. If you hold a room guarantee, you will be assigned a cabin on the day of departure. Invariably, it will be one of the remaining unbooked staterooms, which promise to be among the worst accommodations on board. Instead, pay the extra fee and book an assigned cabin. Make sure, however, you are shown exactly where on the ship the cabin is located. Stay away from rooms that do not have portholes. These inside cabins are usually the smallest and least desirable on board. If for some reason you do get stuck with an unacceptable cabin, ask if it is possible to upgrade once you are on board.

When discussing prices, make sure to ask about extra charges. On most cruises, day trips in ports of call are not included in your fare. If you have not arranged day trips in advance, you may be forced to stay on the ship or to pay a premium by booking a trip at the last minute. Check to see if drinks are included in your fare. While meals are included, drinks often are not, and they can cost upwards of $4 each.

Ask about the cruise line's tipping policy. The industry norm is that you must tip the maid, steward, waiter, and busboy at least $2.50 per person per day. And remember that the more you tip, the better the service you will receive, and the more enjoyable your trip will be. Obviously, include all these extra charges and fees when comparison shopping.

Similarly, ask about cash rebates, free airfare to the port of departure, flat rates for inside and outside cabins, free passages for third or fourth members of a group, and other special offer-ings. Cruise lines don't often advertise their special deals, so it's up to you to uncover them.

Be wary of cruise lines that require you to pay for the entire trip months before your departure—they may be having financial problems. In fact, it makes sense to ask around about the financial standing and reputation of the cruise line before signing any agreements or paying any fees. Pay particular attention to the financial stability of ships not embarking from U.S. ports. A ship leaving from an American port falls under governmental and in-dustry regulatory agencies—such as the Federal Maritime Com-mission, the U.S. Tour Operators Association, and the National Tour Association—which offer passengers refund recourses not open to foreign-cruise passengers.

You can also protect yourself by paying for cruises with a major credit card. If the cruise line goes out of business, you can then get a refund through the credit card company up to 120 days after the scheduled date of departure.

Make sure to get prices from several different sales agents, including the steamship company itself. There is as big a range in cruise prices as there is in airline fares due to promotional gim-micks, commissions, and advance discounts, so it pays to check around. Investigation and research can help insure that your cruise is closer to "The Love Boat" than *Ship of Fools*.

DISABILITY INSURANCE

Protecting Your Stream of Income

The biggest insurance mistake made by most of us is that we carry too much life insurance and not enough disability insurance. Perhaps that's because when most of us think of disaster we immediately assume death. Actually, you have a four times greater chance to become disabled between the ages of thirty-five and sixty than to die. Far too many people simply rely on the disability insurance their employer provides, or on government programs.

Disability insurance is the single most important insurance you can buy. It is possible to absorb other types of losses if you have a stream of income. But if you become disabled and cannot work, you lose your most important financial safety net: the very stream of income that you have depended on to meet both ordinary and extraordinary expenses. I learned this the hard way. In 1978, I was diagnosed as suffering from tuberculosis—contracted, I now joke, from the squalor of where I live . . . New York City's Park Avenue. If not for a disability policy that provided me with $30,000 a year, my family would have been destitute.

Work-related disability insurance generally runs for only a short period of time and is only in force while you are in this particular job. Government programs, while well-meaning, barely provide enough money to live on, let alone maintain your standard of living. The solution then is to purchase additional disability coverage that supplements your existing coverage.

In determining your disability insurance needs and investigating coverage options, you should look at four areas: the size of the monthly payments you will receive if you become disabled; how soon after becoming disabled these payments will begin; how long these payments will last; and the qualifications for benefits. For obvious reasons, the larger the payments, the sooner they take effect, the longer they last, and the more liberal qualifications for benefits, the larger your premium will be. And those numbers can get quite large.

Insurance companies are not gamblers. Since the likelihood of becoming disabled at a young age is much greater than that of dying at a young age, the premiums of disability insurance are much greater than life insurance. That means for you to get the best deal on coverage you will have to make some compromises and decisions.

The first place to compromise is to cut back on the size of the monthly payments. Beware of your initial judgment simply to match your current income—the cost would be enormous. In addition, payments from a disability policy on which you pay the premiums are not subject to income tax. This means that you can begin your analysis with your monthly net, not gross income. Next, analyze your monthly expenses. Go over them with an eye toward cutting corners. How many of them can be eliminated? What luxuries can you do without? What costs won't you be incurring if you are not employed? Determine the minimum income you will need to keep your roof overhead, your belly full, and your insurance premiums paid and insure that amount.

Next, make some projections about how long you could make it without your own disability insurance payments. If you have disability insurance from your employer, find out for how many months it runs. Then, take a look at your savings and emergency funds and figure out how many months that money can keep you afloat. Since the longer it takes for payments to start, the lower your premium, it makes the most sense to take out a policy that starts as late as possible. For example, if your employer's disability policy pays benefits for three months, and your savings can carry you another three months, look for a disability policy that starts paying benefits six months after becoming disabled.

I don't believe it's a good idea to limit severely the length of time your payments will last. If you take out a policy that provides payments for only a year or two and become permanently disabled, you are only delaying, not eliminating, disaster. It makes the most sense to buy a policy that covers you for as long as possible. I recommend that you get a policy that covers you at least until the age of sixty-five.

The final variable in disability insurance coverage is the policy's definition of disability, which describes when you qualify for benefits. Almost every policy has its own definition, each with its own subtle semantics that can severely limit your ability to get benefits. The best definition, and the one I suggest you look for, is that you are disabled if your income goes down as the result of sickness or accident. The standard definition of disability, however, relates to your ability to do the main, regular, or routine tasks of your current occupation, related occupations, or even any occupation. Since you are insuring yourself against loss of income, it makes the most sense that the qualification for benefits be based on exactly that.

With this description of the type of policy you are looking for in hand, call the same independent insurance broker who arranged your life insurance coverage. Explain to him or her that you would like a policy that meets the criteria you've established and would be interested in seeing what's available. Request that they provide you with at least three options.

Once your broker returns with policy proposals look each over carefully. In addition to making sure they meet your requirements, check the provisions of the individual policies.

Avoid policies that have different waiting and benefit periods depending on whether you become disabled from an illness or an accident. Regardless of why or how your income is interrupted, you will still need the same protection.

Take a close look at the renewability provisions of each policy. There are three basic types: class cancelable, guaranteed renewable, and guaranteed renewable and noncancelable. If a policy is class cancelable, it means that the insurance company can cancel all policies in any given group—all policies in Alaska, all policies for fire fighters, or all policies written in 1979, for example. If a policy is guaranteed renewable, it cannot be canceled as long as you continue to pay your premiums on time. However, the insurance company can choose to raise your premiums. The third, and best, option is the guaranteed renewable and noncancelable policy, which cannot be canceled and freezes your premiums.

Another section of the policy to examine carefully is its policy on preexisting conditions. Some companies refuse to cover disabilities arising from conditions that you fail to reveal to them, even if you only suffered from it once when you were five years old. Still others state that they won't pay benefits on disabilities arising from preexisting conditions for the first one or two years you own the policy.

Check the policy's provisions for intermittent disabilities. Better policies will only make you go through the waiting period once each calendar year. Some, however, may require you to wait the entire length of time in each and every instance. This can be disastrous. Let's say you have a policy with a sixty-day waiting period. If you are disabled for forty days, get better, and go back to work for thirty days, then become disabled again, you will still have to wait another sixty days to receive benefits.

Take a close look at any provisions the policy has for waiving premiums. Some companies will pay your premiums for a portion of the time you are disabled, and/or refund premiums you paid earlier.

Finally, it's a good idea also to investigate the policies' clauses regarding partial disabilities, rehabilitation, and potential exclusions—the most common of which are pregnancy and military service.

Insurance salespeople are notorious for trying to add riders, and cost, to basic insurance policies, but in the case of disability insurance there are three such riders that may make sense: social security replacement, option to buy, and cost of living. A social security replacement rider will add the benefits you would have received from social security to your monthly check if the government, for any reason, refuses your claim. An option-to-buy rider guarantees you the right to buy additional coverage in the future. A cost-of-living rider adjusts your benefits for inflation based on some standard index.

As you can see, shopping for disability insurance is not simple. The policies are complex and expensive . . . but they are also very necessary to protect you and your dependents from financial disaster. The cost may be high, but look at it this way: you can get a conservative disability policy that pays you $3,000 a month for less than $40 a month.

DISABILITY INSURANCE FOR POTENTIAL ENTREPRENEURS

It can be very difficult for self-employed individuals to get adequate disability coverage. In order to avoid potentially fraudulent claims, disability insurers require a great deal of income documentation. Entrepreneurs spend most of their time trying to minimize any evidence of income in order to avoid taxes, so they can have a hard time proving their actual earnings. The solution is to plan ahead. If you plan on going into business for yourself, take out a disability policy while you are still employed. While it may not be as much coverage as you'd like, it's better than nothing.

FOR MORE INFORMATION . . .

You can learn more about disability insurance from the following books:
- *The Complete Book of Insurance* by William Kent Brunette
- *The Family Insurance Handbook* by Les Abromovitz
- *Winning the Insurance Game* by Ralph Nader and Wesley J. Smith

DOCTORS

Finding and Selecting Physicians

When it comes to hiring most professionals in this country, we have no problem interviewing them, looking into their backgrounds, or checking their references. This has become the accepted way to select the best person for our needs. But when it comes to finding and selecting doctors, we throw this rational approach out the window.

We treat doctors as demigods. While this is partially our own fault—it is more reassuring to place our lives in the hands of someone who borders on the divine—the medical profession works to reinforce this perceived infallibility through its indoctrination of young physicians and relentless public relations efforts. In order to make a reasoned decision on who best serves your medical needs, you have to knock doctors off their pedestals.

Generally, our physicians are inherited from our parents. We go along with their choices of general practitioners and specialists long after we are mature enough to make our own choices. To a certain extent that isn't all bad: there is a great deal to say for having an established relationship with a professional. As long as you have no problems with the physicians you have inherited from your parents, feel free to remain as their patient. However, if you are uncomfortable with your present physician, find out your present doctor is retiring or relocating. If you are relocating yourself, you have an opportunity to break free from family ties and search out your own doctors.

It is easy to judge the skill of attorneys, accountants, architects, and most other professionals—there are intellectual and physical signs of their effectiveness and third-party opinion can be treated as knowledgeable. Doctors, on the other hand, leave no physical trace of their labors—except for cosmetic surgeons. And the opinions of others who know as little about medicine as you do can't be treated as gospel. That means that while we are perfectly qualified to make a judgment on the bedside manner or personality of a doctor, we can't make a judgment of their professional skill.

The ways around this predicament are to enlist the aid of people who are experts in judging medical skill—the heads of departments at teaching hospitals—and to first select an internist or family practitioner and use them as a source for specialists.

Begin your search for a physician by finding out which hospital in your town or city is considered the best. You can base your selection on reputations, but give priority to teaching hospitals affiliated with major universities. If there is no teaching hospital in your area, opt for a state or regional hospital over a local one.

Next, telephone the head of the hospital's department of internal or family medicine, depending on whether or not you have children. Tell the department head that you are new to the community, are looking for a doctor, and would like their recommendations. Mention that while you are looking for a highly skilled practitioner, you are also concerned with the economics of medical care. Ask for two or three names.

Telephone each doctor's office and say that you are calling on the recommendation of the person you previously spoke with, dropping their name and hospital affiliation. Explain that you are looking for a physician and would like to meet and speak with the doctor. Stress that this will take only about five minutes of the doctor's time and indicate that your schedule is flexible. If a doctor refuses to meet with you, even if for only five minutes, cross the name off your list.

Obviously, there isn't much ground you can cover in such a brief meeting, but it will indicate some important things about the physician. First, their willingness to meet with you at all shows they have not placed themselves on too high a pedestal. It indicates that they are open to answering questions. That's an excellent trait for a professional to have. You want a doctor who will not only tell you how, but will also explain why. Second, once in their office you can make some superficial, but valid, judgments:

- How old is the doctor? Place a premium on experience. Your specialists can be young hotshots, just out of medical school, familiar with the latest techniques and technologies, but your internist or family practitioner should have some seasoning. If you have any questions about how long they have been in practice, ask them directly.
- What is the doctor's personality like? Opt for someone who is serious and businesslike. Technical ability is more important than bedside manner; you are selecting a medical doctor, not a

psychotherapist. It is enough if they ask you about your own medical history—they don't have to express interest in your personal life.

- What does the doctor's appearance tell you? Do not go to a doctor who is obese, who smokes, who smells of liquor, whose hands shake, or who, in any obvious way, does not take care of him or herself. If they don't take care of themselves, they aren't the person to take care of you or your family.

- How difficult is it to schedule appointments? Ask the receptionist how long in advance most appointments have to be made. Almost every doctor leaves some flexibility in his or her schedule to deal with emergencies—make sure this doctor isn't an exception.

- What are their fees? Don't be afraid to ask a doctor what he or she charges for an office visit, for a first physical, and for an annual physical. If all other things are equal, there is nothing wrong with selecting the physician who charges the least.

Do not let yourself be intimidated by the doctors you interview. There are an incredible number of doctors in this country—in urban areas there is even a surplus. While they would be loath to admit it, doctors do compete for patients. There is no reason, then, why you shouldn't shop around and be discriminating.

MEDICAL RECORDS

Your medical records are your property. When you make your selection of a physician, contact by mail all other physicians you have seen during the past ten years and instruct them to forward all your records to your new doctor. Two weeks after sending the letter, follow it up with a telephone call to "check on whether or not" they received your request. Remain firm if your previous doctor's office staff raises objections. Enlist your new physician as an ally, having his or her office staff call and request that your files be forwarded to them. If necessary, make a personal appearance at their office in order to pick up your files. Not only do your past medical records belong to you, but they are an important ingredient in the proper diagnosis and care of present and future medical conditions.

ECONOMIC INDICATORS

Which Numbers and Statistics Are Really Important

In this information-hungry age many Americans are becoming increasingly preoccupied by economic indicators: financial statistics that allegedly indicate the future direction of our economy. Otherwise rational people are basing their personal financial decisions on stock prices, the dollar/yen exchange rate, new home sales, the price of gold, paper-production figures, the consumer spending rate, the money supply, or the prime interest rate, among other numbers. You'll find investors who will tell you with a straight face that hemlines and Super Bowls have to be factored into financial decision-making. So obsessed are we with numbers that special indices, which represent a consensus or average of other selected indices, are now becoming popular.

The media, which is spending more and more time on business news, feeds this obsession by reporting the release of each new number as front-page news. The sources of the numbers only unveil their latest tabulations when they are guaranteed to get the maximum media exposure. Individual economists and business writers all have their favorite indicators on which they base their "scientific" predictions. This self-perpetuating craziness has reached the point where otherwise levelheaded people set their alarm clocks for three A.M. so they can be the first to hear what is happening on the Tokyo stock exchange.

It is perfectly natural to wonder about the future and to search for omens and signs—man has been doing it since the dawn of time. And it's understandable, even admirable, to keep track of the current financial and economic conditions. But it is ludicrous to base your personal financial decisions on a statistic, average, or index. You might just as well consult a palm reader or soothsayer.

Ironically, most economic indicators simply reflect the past attitudes and actions of the American public. All they are indicative of is what you and your neighbors thought and did in the past month or week. It is ridiculous to base your future on your past actions, even if they are cloaked in the mantle of statistical authority.

Rather than watching the numbers and waiting for signs of precipitous drops and meteoric rises in the economy, plan for the real world. The economy isn't filled with booms and busts. It is actually a steady series of shifts, back and forth like a metronome. Be prudent in your finances. Invest and risk based on your own assessment of what you can afford financially and emotionally. Base your financial decisions on the only economic indicators that really matter: how much you owe and how much you have in the bank. Being comfortable with your levels of debt and savings is the single best positive economic indicator there is.

EMERGENCY FINANCES

Dealing With Temporary Setbacks and Shortages

There is no shame in having a financial setback. Everyone, at one time or another, faces financial difficulties: you've lost your job; your spouse has left you; you've had a medical emergency. The only shame is in giving up.

Debt has nothing to do with moral fiber. Take charge of your emotions and keep your spirits high. Depression is contagious and obvious. Don't hide from the world, stop opening your mail, or sleep late as a reward for your travails. Look upon your situation as an obstacle to be overcome, not a problem. It is essential that you face each morning with enthusiasm and vigor. Wake up as if nothing has happened.

The first step in dealing with a financial emergency is to provide for essentials. Draw cash advances on your credit cards and use this cash to stock the pantry, refrigerator, and freezer. Spend only on essentials; luxuries and frills are for those who have money to burn. Look on these advances as a priority loan— perhaps the most important loan you will ever take out.

Next, slow down your payment of bills in order to conserve cash for as long as possible. Since you will be telephoning and speaking to your creditors' collection clerks, it's important to understand their point of view. Collectors must demonstrate to their supervisors that they have intimate knowledge of problems and are on top of situations. This means you will have to engage in an ongoing dialogue, speaking with them on the telephone every one or two weeks. It is helpful to initiate this dialogue by calling when there's smoke but no fire. Almost every legitimate creditor has accessible staff people with the power to offer extended payments as long as they are given a rational reason.

Your first calls should be utility companies—telephone, gas, electric, etc. After food, your ability to communicate and maintaining a comfortable environment are priorities. Be candid, explaining that you've had a financial setback and may be late with your payments. Ask them to mark your file accordingly. Note the name of the person you spoke with and tell them you will call at least twice a month to keep them informed of your status.

If you are a renter, the next person you contact should be your landlord. Say that you have had a financial setback, but don't give too many details. When pressed, cite family medical problems. Explain that you may be late with the rent this month, and stress that you will call later to verify the fact.

With your basic needs taken care of, start calling your other creditors. Tackle finance companies first since they are the toughest and will require the most effort. Other creditors, including credit and charge card companies, are a bit more lenient. Once again, tell them you have had a financial setback. Ask to either skip a payment or pay just the interest charges. Explain that you will stop using the card until your finances are straightened out, but don't destroy or return the card even if they request it.

If you have any insurance payments coming due soon, call your broker and ask him or her to advance it. A good broker, interested in keeping your business—and his or her commission—will be happy to help.

Homeowners' final call should be to the bank that holds their mortgage. Surprisingly, the banker will probably be your most understanding creditor—the last thing they want to do is foreclose on your mortgage—and the easiest with whom to work out an extended payment plan.

With the flow of cash from your limited coffers diminished, examine ways to change your lifestyle. Stop going to restaurants and eat as economically as possible. Take public transportation whenever possible and limit the use of your car. Cut back on entertainment—rather than going out to the movies, rent a videotape and make some popcorn. Cancel your memberships in social or exercise clubs. And stop giving gifts or making charitable donations.

At this point, start a campaign to raise as much cash as you possibly can. Look around the house for unnecessary items and possessions and perhaps consider a yard sale. Scour the attic and safe deposit box for bonds, jewelry, and collectibles that can be converted into cash. Approach your friends and relatives for short-term loans, structured as business transactions with payment and interest spelled out in writing.

Keep in mind that this financial emergency can actually be an opportunity for you. All the cutting back and trimming can help you develop a more frugal, streamlined lifestyle. You'll have a clearer picture of exactly what is essential to you, and what is simply added luxury. Finally, it can prompt you to take stock of your job or career and lead to your finding a better, higher-paying position.

The absence of ready cash because of sickness, casualty, job loss, or layoff has absolutely nothing to do with your worthiness. This is a temporary obstactle to be overcome—nothing more. God has not made a judgment and found you lacking.

TELEPHONE LANGUAGE—CREDIT CARD COMPANIES

The people who answer the phones for these companies are almost robotic; they have little authority. Simply ask them for the rules concerning late payment and stress that you "don't want to create any undue problems" for them, and that you want to keep your "good credit rating."

TELEPHONE LANGUAGE—CHARGE CARD COMPANIES AND UTILITIES

Customer service personnel with these companies have some power and flexibility. Begin your call with, "I want to ask you about your billing cycles." They can identify with this language. Then say, "I'm going to be late and I need to know what I have to do."

TELEPHONE LANGUAGE—LANDLORDS

It is nearly impossible to manipulate landlords. Instead, try to get their sympathy and enlist their help. Tell them that in the x number of years you have lived in their apartment you have "taken care of it as if it were my own home." Explain that you have "had a financial emergency." Don't indicate that you have mismanaged your life or lost your job. Just say that "because of medical reasons my income flow has stopped," or that you have had to "sidetrack money to take care of a family medical emergency." Humbly say that you will stay there "as long as you let me." Keep in the back of your mind the fact that in certain parts of the country you may be able to go six months before being evicted for nonpayment of rent; and if you can begin paying before your deadline expires, you may be able to forgo moving altogether.

WHEN BEATEN TO THE PUNCH

If a creditor calls you before you have a chance to call them, say "I have been trying to call"; "you have been in my thoughts"; "you are the most important person I owe money to"; and/or "I have been afraid to call you."

A CHECKLIST FOR FINANCIAL EMERGENCIES

This checklist is divided into two sections. Regardless of how temporary your financial emergency, you should do all the steps listed in Phase 1 in the order indicated. If your dire straits continue, proceed on to Phase 2, taking each step in the order indicated and moving on to the next step only if your troubles continue.

Phase 1
- Stock your refrigerator and pantry with staples, using cash advances from your credit cards if you must.
- Draw up a list of all your creditors and include how much each is owed and when it is due.
- Telephone your utility company.
- Telephone the telephone company.
- If you rent, speak with your landlord.
- Telephone the issuers of your credit and charge cards.
- Telephone stores with which you have charge accounts.
- If you own a home, speak with an officer at the bank that holds your mortgage.
- Telephone any professionals—doctors, dentists, lawyers—who are owed money.
- Work out an austerity budget . . . and stick to it.

Phase 2
- Close out IRA, Keogh, and other retirement accounts.
- Go to family and friends and ask for loans.
- Ask elderly relatives for inheritances early.
- Scour your home and bank vault for dormant assets that can be converted in to cash.

- Rather than wait for a full-time position in your field to come along, take a part-time job just for the cash.
- Consider selling additional valuable assets (i.e.: cars, boats, jewels, furs, artwork, furniture, etc.).
- Consider bankruptcy.

EARLY WITHDRAWALS FROM 401K PLANS

It is possible to take an early withdrawal from your company's 401K pension plan if you have "an immediate and heavy financial need" and other resources are not "reasonably available." Examples of "immediate and heavy financial need" include: medical expenses for you, your spouse, or your dependents; the down payment on a principal residence; payment of the next semester's or quarter's college tuition for you, your spouse, or your dependents; or to prevent eviction from or foreclosure on your principal residence. Resources that are considered "reasonably available" include: reimbursement or compensation of insurance, reasonable liquidation of assets, stopping elective contributions to pension plans, distributions or nontaxable loans from other plans, and loans from commercial sources. You can withdraw only the amount you elected to contribute to the 401K plan, not from nonelective or matching contributions. And withdrawals are subject to a 10-percent tax penalty on top of your regular income tax rate. In addition, you can borrow against your contributions to 401K plans, subject to IRS regulations and your employer's approval.

EARLY WITHDRAWALS FROM IRAS

You can withdraw money deposited in IRAs at any time, but such withdrawals are subject to a 10-percent penalty on top of your regular income tax rate. The 10-percent penalty is waived if: you're dead (in which case, this waiver is only beneficial to your survivors or your estate), you set up a series of roughly equal payments tied to your life expectancy, or if you have a mental or physical disability that is expected to last longer than a year or lead to your death.

EARLY WITHDRAWALS FROM KEOGHS

Similarly, you can always withdraw monies deposited in Keogh Accounts, which is also subject to a 10-percent penalty on top of your regular income tax rate. The 10-percent penalty is waived if: you're dead (again, this waiver is only beneficial to your survivors or your estate), you set up a series of roughly equal payments tied to your life expectancy, you have a mental or physical disability that is expected to last longer than a year or lead to your death, or you're withdrawing the money to pay otherwise nondeductible catastrophic medical bills. That means catastrophic medical bills not in excess of 7.5 percent of your adjusted gross income.

HOW LONG CAN YOU HANG ON?

In order to determine how long you can weather a financial emergency, you need to take a personal financial inventory. First, compile a list of all your assets. Next, categorize each asset as being readily available, easily convertible, fairly convertible, or nonconvertible unless in extreme difficulty. With your asset analysis complete, tabulate your monthly income from all sources and your total monthly expenses. Subtract monthly expenses from monthly income to calculate your monthly surplus or deficit. If you have a monthly deficit, divide each category of assets by the deficit to determine how long you can stay afloat by disposing of assets. Here's a worksheet to make the process easier:

Assets	Readily Available	Easily Convertible	Fairly Convertible	Non-Convertible
Checking account				
Savings account				
CDs				
Other cash in bank				
Value of savings bonds				
Value of insurance				
Value of mutual funds				
Value of stocks				
Value of bonds				
Value of annuities				
Value of other securities				
Monies owed you				

	Readily Avail-able	Easily Convert-ible	Fairly Convert-ible	Non-Convert-ible
Assets				
Value of home	_____	_____	_____	_____
Value of other real estate	_____	_____	_____	_____
Value of car(s)	_____	_____	_____	_____
Value of collectibles	_____	_____	_____	_____
Value of furnishings	_____	_____	_____	_____
Value of furs and jewels	_____	_____	_____	_____
Value of appliances	_____	_____	_____	_____
Value of other possessions	_____	_____	_____	_____
Total assets	_____	_____	_____	_____

Monthly income

Own income	_____
Income of significant other	_____
Income from children	_____
Gifts or loans	_____
Stock dividends	_____
Interest income	_____
Total monthly income	_____

Monthly expenses

Mortgage or rent payment	_____
Tax payment	_____
Food	_____
Utilities	_____
Telephone	_____
Insurance	_____
Household maintenance	_____
Auto	_____
Debt service	_____
Nonreimbursable medical	_____
Total monthly expenses	_____

Surplus or deficit

Monthly income minus monthly expenses _____

Time frame

Total assets readily available _____ ÷ monthly deficit = _____ months
Total assets easily convertible _____ ÷ monthly deficit = _____ months
Total assets fairly convertible _____ ÷ monthly deficit = _____ months
Total assets nonconvertible _____ ÷ monthly deficit = _____ months

ESTABLISHING CREDIT

Applying For, and Getting, Credit

No one is born with credit. You have to reach out and get it by demonstrating that you can handle money responsibly, and that you are a stable, financially sound adult. The best time to prove that is as early in your adult life as possible.

If you are a graduating college senior, you may find credit card applications in your mailbox. The credit card companies are eager to get their hooks into people as early as possible, so they often run special promotions, providing college seniors with small lines of credit to get them in the habit of using plastic rather than cash or checks. If you receive such invitations, take them up on their offer—but use them to your advantage. In many cases, these introductory cards will have high interest rates. Rather than using them for big-ticket items, buy inexpensive products, then pay your bill immediately. This will help you build up a positive credit-bureau report. Soon, other credit card companies and banks will notice your good standing and seek you out as well. At that point you can pick and choose among them for the best deal.

Most of us, however, aren't lucky enough to be recruited by the credit card companies. We have to go out and obtain credit on our own. And while the process of building up credit can turn into a series of catch-22s—you can't get a loan or credit card without having a credit history, but you can't develop a credit history without a loan or a credit card—it can be done. All it takes is some perserverance and knowledge of the system.

The first step in your campaign to establish credit is to get an application for a gasoline-company or department-store credit card. These are the easiest credit cards to obtain since they are primarily used as marketing tools. But before you rush to complete the application and send it away, it is vital that you examine the form carefully and fill it out with an eye toward maximizing your chances for acceptance.

All credit applications—whether for a credit card or a bank loan—are basically the same, since all lenders base their decisions on the same factors. The purpose of the application is to allow them to judge how stable a person you are. Initially they want to know how long you have lived in your residence, how long you have been at your present job, if you own a car, and if you have a telephone. They will want information about any bank accounts that you have. Lenders also want evidence of a steady stream of income so they can see whether or not you will be able to pay them back.

In an effort to streamline their processing of applications, lenders have developed scoring systems. By giving you a minimal amount of space to write your answers, the lender tries to reduce the information to its most objective level so that a clerk can make the decision whether to grant credit or not. Possible answers are given point values, and if you don't get the required point total, you are rejected. Unfortunately, this scoring has made it difficult for people without any past credit history to get credit.

Scoring is an American scourge today. It is even being used in college and job applications as a substitute for the personal interview. It unfairly discriminates against the young, the elderly, and most of all, women and should be battled at every opportunity.

The secret to bypassing this scoring system, and to giving yourself the best chance to have your credit application accepted, is to turn the application into a window on your life, rather than a score sheet. You can do that by attaching typewritten supplements to the application that provide full and thorough answers to its questions. Supplementing your application in this manner accomplishes two things. First, it takes the application out of the hands of an unthinking clerk. As soon as one of these individuals sees that your application doesn't fit the standard mold that they have been taught to score objectively, they will pass it on to their supervisor, a person qualified to make a subjective judgment. In addition, by supplementing your application, you can turn potentially negative factors into positive ones.

If, for example, you have just moved into your apartment two months ago and write that on the application, you could be seen as unstable. Instead, fill in the blank space with the phrase "see supplement A," and on a separate piece of paper explain that while you have only been in your present home for two months, you recently relocated because of a new and better job, and that you lived at your previous home for many years. If you have only been at your current job for six months, it might also be held against you. Once again, supplement your answer and explain that job-hopping is common in your industry. Then provide a detailed account of how you have progressively moved up the career and income ladder. When filling out questions on your income, remember to include all income, including interest and recurring gifts, in your supplemented answer.

Another way to build up your own credit history is by borrowing someone else's credit. It is possible to have someone who already has good credit standing—perhaps a parent—sign on as a guarantor of your credit application. Almost any lender will agree to a line of credit that is secured in this manner. As long as the credit is in your name and you pay the bills, the credit bureaus will never know, nor report, that the credit is secured.

It is actually easy to ask someone to sign such a guarantee. Simply say to them that you have learned that credit is a catch-22 and that the only credit available to you is the family's credit. Since you will be making all the payments, you are actually just borrowing, not using, the other person's credit. And since it will show up on your credit report, not theirs, it will have no adverse effect on their own credit rating.

A third method of kick-starting your credit life is to take out a passbook loan. Banks are happy to make small loans that are secured by a deposit of the same amount in one of their accounts, which is then frozen until the loan is repaid. Simply borrow the money and pay it back as quickly as possible, and you will have started a positive credit report on yourself.

It is important to realize that the amount of credit you receive initially really doesn't matter. Credit bureaus and lenders aren't as concerned about how much you borrow as they are worried about your demonstrating that you will pay it back. A small credit line is better than none at all. And if you use your credit and pay it back on time, you will find that your credit line will be increased and that other lenders will approach you.

As soon as you have successfully obtained a department-store or gasoline-company card and have begun using it, start looking around for a local bank that offers its own MasterCard or Visa. Approach a bank officer and say that you would like to consolidate all your banking needs. Explain that you will be opening a checking account and a money-market account, renting a safe deposit box, and taking out a credit card. Quite often, local banks grant credit cards much more readily than regional or national banks—particularly if you are a regular customer.

Regardless of exactly how you go about establishing your credit, remember that it is a valuable part of your financial life. In fact, you should check your credit report every year. (See the chapter "Credit Bureau Reports.") Your personal creditworthiness can be the key to buying a home, to launching your own business, to sending your child to college, and to enjoying your life to the fullest. In our society, credit equals stability, and stability in turn equals good character.

FOR MORE INFORMATION . . .

You can learn more about establishing credit from the following books:
- *How to Borrow Money* by Stephen M. Pollan and Ronald and Raymond Roel
- *Conquer Your Debt* by William Kent Brunette
- *The Credit Power Handbook* by Daniel K. Berman

ESTATES

Leaving a Legacy to Your Heirs

For some reason Americans have always considered it prestigious to leave large estates when they die. They believe that the size of their estate is a direct reflection on their financial acumen, their worth as a person, their thriftiness, and their love of their heirs. In fact, the only thing a sizable estate is indicative of is how foolish you are.

Estates are taxed at a higher rate than almost anything else. Your heirs, for whom you accumulated and hoarded and saved for years, may well have to pay a 50-percent tax on their inheritance. That is patently absurd. In addition, there is absolutely no reason for you to conserve your money while you are alive in order to provide for your heirs after your death.

Rather than wait for death to transfer your assets, do it yourself while you are alive. Once you reach the age of sixty, begin to dispose of some of your financial assets by bestowing gifts and transferring ownership to valuable objects or real estate. (For more information see the chapter "Nursing Home Care.") Just make sure that the people who receive your assets agree that they are at your disposal if you need them. Not only will this protect your heirs from high estate taxes and protect your assets from the long arm of medicaid if you must one day enter a nursing home, but it will also give you the pleasure of seeing your heirs enjoy your generosity and of being able to accept their gratitude.

Another way around the estate tax question, and the one that I personally adhere to, is to try to spend all your money while you are alive. Live life to its fullest. Surround yourself with fine furnishing and adornments. Dine out whenever you want. Take in concerts and plays. Travel and see the world. And of course, give gifts to the people you love. There is no shame in being broke when you die. In fact, I believe that to the extent you die with anything substantial in the bank, you have made a mistake. Plan your funeral yourself and make financial provisions for it, and leave enough money to pay your debts. Aside from that, spend away. The last check you draw should be for cash.

WHY YOU NEED A WILL

A will is basically a document that, upon your death, conveys all of your assets in the manner you choose and appoints someone to manage your estate. The states have taken it upon themselves to establish rules and procedures to convey the assets of those who die without wills. The state does charge a fee for doing this, however. In addition, if the state takes charge of conveying your assets, it decides who will manage your estate. If you die without a will, rather than having a friend or relative manage your estate, a political appointee could be placed in charge. I believe that if you've been an active, in-charge person for your entire life, then it's only sensible to try to maintain control of your affairs—to whatever extent possible—after death. In other words: I feel everyone should have a will drawn up.

WHO SHOULD PREPARE YOUR WILL

If you have total assets of $600,000 or more you should have your will drawn up by an attorney who specializes in estates. If your estate is less than $600,000 it's all right to have a good general practitioner prepare your will. The reason for the $600,000 cut-off point is that the federal government does not tax estates under that level. (State tax laws vary, however.) An attorney who specializes in estates will be able to help minimize the tax bite, and therefore maximize the amount your heirs will actually receive.

LIVING TRUSTS

These trusts—very common in states such as Florida and California, which have large elderly populations—allow you to provide for yourself while alive, and then convey your assets privately, according to your wishes, and without paying probate fees, after your death. Basically, what's done is that everything you own— from your insurance policies to your home—is turned over to the trust, which then distributes it both while you are alive and after you die. Living trusts make sense for individuals with sizeable estates who want to save probate costs and keep the size and disposition of the estate private. In order to determine whether a living trust makes sense for you, do a cost/benefit analysis. Determine how much probate would cost and compare this to how much it will cost to have the trust documents drawn up, how much time and/or money it will cost to transfer ownership of all your assets, and how important it is for you to keep disposition of your estate private.

LIVING WILLS AND DURABLE POWERS OF ATTORNEY

A *living will* is a document that outlines what medical care and emergency measures you do and don't want done to preserve your life if you are incapacitated and cannot make your wishes known to your physicians and family. It covers strictly medical matters, including, but not limited to, the use of painkillers, feeding tubes, and artificial respiratory or cardiac aids. Even if your state doesn't yet recognize living wills as legally binding, the fact that you have formally declared your wishes can be crucial if the matter has to go to court. A *durable power of attorney* is a document that gives someone else the power and authority to act on your behalf, regardless of your subsequent disability or incompetence. Its scope can be as broad or limited as you wish, including everything from the removal of life supports to signing checks or selling assets. Bear in mind that in some states, durable powers of attorney must be officially recorded to be valid. In effect, the living will makes your wishes known, and the durable power of attorney gives someone you trust the power to follow those wishes. That's why I urge my clients to have both of these documents drafted simultaneously with drawing up a will.

FOR MORE INFORMATION . . .

You can learn more about wills, living wills, and living trusts from the following books:
- *Loving Trust* by Robert A. Esperti and Renno L. Peterson
- *The Do It Yourself Will Kit* by SJT Enterprises
- *The Essential Guide to a Living Will* by B. D. Colen
- *The Living Trust Handbook* by David E. Miller
- *Understanding Living Trusts* by Vickie and Jim Schumacher

EXTENDED WARRANTIES AND SERVICE CONTRACTS

Taking Out Insurance on Your Purchases

Salespeople today take a double-barreled approach to consumers. First they sell the product, then they sell a service contract or extended warranty. Sales of these product-insurance policies topped $1 billion last year and involve everything from autos to appliances.

Retailers push these contracts because there is often more profit in the sale of them than in the product itself. Generally there is at least a 100 percent markup on service contracts and extended warranties. This can be an incredible boon to a retailer in a competitive industry that works on small margins.

Product-insurance policies fall into two different categories. Some retailers who have their own service facilities peddle their own. Other dealers, usually those who do not offer in-house repairs, buy contracts at wholesale from large companies that handle the administration of the service program. These administrator companies then either reimburse the dealer for repairs made or arrange to farm the work out to repair shops. Both types of contracts cover the cost of most repairs (parts and labor) and sometimes provide for the replacement of equipment with chronic problems.

These agreements are often complex documents with page after page of provisions and clauses. If you are considering the purchase of a service contract, you should first check to see if there is a deductible. Then try to figure out exactly what is and isn't covered. If something is not mentioned in the contract, then it isn't covered.

Look for mandatory maintenance, which may involve additional fees. Find out if it is possible to buy the contract at a later date, perhaps after the manufacturer's warranty expires. See if you can determine exactly who is responsible for fulfilling the terms of the contract—the dealer or the administrative company—and investigate their reputation.

Check if the contract provides for in-home service, or if the product must be brought to a shop. If you must carry the product in, where would you have to bring it? Finally, ask what happens if you move. Will your contract only be valid with this particular dealer or repair shop?

Try to compare the cost of the service contract with the cost of potential repairs. For example, a one-year service contract for a small television costs on average $30, while repairs would run $35 per hour; a one-year service contract for a personal computer runs approximately $80, while repairs cost $50 per hour.

While extended warranties and service contracts sound like good deals when the salesperson pitches them to you, they generally don't stand up to close scrutiny. Generally, if a product doesn't break down within the period covered by the manufacturer's warranty, it isn't a lemon, so you can assume that it will have an acceptable service life. If a salesperson touts the product's reliability to you, how can they then justify selling you an extended warranty? It makes more sense to spend a little bit more up front and buy the most reliable product you can afford.

Finally, the mathematics of the purchase don't work. Let's say you buy a videocassette recorder for $300 and a service contract for $40 per year. After maintaining the contract for three years you have already paid $120. At that point you are betting that the repairs will cost more than the $120 you have already invested in the contract, which is unlikely. And even if they did, wouldn't it make more sense just to buy another one?

Buying a service contract or extended warranty almost never works out to be cheaper than simply paying the repair bill yourself. Even if you put a product through heavy use, or if your budget won't allow for a surprise repair bill, it makes more sense to select the best product you can afford and then rely on the manufacturer's reliability and your own judgment.

FINANCIAL PLANNERS

Selecting Someone to Help Manage Your Money

Icreasingly Americans are turning to financial planners to help manage their investments and savings. Accountants, excellent at keeping track of your money and advising on tax strategies, are not always well versed in the wide range of investment options available. Attorneys, expert on the legal and contractual ramifications of investments, may not have the financial savvy to provide sound guidance. Financial planners have emerged to fill this professional gap. They study and evaluate the multitude of financial products now available and can guide consumers to the products that best suit their needs.

Unfortunately, financial planning is one of America's newest professions and as such, is still formulating its codes of ethics and standards. At present, there are no specific qualifications required before you can call yourself a financial planner. The initials CFP—which stand for certified financial planner—after a person's name indicate that he or she has graduated from an eighteen-month training course at Denver's College of Financial Planning or one of the colleges that have purchased a franchise from the college . . . but that's all the initials indicate. They do not represent adherence to an accepted code of ethics and standards. Anyone can become a certified financial planner, and many salespersons—such as insurance agents and stockbrokers—are using the title to wrap their selling efforts in the garb of professional advice. All that's required to register as an investment advisor is to pay a small fee to the Securities and Exchange Commission and sign a statement swearing never to have violated any securities laws. Until the profession institutes a code of ethics and standards, and begins to police itself, vigilance will be left up to the consumer.

One way to find a financial planner who is accountable is to look for those with either an accounting or legal background. Besides indicating a solid financial and educational background, it makes them accountable for their actions. If they are CPAs or members of a bar association, they must adhere to accepted standards of behavior and a code of ethics in order to keep their licenses. At the very least the financial planner should have at least a master's degree in business or finance.

Financial planners earn their living in one of two ways: by charging an hourly fee for their services like other professionals; or by earning a commission on the sale of financial instruments. Make sure you work only with a planner who charges an hourly fee. Those who work by commission are more interested in matching you up with one of their products than in tailoring a plan that suits your needs. They are salespersons in disguise. Similarly, avoid financial planners who work for one specific company, or who specialize in one particular type of financial instrument. Their advice is automatically biased toward their company's products or their specialty. Request printed verification of the planner's fee structure and study it before making a final decision.

Keep your eye out for independent planners or those with small firms. They are more apt to have expertise in dealing with middle-class investors. Large financial-planning firms often specialize in preparing complex packages for highly paid corporate executives or extremely wealthy investors. Only consider hiring planners who have at least five years full-time experience. You do not want someone to learn the ropes using your life savings.

Searching for a financial planner is one time where it is better to ignore recommendations from friends, coworkers, and relatives and stick with names supplied by your existing professional team. Tell your accountant and lawyer exactly what you are looking for in a planner, and ask them to make some recommendations. Contact your banker and ask for his or her input as well. This should help you avoid fly-by-night operators or salespersons since the accountant, attorney, or banker is putting his or her reputation and judgment on the line by making such a recommendation.

Once you have developed a list of potential candidates, put them through the same interview process you use when selecting the other members of your professional team, and seal your relationship with an engagement letter.

Financial planners can be of tremendous help in establishing a savings and growth investment plan and in laying the foundation for retirement, and therefore, they are an excellent addition to your professional team. But since their profession is still in the early stages of development, without a solid and enforceable code of ethics and behavior, it is especially important for you to find someone who suits your needs, whose judgment you trust, and who can withstand the intense scrutiny of a thorough interview and reference check. But while their input and advice can be invaluable, you must not simply place your finances in their hands. In the final analysis, you are responsible for your own finances.

AVOIDING MONEY MANAGEMENT MISTAKES

I firmly believe that everyone should manage his or her own money. No advisor, regardless of how caring or intelligent, can take care of your finances as well as you can—as long as you avoid these all-too-common mistakes:

- Investing in something without understanding it fully. Never agree to buy something unless you understand exactly how it works, what the risks are, and what the potential rewards are. The magic question to ask a salesperson is "Why?"
- Forgetting to keep tabs on your investments. Don't hide your head in the sand. Read the financial pages every week to see how your investments are doing. Don't overdo it and be misled by the knee-jerk reactions of the stock market or one-sixteenth shifts in price, however.
- Not setting goals and limits to stock purchases. When you buy a stock, establish one price at which you would be happy to sell and take a profit, and another at which you would take the loss and sell. When either price is reached, take the appropriate action.
- Making investments for tax purposes. While tax shelters may provide you with write-offs, they may also lose you a great deal of money. Your first consideration has to be the integrity of the investment.
- Basing investments on other people's experiences. Just because your brother made a bundle in pork bellies doesn't mean you should make the same investment. Everyone's circumstances and personality are different. Your investment decisions should be custom-made.

DEALING WITH STOCKBROKERS

One of the biggest mistakes stock investors make is believing that their stockbroker is a good source of financial advice. On the contrary, stockbrokers are salespeople, and like other salespeople, some are honest and some are dishonest. Unscrupulous brokers—known as churners and burners—will try to persuade you to buy and sell constantly since they earn a commission on every transaction. Similarly, some brokers engage in "cold calling." They telephone people at random offering "inside tips" on good stocks to buy. At most you can count on your stockbroker to carry out your buying and selling orders, to provide you with research on specific stocks, and to furnish you with the latest price information. They should not be used as sources of advice. The decision to buy or sell a specific stock must be based on your own research and judgment, not on the whims of your broker.

STEERING CLEAR OF FINANCIAL-PERSONALITY ANALYSES

Some financial planners, with the assistance of psychotherapists, have taken to using personality testing in their practices. The catch is that rather than using psychological insights to get a clearer understanding of their clients' needs and wants, they are using them to pinpoint which products and what type of sales appeals clients will be most apt to buy—regardless of whether it is in their best interest. If any financial planner asks you to take a personality test, get up from your chair and walk out the door.

FINE PRINT

Heinous Clauses in Innocuous Agreements

When we enter into formal contracts with other parties—if we are prepared and knowledgeable—we can spot potential problems lurking in the fine print of the agreements. But most of us don't realize that we enter into hundreds of less formal contracts each week, and that they too contain fine-print clauses that take away our rights and limit our recourses.

Almost every time a dollar changes hands, or services are performed, an enforceable contract is created. The process of creating a contract can be extremely subtle. Legally binding agreements do not have to be in writing and can be formed by shaking hands, verbally agreeing to something, or even just accepting a receipt or claim check.

Because we live in such a litigious society, businesses use every possible self-protection device. That has resulted in a trend toward making written agreements even more complex, and making subtle nonwritten contracts more subject to restrictions and provisions often hidden on the back of receipts or posted on signs. While these efforts by businesses are understandable, they are often blatantly unfair to the consumer, and sometimes even illegal.

The preparers of contracts containing these illegal clauses are well aware that they wouldn't be able to enforce these provisions in a court, but they know that the mere presence of the clause will scare off 90 percent of the people affected and keep them from ever challenging it. Of the remaining 10 percent, 5 percent will settle out of court, and only the remaining 5 percent will take the matter to court.

The best way to avoid being bound by unfair or illegal clauses is to be aware of their presence and to challenge them before entering into the agreement. Read everything you are asked to sign before signing, including the fine print. If the contract involves a sum of more than $500, consult an attorney before signing it.

Most importantly, remember that there is no such thing as a

standard contract. You are completely within your rights to try to negotiate, cross out provisions, lengthen the amount of time you are given to do things, and to change any language you don't agree with. On the other hand, the other party has the right not to accept your changes and to call off the agreement or transaction.

Another way to avoid particularly heinous clauses in agreements is simply to state your refusal to accept certain provisions. For example, you can tell the other party, "Under these conditions I am forced to sign this agreement, but that doesn't mean I accept all its conditions." If you are pressed for time, you can state, "It is unreasonable to expect me to read the whole agreement under these conditions, so I cannot be bound by any unreasonable clauses." Even a simple "I don't understand this agreement" is likely to stand up in court if your disagreement ever gets there.

Here are some truly heinous clauses to look for in seemingly innocuous agreements and some ways of diffusing them:

AIRLINE TICKETS AND BAGGAGE

Airlines make every effort to limit their liabilities. The fine print in your agreement with them, which may appear on the back of the ticket or on the envelope containing the ticket, contains language that lets the airline off the hook if there are changes in time of departure or arrival or even final destination. Another provision gives the airline the right to overbook a flight and force ticket holders off the plane. Further clauses obligate the passenger to present a claim for damaged or lost luggage within seven days, and to provide proof of the value of the luggage and its contents.

Unfortunately, you can do little to remove these clauses. Even if you can convince an airline representative to cross out the offending clauses, another clause in the ticket states that no oral changes are binding and that airline representatives have no right to make changes to the agreement. Your only defense is to be aware of airline rules. First, before anyone can be bumped from an overbooked flight, the airline must solicit volunteers. Second, even if you are forced off the flight, the airline must provide you with a seat on the next available flight and compensate you in some manner. The form of compensation varies from airline to airline, but may include a stay at a hotel, a free meal, or a reduced-rate ticket.

AUTO PURCHASE AGREEMENTS

A standard clause in auto purchase agreements states that the purchase price is based on the date of delivery, not the date of purchase. This clause can spell trouble if you are not buying a car already on the lot. The price and provisions of the agreement you signed may no longer apply when the car actually arrives. For example, on the day you signed the purchase agreement there may have been a $1,000 rebate in effect. If it expires before you accept delivery of the car, the rebate no longer applies. Similarly, if a manufacturer's price increases between the time you order the car and the time you take delivery, you will have to pay the higher price.

You can avoid this trap by striking out the clause before you sign the original agreement, or if the dealer won't let you cross out the clause, state loudly and clearly your understanding that the price you agree to now will be applicable whenever you accept delivery of the car.

AUTOMOBILE RENTAL AGREEMENTS

Many auto rental contracts contain a clause which states that you are responsible for all damages to the vehicle in case of an accident if you do not accept, and pay, the rental company's insurance charge. Other clauses may require you to waive your right to a jury trial; waive your right to a countersuit; and appear in a legal jurisdiction of the rental company's choosing. Adding insult to injury, if you use the express checkout procedure, you may not even have a copy of the agreement or a receipt.

Don't fall for the insurance clause. It is a sales trick to get you to buy the company's insurance. Your own auto insurance or your credit card company provides better coverage than the rental car company, and it costs nothing. Strike out and initial any other heinous clauses in the agreement as evidence that you did not want to be bound by them.

HEALTH CLUB AND EXERCISE STUDIO MEMBERSHIP AGREEMENTS

The most offensive provision fund in health club and exercise studio membership agreements is that you may be locked into a long-term contract that offers few opportunities for you to cancel it. The business may move to another location, or you could become physically unable to use the facilities, yet you would still be bound to pay monthly fees. What few cancellation rights are offered often stipulate that you provide up to three months' notification.

The solution to this is to refuse to sign any membership agreement that stretches more than three years. In addition, make sure that you have the right to cancel your membership and receive a refund if the studio moves or you are physically unable to use its facilities. If you are signing an agreement with a studio that has not yet opened its doors, make sure that there is a clause stating that any deposits you make must be placed in an escrow account and cannot be used for preopening expenses. Add language that says that if the studio does not open by a specific date, you are entitled to a refund of your deposit payments.

PARKING LOT TICKETS

Owners and operators of parking lots and garages try to limit their liability by posting signs around the premises and printing disclaimers on the backs of their tickets. The most common disclaimer is that the lot or garage is not responsible for the theft of anything left in the car. Other clauses may require you to make a damage claim before leaving or to have the car repaired at a place of the owner's choosing. Some of the more legally astute operators add provisions placing the burden of proof on you, limiting the time within which you can take legal actions, and limiting their total liability to an obscenely low figure.

Despite all their efforts, and regardless of what their tickets or signs say, parking lot or garage owners and operators are liable for any damages or losses that result when your car is in their care . . . if they are in possession of your keys. The only added step you should take to protect yourself is to put the attendant on notice either that there is something fragile about the car or that there is something valuable inside it.

SPORTS TICKETS

On the back of every sports ticket there is a printed statement limiting the stadium's liability and stating that the ticket holder assumes all the risks of entering the facility.

This disclaimer sounds more impressive than it really is. While you do assume some risks, such as those common to the event, you do not assume all risks. You do assume the risk of being hit by a hockey puck, since that is part of the game. But you do not assume the risk of being hit by a skater's stick if he angrily climbs in the stands to attack a heckler. If that happens, the player, the team, the stadium, and the league can be held liable.

CERTIFICATE-OF-DEPOSIT AGREEMENTS

Many times certificate-of-deposit agreements contain a provision stating that the bank is allowed to roll over the investment at the current rate of interest for the same period of time as previously if you do not take any action. That can be disastrous if you had locked your money up in a three-year CD when rates were high and have had it rolled over into another three-year instrument when rates are low.

You can work around this provision by simply sending a letter to your bank telling them that none of your investments are to be rolled over without your specific instructions. Instruct them to place your investment in a money market account if they do not receive specific instructions from you.

SECURITIES BROKERAGE AGREEMENTS

Invariably, these contracts force you to waive your right to trial by jury and submit any dispute to an arbitration panel—a panel stacked in the brokerage house's favor. In addition, some of these agreements give you only five or ten days to contest a mistake in your account statement. Finally, these documents may also contain a provision requiring you to pay a minimum fee to the brokerage house if your account didn't generate a certain amount of commission fees.

There is probably no way you can avoid the waiver of trial by jury. Your only hope in that regard is that many states are in the process of making such a waiver illegal. If you have substantial leverage with the brokerage house, you may be able to eliminate the minimum-fee provision. Even if you are only an average customer, you should be able to increase your time to contest possible mistakes to at least thirty days.

ADDING A MAGIC WORD

The simple insertion of one word into the language of a contract can make all the difference in the world. Every time a contract mentions that you have a specific number of days within with to take an action, insert the word *business* before the word *days*. The added two days that often result can help give you some breathing room.

THE UNIVERSAL RIDER

The following rider, if added to a contract, can help protect you from even the most heinous of clauses or provisions:

"We are about to enter into a business transaction that I expect you to conduct in the customary way. I will not agree to any provision of any document or posted sign unless you point it out to me and tell me you will not do business unless I agree. In any event, I do not agree to any waivers, releases, exculpatory clauses, jurisdictional matters, private periods of limitation, arbitration, payment of legal fees, or other costs or limitations upon your obligations and liabilities to me. Our mutual obligations are to be dependent on each other."

FOR MORE INFORMATION . . .

You can learn more about the fine print in contracts from the following book:
- *Sign Here?* by Mari W. Privette

FIRING EMPLOYEES

Doing It as Painlessly as Possible

It is never easy to fire someone. More often than not, you, as the person who did the hiring, are at least partially to blame for the problem. You are confronted with having to fire someone because you made a mistake in hiring him or her. That means that unless the employee has stolen from you or your business, you have an obligation to make things as painless and easy as possible for those you fire, and a responsibility to do everything in your power to speed their reentry into the job market. Of course, if you are firing for cause, you owe the employee nothing except a quick kick out the door.

A firing should be carefully planned. If at all possible, it should take place on a Friday afternoon. Not only does this ease bookkeeping and give some closure to the relationship, but the weekend gives some cushioning and reflective time to the fired employee.

Provide as much severance pay as possible, taking into consideration how easy or difficult it will be for the person to find another job. Look on severance pay as a way to make up for your mistake in hiring him or her in the first place.

It is important for all concerned that the firing be a quick and clean break of relations. That's why it is best to ask those fired to clean out their desks and leave right away. Don't allow former employees to use office facilities in their job searches—their presence will only lower the morale of others. If you feel compelled to help them, just add another week's pay to their severance checks. The longer they stick around after being fired, the more damage they will do to your operation.

Make your determination on severance pay prior to your meetings with them. Additionally, compose letters of reference and have them on hand when you call them in. Be cordial and straightforward. One good approach might be: "I'm sorry but our relationship is not working out. I am sure you are as aware of that as I am. Therefore I would like you to leave today. Here is a severance check and a letter of reference. I wish you the best and please feel free to use me as a reference."

While this approach may appear cold, it is in your best interest to make this discussion as short as possible. If you believe that there will be some type of emotional outburst, have another person—perhaps the individual's direct supervisor—on hand. People are much less likely to become emotional when there is a third party in the room. Remember, when you hire someone, you assume a responsibility that you then discharge when you fire them. It is your obligation to provide them with as much severance pay as you can afford and to remove them from the scene as quickly and quietly as possible.

FIRST JOBS

Looking for a Stream of Income Rather Than a Career

Most of us believe that, after graduating from college, we must go out and find a job in the field we have just spent four, or more, years studying—thereby justifying all the time, effort, and money that went into our acquiring a degree. If you are totally convinced of what you would like your career to be, that is a good decision. Since the one thing college couldn't supply you with was on-the-job experience, go out and find an entry-level position—whatever the salary—and get the hands-on knowledge and experience you will need to move further in your chosen career.

But if you aren't sure of what you want to do with the rest of your life, don't fall into the trap of looking for a job in a particular field simply because that is what is expected of you. It is absurd to think that someone at the age of twenty-one with no experience in the "real world" should know what he or she wants to do for the rest of his or her life. No golden rule says that your first job has to be the first step on your career path.

If you aren't sure of what you would like to do, look for jobs that provide a good stream of income, regardless of what future prospects they offer. And while you are working at your income-producing job, continue to think about and investigate your options. You can even hop around from field to field, looking for something that suits your personality and skills.

Of course, you can't become lazy during this period of your life and stop looking for a career. At some point, as your income reaches a certain level and your obligations and responsibilities grow, you will become locked into a field not of your own choosing. Entry-level positions for people on clear-cut career paths are notoriously low paying. In effect you are exchanging money for experience, putting in your dues, and looking for advancement. That is a trade-off that is much easier to pull off when you have few responsibilities.

This trade-off does not have to take place as soon as you leave college, however. It can be put off one, two, or even five years, until you have a firmer handle on exactly what you need and want from life. Your goal should be to put off making a decision until you are sure of what career you'd like to pursue, and then to devote all your energies to its pursuit. Don't wait for 100-percent certainty—it may never come. Simply go with your gut instincts. Even if you make a mistake, it's possible to shift careers: I've done it many times.

I became an attorney really by default. When I was in high school and college, my true love was the media. I had my own little radio show and loved giving advice and offering opinions. But one day I received a scholarship to law school. Considering my family's economic background, and the opportunities law school presented, I took the scholarship. But once I became an attorney, I wasn't completely happy. I still looked for other things to do. I became a real estate entrepreneur, then president of a Small Business Investment Corporation, and then a banker. It wasn't until I was forty-eight years old and had left my job for health reasons that I realized what I really wanted to do with my life was to be a legal/financial advisor, and to give advice through magazine articles and books, and on radio and television. It took me thirty years to get back to what I wanted to do when I was eighteen years old. I don't want you to have to wait that long.

FOR MORE INFORMATION . . .

You can learn more about finding a first job from the following books:
- *Careering and Re-Careering for the 1990's* by Ronald L. Krannich
- *Do What You Love and the Money Will Follow* by Marsha Sinetar
- *Guerrilla Tactics in the New Job Market* by Tom Jackson
- *The Job Bank Series* by Bob Adams, Inc. Publishers
- *What Color Is Your Parachute?* by Richard Nelson Bolles
- *Wishcraft: How to Get What You Really Want* by Barbara Sher

FUNERALS

Arranging Dignified yet Economical Farewells

The topic of death is—or at least should be—more open to discussion today. Just as our customs surrounding birth and marriage have evolved, reflecting society's changing attitudes and beliefs, so should our customs surrounding death and dying.

That doesn't mean, however, that the arranging of a funeral is a simple or easy task. Not only does it involve such sensitive and emotional issues as embalming and cremation, but it is often the third-largest expense most Americans will ever face, topped only by the purchase of a home and an automobile. In 1988 approximately $8 billion was spent on funerals, and the number continues to rise each year by about 7 percent. Today, a traditional funeral costs between $3,000 and $6,000—and that doesn't include the $500 to $1,500 required for a cemetery plot.

Making it even more difficult is the fact that Americans are facing these numbers when they are at their most vulnerable. They have lost a loved one who may or may not be the family's primary wage earner. Speed is often of the essence, if not due to religious requirements, then due to the pressures of having to remove the body either from the home or a medical facility. Few people ever make known their wishes for their own funerals, and fewer still make the necessary provisions, so the survivors are left with having to make decisions for them. Finally, the funeral industry has more than its share of shady salesmen eager to take advantage of grief and suffering.

The key to overcoming these seemingly insurmountable obstacles is to have the right attitude. Unless you have been given specific instructions by the deceased—either verbally or in writing—you are acting as the agent of the deceased's estate, not the deceased themselves. Bear in mind that the deceased is totally unconcerned about the event and will never express his or her disappointment. Your obligation is to spend the estate's money as prudently as possible. The cost of the funeral is not an indication of how much you love or respect the deceased. Love and respect are demonstrated by how much you feel, not how much you pay.

Far too many people limit their options by immediately selecting one particular funeral home—either because of family history or proximity—and placing their loved one, and their open
wallets, in the funeral director's hands. Instead, it is incumbent
on you to do some comparison shopping. Realizing the pressures
that consumers are under, the Federal Trade Commission has
passed regulations that require funeral homes to provide price
information to consumers over the telephone.

Call all the funeral homes in your immediate area for price
information. There is no such thing as a Jewish funeral home, an
African-American funeral home, an Italian funeral home, a Cath-
olic funeral home, an Irish funeral home, a Protestant funeral
home, or a Hispanic funeral home. These ethnic associations are
marketing techniques, nothing more, and should have no impact
on your selection.

Explain to the funeral director exactly what you are looking
for. Simple and traditional arrangements not only cost less, but
are also more dignified. Steer clear of funeral home packages,
which are often padded with unnecessary and expensive add-
ons. Instead, buy à la carte. Be candid with the funeral director
about your ability to pay, and remember that all prices are negotiable. If you have any doubts about the value of shopping around
and negotiating, you should pay careful attention to this list of
funeral products and services and their price ranges:

Body preparation	$50–250
Casket	$200–25,000
Chapel	$75–200
Clergy	$25–350
Clothing	$25–100+
Coordination of service	$100–350
Cremation	$150–950
Embalming	$100–400
Entombment in mausoleum	$1,500–25,000
Flowers	$10–1,000+
Funeral director fees	$350–2,000
Headstones	$800–15,000
Hearse	$100–125
Limousine	$75–125
Long-distance shipping of remains	±$2,500
Motorcycle escorts	$75–150

Music	$15–100+
Niche for urn	$150–8,000
Refrigeration of body per day	$50–125
Traditional burial cemetery charges	$900–11,000
Transporting remains to funeral home	$50–300
Urn for Cremains	$25–300
Utility or lead car	$50–100
Visitation room	$50–300

Packages

Standard package	$750–2,000
Luxury package	$2,000–4,000
Direct cremation	$350–1,000
Immediate burial	$425–1,250
Memorial Society direct cremation	$150–600
Memorial Society immediate burial	$400–857

When considering what products and services you will require, bear in mind that embalming is not necessary for either health or sanitation reasons and has no long-term preservative effect on the body; that caskets and vault liners, regardless of their construction or composition, do not preserve the body or prevent decomposition; and that you do not need to buy a casket for a cremation—a simple cardboard box should suffice, or if the body is to be viewed, a casket can be rented from the funeral home for between $250 and $500.

I believe that the most positive way to deal with death, provide a conduit for profound feelings and memories, and to say final farewells is to arrange for the speedy disposition of the body—through direct burial or immediate cremation—and to hold a memorial service, without the body present, and at a place that holds meaning for everyone involved. Much of the overspending at funerals involves showing family and friends how we have cared for the body of the deceased through embalming, clothing, and elaborate caskets. This is eliminated by not having a public display of the body. In addition, by not having the body present at a memorial service, everyone involved is given a chance to center their feelings and memories on the life of the deceased, not on their death.

Finally, let all this information serve as the jolt that finally convinces you to prearrange your own funeral, either by joining a memorial society, telling your family and friends of your wishes, or by drafting a letter expressing your desires. Prearrangement will save money and keep your family from having to go through the pain and turmoil of having to do it for you.

GIFT GIVING

Taking the Hassle out of December Shopping

December gift giving has become an expensive and time-consuming chore. When the occasion involves just one purchase, such as a birthday or anniversary, shopping for the right gift is usually both fast and enjoyable. But when the occasion involves buying multiple gifts for very different individuals, the process can be a strain on both your budget and brain. Here are some tips for taking the stress out of this yearly headache.

Begin by making a list of everyone you will be shopping for, including family, friends, and business associates. The family and friends portions of the list are easy . . . it's when you get to business associates that problems often come up. Definitely add your immediate staff to the list, but only give gifts to all employees if bonuses aren't given. Make sure to include important clients, customers, and consultants. There is no reason to give gifts to your superiors or your professionals. If you made a list last year, check it first for changes in personnel, and second for deletions. Just because you gave some a gift last year doesn't mean you have to perpetuate the practice. Write down the home addresses of all those on your list and have gifts sent to them there. Not only will this eliminate the problem of lugging boxes and bags home from the office, but it will sidestep any possible envy.

Deciding on a budget for gifts to family and friends is a personal decision. But don't overspend—it really is the thought that counts. In addition, there is absolutely no reason to increase the amount you spend on gifts each year. Thankfully, business gift giving has some guidelines. The IRS allows you to deduct up to $25 for each business gift. If you spend any more than that, include holiday gifts in your advertising and promotion budget. It is customary to spend $15 to $25 on gifts for your staffers, but top assistants might merit a little more. Most companies spend approximately $50 on their regular customers, but an important client might merit a gift closer to $100 in value. Of course, take your company's overall size into consideration. No one expects a home-based consultant to send the same gift as a Big Eight accounting firm.

Shopping this time of year can be stressful and time-consuming. After Thanksgiving you should avoid stores all weekend long and on weekdays between noon and five P.M. If you can, use a department store's corporate gift department or personal shopper. While catalog shopping usually requires placing orders well in advance of the holidays, some mail order companies will ship gifts by Federal Express or UPS Air.

Your gift selection should reflect the recipient's tastes and interests, not your own. Avoid gift certificates and cash, items with company logos, and works of art. Enclose handwritten note cards rather than your business card. Make a note of some salient fact about each person on your list—for example, loves to cook, avid skier, frequent traveler. When shopping for children, avoid fads and stick with classic books or videotapes. If someone enjoys imbibing, opt for wine or champagne, not liquor.

Memberships and subscriptions are often excellent choices since your thoughtfulness will be remembered over and over again. Personalized gifts—monogrammed, etched, or engraved—show that you thought enough to plan in advance. Books work well for almost everyone, as long as your selection reflects the recipient's interests. When in doubt, stick with traditional gifts such as scarves, fountain pens, umbrellas, and picture frames. Even better, give a gift that truly reflects the meaning of the season and make a contribution in the recipient's name to a worthwhile charity.

GOVERNMENT

Getting Elected Officials to Work for You

Americans are always griping about how little the federal government does for them, despite all the dollars they pay in taxes, yet nine out of ten people never write or telephone their elected representatives. Most of us feel that Washington is another world, and that our elected representatives are too busy dealing with grave and important matters to bother with the problems of one lone constituent who didn't donate $10,000 to their reelection committee.

This common feeling is completely unfounded, however. The single best way to get action out of the federal government is to write a letter. But for this simple technique to work the letter has to be directed to the right place and written in the right manner.

First, regardless of what your problem is, and what part of the vast federal bureaucracy it involves, bypass the civil servants who work in government agencies and write directly to your congressional representative. Congressmen rely on the support of their constituents to keep their jobs; civil servants do not. As incredible as it may sound, you will get more attention and service from a well-known congressman than from an unknown midlevel clerk in an obscure agency.

Your letter should be written on your personal or business stationery, so that it stands out from all of the bulk mail and form letters that the congressman receives. Begin your letter by clearly stating exactly where you live and that you are a constituent of the congressman. Be polite, clear, and concise, and concentrate on one particular issue. The letter should read like an appeal for help, not a litany of complaints and threats.

Don't be disappointed if you receive a response from a congressional aide rather than directly from the congressman—aides generally handle the bulk of constituent service work and often have quite a bit of clout. If you receive a form letter in response to your personal letter, feel free to write back and complain. Explain that you are disappointed in receiving a form letter, and that the congressman has not answered your question or addressed your concern.

If you still don't receive an adequate response, pick up the telephone and try contacting the congressman directly. Feel free to badger and prod your elected representatives continually until you get the response you want. Remember, they work for you.

SAMPLE LETTER TO A CONGRESSIONAL REPRESENTATIVE

Dear Representative Smith:

I have been a resident of the Sixth Congressional District for twenty-five years. I have always respected and admired your efforts on behalf of your constituents. At this time I must reach out to you for help. Six months ago I mistakenly flushed my social security check down the toilet. I have been trying to get the Social Security Administration to issue a replacement check to me, but all of my inquiries have been met with callous and unresponsive behavior on their part. I am hoping that you can use your good offices and take time out of your busy schedule to help me resolve this problem. I look forward to hearing from you or your staff soon.

CONTACTING YOUR CONGRESSIONAL REPRESENTATIVE

Letters to members of the House of Representatives can be mailed to either their local offices—the addresses should be listed in either the front or rear of your local telephone directory—or directly to the U.S. Capitol, Washington, DC 20515. Local and Washington, DC, telephone numbers of representatives should be listed in your telephone directory as well. They can also be obtained by calling the Capitol Building at (202) 224-3121. If you don't know your representative's name, telephone your local newspaper.

GRATUITIES

When, How Much, and Whom to Tip

Tipping in America has changed dramatically in the past twenty years. Tips originated as cash rewards for providing exceptional service. Today, however, many businesses—notably restaurants—underpay their employees, assuming that tips from customers will supplement their income.

In addition to tipping's becoming required, there are no real rules to go by. In some restaurants, tips are incorporated into your bill as an added surcharge. Other restaurants place all monies collected as tips into a pool, which the employees split. Some greedy employers even require employees to kick back a portion or all of their tips.

The solution to all the confusion surrounding tipping in restaurants is to follow some simple rules:

- If a restaurant incorporates a service charge into your bill, do not leave a tip regardless of how stupendous service was.
- Never tip because you've been intimidated either by the waiter/ waitress or the maître d'. You are entitled to normal, courteous service.
- Since restaurants chronically underpay employees, automatically leave a 10 percent tip. Consumers should not be responsible for filling in the salary gap created by greedy restaurant owners. An automatic 10 percent helps supplement the waitress's or waiter's income while reinforcing the notion that a tip is really for extraordinary service.
- If restaurant service is above average, tip 15 percent. If service is exceptional, make it 20 percent.
- If you are waited on by many people—captain, waiter, busboy, wine steward, etc.—simply leave one total amount of 20 to 25 percent, which the staff can split up themselves.
- If you are charged for checking your coat, do not tip the attendant; otherwise, tip $1 per coat. If you see a metal strongbox at the coat-check window, be wary: that generally means that management, rather than the employee, is collecting the tips.

- If you are drinking at the bar, a 15 percent tip for the bartender is appropriate. However, if you are asked to sit at the bar while waiting for a table, you do not have to order a drink or tip the bartender. If you do order a drink while waiting for your table, ask the bartender to put it on your dinner check.
- Never tip the maître d' if he or she is also the owner of the restaurant. If you want to improve your chances at getting a good table, $20 concealed in a handshake may help, but it's no guarantee. If you wish to become a favored regular, an occasional $10 or $20 slipped to the maître d' will nurture goodwill.
- If you are unhappy with the service at a restaurant, discuss your problem with the waiter or waitress, and if necessary, speak to the manager. Stiffing is really not appropriate unless the service is utterly abysmal.

Unfortunately, in today's world, tipping has become expected and is used by employers as an excuse to pay lower salaries. Even though you didn't hire these people, you have been forced to pay what amounts to a sizable portion of their salary. But that doesn't mean you have to go overboard. Leave a standard 10 percent tip to assuage your guilt, and only add to it if you receive more than minimal service.

TIPPING IN BEAUTY PARLORS AND BARBERSHOPS

While tips may vary based on how exclusive the shop is, the following are accepted standards: haircutter—10 to 20 percent of the bill; manicurist or pedicurist—15 to 20 percent of the bill; hair coloring or permanent—10 percent; hair washer—$1 to $2.

TIPPING HOTEL PERSONNEL

Gratuities for hotel personnel often depend on the size and exclusivity of the hotel and the length of your stay, but these are some rules you can go by: bellhops—$.50 to $1 per bag; maid service—$1 per day, but only for stays of more than one night; room service waiter—15 percent of bill; concierge—based on whether or not services are used, $5 to $20 upon arrival ensures attentive service.

TIPPING SKYCAPS

It is traditional to give these airport personnel $1 per bag; more if the bags are extremely large or heavy, such as trunks, crates, or cartons.

TIPPING TAKE-OUT FOOD DELIVERY PEOPLE

Giving these people $.50 or $1 is sufficient, but 10 to 15 percent of the bill may be more appropriate if you are a regular customer.

TIPPING VALET PARKING OR GARAGE ATTENDANTS

Normally you should give these attendants $.50 per car, but if you are in a major city, $1 is more appropriate.

TIPPING TAXI DRIVERS

Ten to fifteen percent of the bill is the traditional tip for a taxi driver, but if they drive dangerously, are obnoxious, or don't help you with your bags, stiffing is entirely appropriate.

TIPPING NEWSPAPER DELIVERY PEOPLE

Most people give $.50 per week, but only if service is acceptable. One month's fee is a standard Christmas tip.

TIPPING APARTMENT PERSONNEL

Gratuities in apartment buildings depend on the size and quality of the building, but these are some general guidelines: superintendent—Christmas tip of from $25 to $100, other special work may merit from $5 to $20 per job; doormen—Christmas tip of from $10 to $50, helping with small packages does not merit a tip, but aid with a large load merits from $5 to $10. Tips may be given quarterly rather than just at Christmas, if the building staff turns over often.

HEALTH INSURANCE

Selecting the Best Type of Coverage

Health insurance costs are skyrocketing, creating a crisis environment in which both businesses and individuals are searching for any way to cut down on their exorbitant monthly premiums. And until the medical profession and the government finally come around and realize the pressing need for some form of national health insurance, the situation will only get worse.

The simplest method to cut down your health insurance bill is to increase your deductible and become more of a self-insurer. Since the real purpose of health insurance is to provide a safety net in case of catastrophe, it makes sense to take a policy that has as large a deductible as you can afford—$500 or $1,000, for example—and be prepared to foot up to that amount of medical bills yourself. But this effort at self-insuring doesn't offer enough savings for some businesses and individuals. This has led to the creation of two new forms of medical coverage—the health maintenance organization (HMO) and the health insurance plan (HIP)—that carry lower premiums.

The traditional form of health insurance is called major medical. Under this type of plan, the policyholder selects his or her own physician, pays the bill, and then submits a claim to the insurance company, which may then reject the claim, apply the amount to the policyholder's deductible, pay a percentage of the bill, or pay the entire amount. Whatever the case, the selection of the care-giver is up to the policyholder.

HIPs are medical plans that have a select list of member physicians, who provide care to policyholders. In order for care to be covered by the insurance plan, it must be given by a member physician—except in some emergency situations. HIPs have become a way for new doctors to market themselves and gather patients.

HMOs are medical plans that bring under one umbrella a cooperative group of physicians who have various specialties. These doctors are willing to accept medicare, medicaid, or to take their share of a yearly fee collected from policyholders. HMO physicians make a profit by keeping their overhead and expenses low.

The problem with HIPs and HMOs is that in exchange for lower fees they break down the doctor-patient relationship. Unfortunately, some HIP physicians become insensitive dictators, since they have a captive market of patients. HMOs often turn into impersonal assembly line dispensaries in which the doctor tries to maximize the number of patients he or she sees in a day in order to maximize profits. In both cases, the practitioners are no longer in competition with other physicians and so can become even more imperious and condescending to their patients. While we all too often elevate doctors to the status of demigods, at least by retaining the option to go elsewhere for care we prevent them from acting like total immortals.

HIPs and HMOs should be treated as a last resort, when it is absolutely impossible for you to afford major medical coverage. If you must lower your health insurance costs, rather than opting for either of these types of coverage, increase the deductible on your major medical policy and solicit bids from as many legitimate health insurance providers as you can find. Explore the option of joining a professional organization that offers medical coverage to its members. The doctor-patient relationship is at the heart of good medical care and should not be readily sacrificed for cost savings.

FOR MORE INFORMATION . . .

You can learn more about health insurance from the following books:

- *The Complete Book of Insurance* by William Kent Brunette
- *The Family Insurance Handbook* by Les Abromovitz
- *Winning the Insurance Game* by Ralph Nader and Wesley J. Smith

HOME-BASED BUSINESSES

Combining Entrepreneurship and an Improved
Lifestyle

More than 13 million Americans have found that by launching a home-based business they can substantially cut back on the amount of money they will need while simultaneously improving their quality of life. A home-based entrepreneur can work in an environment that encourages, rather than discourages, creativity; bring family and career goals back into proper balance; live and work anywhere that has telephone service; and continue to work no matter their age or physical condition. Many futurists predict home-based businesses will leap in popularity in the coming decade since they answer two increasingly important needs for Americans: financial independence and family stability.

While technology has progressed to the point where almost every business could conceivably be based in a home, legal restrictions on the use of residential property rule out using your home as the base for a retail, manufacturing, or wholesale business. That doesn't necessarily limit you just to starting a service business. Ingenuity is the rule with home entrepreneurship, and many savvy individuals have been able to come up with legitimate ways around possible restrictions. Traditional retail sales may be out of the question, but mail order catalog operations can easily be run from a home location. Similarly, a home office can serve as the nerve center of a wholesale or manufacturing business that has separate storage and factory facilities.

Even though home entrepreneurship lends itself to innovative and inventive business approaches, it is still necessary to follow the same principles and practices as other traditional entrepreneurs. The only shortcut open to home-based entrepreneurs is that they need not find a location, come up with deposits for a landlord, or pay a monthly rent. You still have to come up with a good idea, draft a solid business plan with sound financial projections, put together a team of professional advisors, acquire sufficient seed and operating capital, set up a system of financial management, and launch an effective marketing program. Any shortcuts you take in the process are foolish and will only speed up your reentry into the job market.

The home-based entrepreneur faces three unique problems in establishing and maintaining a business: furnishing and equipping an office; clarifying his or her tax status; and overcoming discriminatory and disruptive attitudes.

FURNISHING AND EQUIPPING THE HOME OFFICE

The single most important thing when equipping a home office is to keep your plans realistic and affordable. A home office is imperfect by its very nature; compromises will have to be made in order for both home and office functions to coexist peacefully. Remodeling and construction, a potential way to avoid compromises, are so expensive that they basically eliminate the financial advantages gained by operating from your home. In addition, money spent to remodel your home to make it more officelike will never be recovered in the sale of the home.

Even though perfection is out of the question, there are certain minimum standards you should set. Look for an area that measures at least 144 square feet (twelve by twelve), has its own door, and is outside the normal daytime flow of family traffic. It should have a window and be easily heated and cooled. Try to locate your office near the convenience of a bathroom, but away from the temptation of the kitchen.

With a site for your office selected, the next step is to buy furniture and equipment. Many home entrepreneurs, in an effort to compensate for lingering feelings that a home-based business isn't a "real" business, overspend on their furniture and equipment. Don't fall into that trap. Buy only what you need and can afford based on your budget and projections. The three most important rules for buying home office furniture and equipment are:

1. Buy only as much as you need;
2. Durability is the priority; and
3. All other things being equal, buy the smaller product.

The most important piece of equipment in any home office is the telephone. Since no one expects to get a busy signal when calling an office, have two lines installed, or if that is too expensive, get call waiting. Conference call capability is great, but worthwhile only if you will use it at least once per week. Call forwarding, on the other hand, is totally unnecessary.

Choose reliability over gimmicks when buying a telephone. Hold buttons and speed dialing are sensible features to look for. Speakerphones, however, are simply for ego boosting. If you intend to have clients come to your office, buy a separate extension telephone for their use so they don't have to sit at your desk to place or take a call. Finally, forget about car telephones. They are dangerous, expensive, and unnecessary. Use telephone booths instead.

After buying a telephone, find yourself a telephone answering machine. Look for a two-line, voice-activated, remote-controllable unit that lets you vary after how many rings the machine answers the call.

Your next purchase should be a typewriter or a computer. If you are having problems deciding which to buy, go with the computer—the added capabilities will more than make up for the added cost in the long term. Buy a laser printer—they are quick, quiet, and turn out exceptionally professional-looking documents. Their cost can be offset by using them to produce letterheads, printed envelopes, business cards, graphics, transparencies, and promotional materials. If you can't afford one, opt for a letter-quality printer; dot-matrix units generally do not produce business-quality printouts.

Facsimile machines are a must today. Don't get caught spending big bucks on a high-speed machine. Instead, spend your money on features such as a document feeder and a built-in page cutter. You only need a facsimile machine with memory if you regularly send messages overseas.

Don't buy a photocopier unless you spend more than one hour per week at a copy shop. Avoid using your facsimile machine to make copies since the paper is expensive and the copies fade quickly. If you must buy a copier, opt for a small workhorse with few bells and whistles. The more features it has the more often it will break down.

The single most important piece of furniture in your office is your desk chair. You will be spending more than eight hours a day in it, so make sure it's comfortable. Forget about using an old kitchen chair. Your desk, on the other hand, can be a converted dining room table. Don't worry: no one intelligent is going to measure your professionalism by your office equipment or furniture. Only buy as many filing cabinets as you need. Excess files can always be stored in a closet, garage, or attic. In addition, buy only as many supplies as you need. Bulk discounts might be alluring, but they are only for people who have extra money and storage space.

CLARIFYING THE TAX STATUS OF A HOME BUSINESS

The second obstacle peculiar to home businesses is their tax status. Surprisingly, the IRS rules and regulations governing home businesses are fairly straightforward. In order to deduct expenses for the business use of your home, you must actually be engaged in a trade or business. You are only allowed to deduct that portion of your home that is exclusively and regularly used as either a principal place of business or as a regular meeting place.

You are allowed to deduct expenses that are both directly and indirectly related to your business, but not personal expenses. Direct expenses are those that benefit only the business portion of your home, while indirect expenses are those that benefit both the business and nonbusiness parts of your home. The formula for determining how much of the total indirect expense is deductible is simple: divide it by the percentage of your home used exclusively and regularly for business. For example, if your heating bill for the month is $500 and you use 10 percent of your home for business, you can legitimately deduct 10 percent of the $500 expense, or $50. The IRS does not place a limit on the total amount of your deductions as long as they are less than, or equal to, your gross income. There is no record-keeping system required by the IRS. All you need is proof that you actually used your home office exclusively and regularly for business, and that you actually spent the expenses you are claiming.

OVERCOMING DISCRIMINATORY AND DISRUPTIVE ATTITUDES

The third obstacle unique to home-based entrepreneurs is to overcome the discriminatory and disruptive attitudes toward home businesses. Surprisingly, the first place to look for such problem attitudes is inside yourself.

Home-based entrepreneurs must be self-disciplined. Procrastination can bankrupt a business, and workaholism can destroy a family. The best way to avoid these two problems is to establish cues for starting and stopping work. Select a specific cue that signals you to begin your workday—a certain program coming on the radio or television for example—and another that signals the end of your day, perhaps leaving to pick up your spouse at the train station. In addition, establish routine behaviors throughout the day. Act as if you were in an informal, public office. That means getting washed and dressed each day, and having lunch and coffee breaks at a specific time. Become a fanatical scheduler and list maker, even noting errands and minor tasks on your calendar. Make it a rule to return all telephone calls the same day they are received, or at least the first thing the next morning. The flip side of all this obsessiveness is that once you leave your office, you should put your work behind you. Establish regular business hours and stick to them. If someone calls before or after those hours, let the answering machine pick up. No one expects a traditional businessperson to be available twenty-four hours a day, so why should you be any different?

Many times, the attitudes of family and friends can also disrupt a home-based business. They may feel that since you are working from your home, your business is somehow less demanding than a "real" business. They may feel free to drop in for a visit or to call frequently to chat. The only way to deal with family and friends is to be honest from day one. Tell your family and friends that you want them to act as if you were working in a formal office. Schedule friendly lunches the same way you would business meetings. If you are in the middle of working when someone calls to chat, tell them the truth and say you will get back to them after you are done.

Don't be misled into thinking that working at home will allow you to be a primary care-giver for your children. It is impossible to devote your time to both a business and a child; and in the attempt, one or the other is bound to suffer. Young children are not capable of differentiating between working and not working if both take place in the home. You will need some form of child care during your working hours. Older children will have to be given clear ground rules explaining when they can and cannot come into your office.

The final obstacle unique to home-based businesses is the discriminatory attitude of some clients toward them. Regardless of how well equipped or professionally designed your home office is, some clients will treat you less seriously simply because of your location. The best way around this bias is to schedule all your business meetings somewhere other than your office. If possible, arrange to meet clients at their offices. When protocol dictates that you host the meeting, hold it at a private club, hotel, or restaurant. When further camouflage is required, purchase space at a private postal drop or rent a post office box.

Because of this innate bias against home-based businesses it is essential for you to be as professional as possible in all your dealings with clients and customers. The image you project in your clothing, letterhead, business card, and even answering machine message should be traditional and conservative. If clients persist in questioning your professionalism and haughtily ask why you work from your home, use one of these retorts: "My clients prefer the privacy and confidentiality that my location offers"; "My clients prefer the relaxed atmosphere and personalized service I can offer from my home"; "It's more expensive for me, but it lets me spend more time with my family"; or, "The ambience helps me concentrate and be more creative."

FOR MORE INFORMATION . . .

You can learn more about home-based businesses from the following books:
- *How to Set Up and Operate Your Office at Home* by Robert Scott
- *The Home Office Book* by Mark Alvarez
- *Working from Home* by Paul and Sarah Edwards

HOME EQUITY LOANS

Borrowing Against Your Most Precious Asset

The most feared phrase in the language of homeowners used to be *second mortgage*. Those two little words have always conjured up images of a shylock's throwing a struggling family out of their home into the snow-covered street. Most banks scorned second mortgages as an evil tool used by shady lenders to take advantage of marginal borrowers. Despite all this past history, astute, financially secure Americans have been jeopardizing their financial futures by taking out second mortgages on their homes. That's because by renaming these sinister second mortgages "home equity loans" bankers have successfully swept all the well-meaning myths under the rug.

For the past decade, bankers clamored after home equity loan business when they realized that these double liabilities were doubly secure, since the average American would sooner sell his soul than lose his home. Many once-conservative financial institutions became disappointed with the yields from mortgage loans made in the sixties and early seventies. Bank money was tied up in mortgage loans that were paying single-digit interest, while out in the marketplace, new loans were commanding double-digit interest rates. In order to increase the yield on mortgage monies, banks encouraged homeowners to refinance their homes. Today, a home equity loan is the easiest, most accessible source of financing available to Americans.

Full-page, come-hither ads proclaimed that interest rates on equity loans were low and that borrowers could simply write a check to themselves. Interest, the ads preached, was only charged on the amount the borrower withdrew. That was all true; however, while rates may have been lower than on installment loans, they were still variable and often had no ceiling. No mention was ever made of the fees and costs—sometimes over $1,000—in starting up the loan accounts. In addition, repayment schedules often included a large final balloon payment. Finally, banks did everything possible to downplay the inherent danger of a home equity loan—that you are risking the single most important asset you possess.

Despite advertising claims to the contrary, the federal government has not validated home equity loans. They simply have made them more attractive by restricting the deductibility of other forms of interest payments, while retaining the complete deductibility of interest paid on equity loans up to $100,000. In fact, the feverish promotion of home equity loans by banks has drawn attention from Congress, which has enacted legislation to provide some measure of protection to the consumer. But still, the onus remains on the consumer to be a savvy borrower.

First, it is essential to understand the risks of borrowing on the equity in your home. Remember, this is your single largest asset, and more than likely, it will provide the bulk of your retirement monies. There are some instances when it makes sense to take out a home equity loan—specifically, three:

1. To pay for college educations for you or your children;
2. To pay for improvements to your home, which add to its value; and
3. To provide the seed money for starting your own business.

In each of these cases, you would be using the funds from a home equity loan to invest in your future. Please note: these are all equity, not ego, investments. It can be very tempting to use a home equity line of credit for a host of different things, especially since banks make it so convenient. However, it is the height of stupidity to use a home equity loan to pay for luxuries. Never risk your home for a fur coat or a European vacation. Take out a home equity loan only for one specific purpose, and limit the amount you borrow to the amount needed for your goal. If you are renovating your home for $25,000, limit your borrowing to that amount; don't take out another $10,000 for new furniture or a state-of-the-art audio/video system.

Shop around for a home equity loan just as you would for a first mortgage, using the same checklist. Remember, the single best way to cut through all the confusing numbers and information thrown out by banks is to ask for and compare the annual percentage rates (APRs) of different loans. Find out if there are limits, or caps, on the amount a variable interest rate can increase each year or during the lifetime of the loan. Investigate the charges and fees involved in the loan. Some banks charge transaction fees for each check written, while others charge a flat annual fee. Determine whether the loan is amortizing or nonamortizing. Monthly payments on an amortizing loan cover principal as well as interest, while nonamortizing loan payments cover only interest. At the end of a nonamortizing loan the borrower will have to pay the entire principal borrowed in one gigantic balloon payment. If you don't have the cash for the payment, you either refinance it—incurring more fees and interest—or default on your loan and lose your home.

Home equity loans are two-edged swords: used intelligently they can revolutionize your life; used foolishly they can lead to financial ruin. The secrets are to use them only for equity investments, use only as much as you need, and to shop around for the best deal.

USING HOME EQUITY LOANS TO REDUCE YOUR DEBT LOAD

If you're paying a substantial amount of nondeductible interest on debts—either because you've run up big balances on your credit cards or have taken out large installment loans—you can reduce your burden somewhat by taking out a home equity loan— on which you can deduct interest charges—and use it to pay off your nondeductible loans. In effect, you're transforming a handful of high-cost loans into a single lower-cost loan. It's a great way to get out from an oppressive debt load . . . but there's a catch. YOU MUST STOP ALL FURTHER BORROWING. If you continue to build up outstanding balances on your credit cards or take out additional nondeductible loans, you will have built a house of cards that could come crashing down, burying you under an insurmountable monthly debt load, and, since you've pledged your home as collateral for the loan, leading to the loss of your home!

INSPECTING A RENTAL HOME OR APARTMENT
Preliminary Tests You Can Do Yourself

If you are seriously considering buying a home, it is essential that you have it professionally inspected. Only an experienced inspecting engineer will be able to look below the surface and report on potential problems with a structure. But if you are renting rather than buying, it is generally too expensive to call in a professional. That means you'll have to do the inspecting yourself.

When you are out looking for a place to live, always let the real estate broker do the driving. It is his or her job to rent these homes, not yours, and they will probably know the neighborhoods better than you do. In addition, having the broker drive will free you up to ask questions, make observations, and take notes. Even if you trust the broker, always keep your personal judgments to yourself. After all, real estate brokers and agents work for the owner, not the renter.

Dress conservatively when looking at houses or apartments. You should be wearing neat, clean, appropriate garb befitting someone who is involved in serious business. Request that the broker show you no more than five homes or apartments in any one day, and that the five residences be close to each other. It can be difficult to remember the details of any more than five different places, and you want to spend your time actually looking at residences, not sitting in traffic. Try to start your trip as early in the day as possible. You don't want darkness to obscure your inspections and observations.

Bring a shoulder bag or briefcase along with you on your visits, and pack in it an instant camera and film; a small tape recorder; a tape measure; a compass; pens and pencils; a notepad; and a list of your needs and wants. Your first visit to residences will be short—probably no more than thirty minutes—but you will want to be able to make the most of your time.

En route to a potential home, study the immediate area. Is it completely residential or are there stores, or worse, factories, nearby? How far away are stores, schools, major highways, and public transportation sources? If you see anything disturbing, such as a nearby garbage dump or sewage treatment plant, have the broker turn around.

Try to learn from the broker or agent how long the property has been up for rent. Ask why the home is being rented, and what type of person the owner is. The more information you can glean from the broker the fewer unhappy surprises you will have later. Remember, the broker and the owner aren't going to reveal negative factors—you'll have to ferret them out.

When you first pull up to the residence, don't let the broker rush you inside. Instead, take a look around the exterior. What does the property and landscaping look like? Are the outdoor facilities well cared for? Are there streetlights nearby? Does the property have adequate outdoor lighting? What is the condition of the driveway, the sidewalk, and the steps?

Only after you are satisfied with the exterior should you take the big step and cross the threshold. Pay attention to any public spaces you must pass through on the way to the residence. Look at the lobbies, hallways, laundry rooms, trash disposal areas, basements, and elevators of multifamily dwellings. The condition of an individual apartment is indicative of the current occupant's taste and cleanliness. The appearance of the common areas, on the other hand, is indicative of the quality of the landlord or managing agent. Ask the broker, a doorman, or other occupants you see, about the quality of the building staff.

Once you enter the residence in question, take a preliminary walk around the interior. Leave specifics about individual rooms aside for the moment and instead, concentrate on how the floor plan works. Take out your tape recorder and describe what you are seeing. Describe the number, location, and size of windows and doors. Look for the often overlooked details such as linen closets, coat closets, and storage areas. What is the condition of the walls, floors, and ceilings? Once you have walked through the entire residence once, start over again in the kitchen. But this time look for details.

Is there room to eat in the kitchen? How much counter space is available? Is there ventilation? Where are the windows, if any? How much cabinet space is there? Are the appliances in working order? Measure the room and make a note of the location of electrical outlets, light fixtures, and switches. Move to the bathroom next. Is there a window or ventilating fan? Does it have a combination shower/tub or stand-alone shower? Test the water pressure. What happens to the water pressure when you flush the toilet? Drop a wad of toilet paper in the tank and check to see how long it takes to flush. Fill the sink with water and see how long it takes to drain. Are there electrical outlets near the sink, and are they grounded? Is there room to add laundry facilities to either the kitchen or bathroom?

Once you have completed your inspections of the kitchen and bathrooms, move on to the other rooms. How is the light coming into a room? How close is the bathroom? Will your furniture fit in the room and where will it be located? Measure the room, and note the window locations and using the compass, their exposures. If there are rugs on the floor, lift them up to look for damage. Keep your eyes out for mirrors or any furniture or fixture that appears out of the ordinary—it is probably there to obscure something. Are there sufficient electrical outlets and light fixtures in each bedroom?

Is there a den or family room in addition to a living room? Does it have outdoor access? Will it be large enough to combine informal entertainment with informal dining? What does the living room look like? How many people do you estimate could comfortably sit in the room? If there is no family room or den, the living room must be large enough for both formal and informal entertaining. Does the home have a separate dining room or a dining area? Does it have access to both the living room and the kitchen? How many people can be seated in the room comfortably?

In fact, you should ask to see the fuse box. Obviously, circuit breakers are better than fuses, and if you see any signs of pennies or aluminum foil being used to bypass fuses, assume you are standing in a fire hazard. After examining the fuse box, inspect any basement or attic spaces. Look for insulation and signs of water damage.

While inspecting the residence, don't express your opinions or findings to the broker or owner. Remain stoic and simply record your observations in your notebook. If pressed, explain that you will be making judgments only after you have had a chance to look over all the information you have collected from all five residences you are going to look at. Tell the broker that you will contact them the next day with your opinions.

A thorough personal inspection of a rental home or apartment takes no more than thirty minutes. When you consider the number of headaches and problems it can help you avoid, it really is worth the effort.

FOR MORE INFORMATION . . .

You can learn more about inspecting a home or apartment from the following book:

- *How to Inspect a House* by George Hoffman

INSTALLMENT LOANS

Borrowing to Buy Big-ticket Items

Taking out an installment loan is generally the best way to buy big-ticket items such as cars, furniture, and major vacations. In some instances it even makes sense to use installment loans as a substitute for your credit card since your interest expense will usually be much lower. Installment loans may also be the only unsecured bank loans an American can get to start a business. But to take full advantage of the opportunities offered by installment loans, you have to be able to tell a good deal from a bad one.

There are two major types of installment loans: personal loans and secured loans. A personal loan is simply that, a three- to five-year loan based on your personal stream of income and credit history. A secured loan is one in which the lender has a security interest or lien on the property you are purchasing—usually a car, boat, or aircraft—which is surrendered once the loan is repaid three to five years later. Personal loans generally carry a higher interest rate than secured loans, but they do offer you the opportunity to use them for whatever you wish.

Even though these loans are common, they are complicated documents that can vary widely from bank to bank. For instance, there are actually many different ways to calculate and express interest—some taking into account all the costs, others ignoring or obscuring them—and different banks use different techniques. Another way that installment loans may vary from bank to bank is the way finance charges are computed. If you are taking out a loan for $25,000, for example, your finance charge may be $1,000. That means that you actually have $24,000 to put in your pocket. Some banks charge you interest based only on that $24,000 you actually receive, while others charge you interest on the full $25,000. Banks also differ in their specific requirements for loans. One bank may refuse to make loans to self-employed individuals, while another actively pursues their business. Finally, banks that offer variable-rate installment loans may tie their rates to different indices with different degrees of stability.

It is also important to understand that banks are in competition with each other to get your business. They will do anything they can to convince you to borrow money from them as opposed to the bank across the street. Installment loans are, in fact, very profitable for banks. That being the case, banks present their loans in the best possible light, making them appear to be better deals than they actually are. In order to help sort your way through this maze, you have to be an intelligent shopper.

Comparison shop several banks, including regional, ethnic, and local banks as well as the major players. Find out the loan's annual percentage rate (APR)—the actual interest rate you will be paying, which, by law, the bank must inform you of—and use that as your base for comparisons. Inquire about each bank's specific requirements for loan approval. Specifically ask how much each monthly payment will be. Get information on exactly how finance charges are computed. If you are interested in a variable-rate loan, ask for information on the index used, then research its past behavior.

When you are looking for an installment loan, it might even be wise to shop different branches of the same bank. Branch managers have some discretion when it comes to overriding credit and scoring decisions. A branch manager of a bank in an artsy area, for example, may be more willing to write installment loans for self-employed individuals than another branch manager of the same bank who is in an upscale neighborhood or town.

Since the decision of whether or not to make the loan is based on the borrower's ability to make monthly payments, it is possible to turn a rejection into an acceptance simply by asking for less money, or having the loan spread out over a longer period of time. Remember, however, that most loans contain prepayment penalties, which could inhibit your ability to pay the loan back early.

Beware of solicitations you receive right after the holiday season stating that you have been preapproved for a loan. Invariably these loans carry the highest rate. Before actually applying for any installment loans, it makes sense to check your own credit report. Finally, prior to signing any loan agreement, make sure you read the document thoroughly and understand every provision, including those in the fine print, and make appropriate changes to clauses that trouble you.

INSTALLMENT LOANS AS CREDIT ENHANCERS

One excellent way to use an installment loan in order to establish or enhance your credit is to explain to a bank officer that you are looking to establish your credit and would like to take out a small installment loan from the bank. Tell the banker that you would like the loan monies to be placed in a savings account in the bank, and that the banker may hold the passbook as collateral. Banks will leap at the chance to make such a secure loan. Make the first four or five payments on your own, and then tell the bank that you would like them to use the money in the savings account to pay off the balance of the loan.

INTERVIEWING PROFESSIONALS

Judging Their Personalities, Abilities, and Ethics

Most of us would never think of leaving our child with a baby-sitter without first sitting down and having a long talk with the person, making a judgment of his or her maturity, compassion, and honesty. Yet we routinely hire professionals—people whom we pay to baby-sit for our health, legal rights, and finances—without first interviewing them. In fact, many people approach this important process with a "chain store" mentality. They rely on the glib promises of newspaper ads, television commercials, and storefront signs. Or worse, they believe that their professionals should fit the stereotypes they see portrayed on television programs—they think their lawyer should be Perry Mason and their doctor Marcus Welby. Even those of us who ignore advertisements and stereotypes and rely instead on personal recommendations hesitate to interview potential professionals due to vague feelings of inadequacy in the face of authority.

In order to get the best professional help possible it is vital to cast aside your feelings of inadequacy. While professionals are, in most cases, highly educated and skilled individuals, that does not make them any better than you. Regard them as your hired guns—people whom you are employing to do a job for you. If you have a difficult time accepting this notion, just remember that *you* are paying *them*.

When looking for any professional, begin by soliciting recommendations from friends, coworkers, and relatives who are from the same socioeconomic group as you. An attorney who did a fine job arranging the estate of your wealthy maiden aunt may not be the person to draw up your simple will. The accountant who prepares your mother's simple tax return may not be the best individual to put together your much more complex return. The interior designer who decorated the mansion of your employer isn't necessarily the right person to help you decorate your two-bedroom apartment.

Once you have compiled a list of potential candidates, telephone each and ask for an appointment to interview them. State that you are contacting them on the recommendation of your acquaintance, and drop their present client's name. Professionals are often hesitant to deal with people who "come in off the street." Mention that you require only a few minutes of their time and do not expect to pay for this initial visit. If the professional in question balks at meeting with you or insists on charging for the visit, scratch his or her name off your list. Any professionals who feel that they are above being interviewed, or who view their time as so precious that they cannot even spend a few minutes with a potential client without charging for it, are not going to be responsive to or concerned with your needs.

Insist on meeting with professionals at their place of business. (The only exceptions are an interior designer or an architect being used for reconstruction or restoration, both of whom should be invited to your home in order to get a feel for their ideas.) Look around the outer office. Is it orderly or confused? Try to get an impression of the support staff. Do they seem to be mature individuals who are happy at their work? If possible, greet and speak with the support staff. In many cases you will be dealing with them more frequently than with the professional. Observe how the professional treats his staff and how smoothly the office runs. If you are not taken on time, assume that the office always runs late. That isn't unusual for a busy professional office, but any unexplained lateness or a delay not apologized for indicates that clients are not treated promptly and courteously.

Once inside the professional's private office try to make mental notes of what you see. Are there diplomas and professional citations on the walls? Are photos of family members displayed prominently? The former indicates pride and peer approval, the latter, a sense of priorities. Does the office seem organized or chaotic? Don't place too much emphasis on the style or quality of the furnishings, unless of course you are meeting with an interior designer. Similarly, common sense will dictate whether it's important to consider the attire of the professional. While good grooming is a must for anyone in business, standards of dress differ from profession to profession.

Begin your interview of the professional by thanking them for seeing you and reiterate that you are there on the recommendation of their client John Doe. Be candid and explain exactly what you are looking for in a professional. Don't hide or hold back any pertinent information. Ask the professional if they have experience dealing with individuals like you or in your situation. Don't be satisfied with a simple yes or a nod. Get specific examples and ask for names and telephone numbers as references. Feel free to take notes throughout the interview.

If the professional constantly interrupts your interview by taking telephone calls or by barking out orders to his or her staff, think twice about hiring him or her. An occasional interruption is probably unavoidable in a busy office, but a pattern of insensitivity is unforgivable.

Don't be impressed by professionals who claim to have inside influence or who offer nontraditional treatments or programs—they are in all probability crooks or con artists.

Ask about the professional's education, experience, and background. Find out if they regularly update their knowledge through continuing education. The more experienced a professional is the better, and continuing professional education is worth more than a degree from a prestigious university. If at any point the professional uses a word or phrase that you don't understand, ask for an explanation. Don't be embarrassed: no one can possibly know the jargon of every industry or field.

The magic question to ask throughout your meeting with the professional is "Why?" It is easy for a professional to explain how they do things, but only the best will be able to explain why. Their ability to demystify their business and take you by the hand through a process is invaluable.

Make sure to ask about the professional's fees. Get specific information such as how much he or she charges per hour, how much they charge for work done by their staff, and how often they bill. If you are contemplating a specific task or project, ask for an estimate of total costs. Feel free to negotiate fees with the professional, but only if you truly cannot afford them. Experienced, caring professionals may be willing to make alternative arrangements—such as stretching out the billing period or promising to do as speedy a job as possible—but only if you do not characterize their fees as being too high. A criticism of their fees is a criticism of their skill and ability and will be met with stony indifference to your position.

It is important that you try to get a feeling for how the professional will handle your particular case. But this must be done subtly. A professional will rightly feel annoyed if he or she senses that you are looking for free advice. Instead of asking specific questions relating to your situation, couch your questions in hypothetical language such as, "Have you ever had a case that involved. . . ?" Ask the professional what problems they have encountered in these types of situations, how they have solved them, and how long the process took.

Throughout your interview try to establish some personal rapport with the professional. Skill is no replacement for chemistry between a professional and client. Do you feel comfortable with this person? Do you trust them? Do you believe what they are saying? Do you sense that they care about you as an individual? Did they do anything that turned you off? Some professionals drop names of famous clients and make hazy promises of what they can do for you. Those are the people you want to avoid.

Don't be turned off by a professional who admits to not knowing the answer to a particular question. No professional is an expert in every aspect of his or her field. If they are willing to find out the right answer or enlist the aid of another expert, that is sufficient. Actually, their honesty in admitting ignorance of a particular subject or issue is a plus.

Ask for the names and telephone numbers of the professional's three most recent clients in similar situations to yours. A simple request for references will be met with the names of the professional's friends, who may not necessarily reflect the true feelings of his or her clients. Graciously thank professionals for their time and promise to get back to them as soon as you have made a decision.

After each interview jot down your overall impressions. As soon as possible, contact the references and ask them about their relationship with the professional. Rather than asking general questions, dig for specific information. Was the professional courteous? Were they easy to get through to on the telephone? Did they return calls promptly? Did they stick to, or come close to, their estimates of time and money? Were their services satisfactory? Would the client hire the professional again? Once again, jot down their responses.

Go through this process with every potential professional on your list. At the conclusion of your search go back to your notes and refresh your memory about each candidate. When making a decision, try to balance experience and expertise with compassion and humanity. Once you have made your selection, immediately send a letter to all the other candidates informing them that you have selected someone else, but thanking them for their time. Then notify your choice of your decision by sending him or her an engagement letter.

Regardless of how confident you feel about a professional's abilities and character, the terms of your relationship should be defined in a formal engagement letter. Request that the professional prepare a letter that clearly defines the services he or she will perform for you and the responsibilities he or she will have. If any of his or her functions will be contingent on you, this should be spelled out. The letter should state fees, including hourly rates for various staff members, billing frequency, and an estimate of the total cost. It should also include a description of the timetable mentioned in your discussion, noting scheduled dates for various steps or stages to be completed. The letter should state that a status summary will be included with each bill, describing results and projections. Finally, it should include a termination clause which states that if you are not completely satisfied with the relationship, you may disengage at any time. If it isn't already present, add a statement that if the relationship is terminated, the professional is required to release all pertinent documents and working papers.

Good professional help and advise is essential to making it in our increasingly complex world. In order to insure that you are adequately represented you have to take charge of the selection process yourself. In the final analysis you, not your professionals, are responsible for your own well-being.

FINDING PROFESSIONALS WHEN YOU'RE NEW IN TOWN

The best way to find professional help is to ask another professional for their recommendations. For example: when you need an attorney, you can ask your accountant for the names of three or four good lawyers. But when you're new in town, you don't have an initial source for recommendations. Rather than rely on the telephone directory, strike up a relationship with an officer at the local branch of your new bank. He or she should be more than willing to recommend three or four candidate accountants. Once you've lined up your accountant, ask him or her for the names of three or four candidate attorneys. With both an accountant and attorney now on your team you'll be able to count on recommendations for any other professionals you might need.

INVESTMENTS AND SAVINGS

Increasing Your Net Worth Annually

O ne of the most commonly asked questions of financial advisors—including myself—is "What do I do with my money." Of course the answer varies, depending on the age and circumstances of the person asking the question. I firmly believe that our financial lives should be treated as a continuum, not as a path leading to an end called retirement. By actively pursuing a plan of increasing your net worth each year, while making provisions for responsibilities and obligations, you will automatically be planting the seeds for a comfortable old age, whether or not you choose to stop working.

The plan I suggest to my clients is always custom-tailored to their individual needs and their feelings about risk and reward. While it is impossible to offer a customized plan to each and every reader of this book, I can outline the basic steps.

I tell young people that before they begin investing, they must first build a sound foundation for their financial lives. That means obtaining adequate insurance coverage—enough casualty insurance to take care of their personal property, enough fire to take care of their real property, and enough disability to take care of their stream of income—and establishing an emergency fund of enough money to cover their expenses for between three and six months, which should be kept in an interest-bearing money market account.

I believe that the single most important investment anyone can make is to buy their own home, since home ownership offers incredible emotional and psychological advantages as well as financial benefits. That's why I stress to my clients that they should buy as valuable a home as they can, as early in their life as they can. The home serves as the core asset for the rest of our lives, helping to finance other ventures and purchases that increase our wealth and improve our lifestyle. It also invariably grows in value, helping to increase our net worth.

If clients have or plan on having children, already have a firm financial foundation, and own their own home, I advise them to establish a fund—usually based on zero-coupon bonds—for their child's future needs. Simultaneous with their establishing a child's fund, I help them find a way to begin putting some of their income into mutual funds as a way to build up their net worth as efficiently as possible.

Mutual funds offer the investor an incredible service. None of us has the time to analyze individual companies. And even if we do have the time, our knowledge is not sufficient to make judgments on different industries. Mutual funds do all the hard work for us. Professional fund managers, whose incomes are tied not to sales but to the performance of the fund, are continually analyzing a vast array of individual companies and industries, making informed judgments and offering blended, compatible investment packages. They take a huge body of investment information and cut it down into bite-sized, easily digestible morsels.

Buying into a well-managed mutual fund is much better for the average investor than building up a portfolio with the assistance of a stockbroker. Investing in one or a handful of companies is risky—it's like putting all your eggs in one basket. And basing your financial decisions on the advice of a stockbroker whose income is predicated on the sale, not the performance, of investments is simply foolish.

That doesn't mean that investing in mutual funds is simple. There are so many funds out there today, each with their own specialties, that the selection process becomes almost as dizzying as picking out an individual stock. The way around this problem is to enlist the assistance of yet another professional—an independent financial planner—who can help steer investors in the direction appropriate for them. Still, the individual investor must do research on fund performance—but thankfully, many major business and consumer magazines are now doing exhaustive annual studies of mutual funds.

My advice is to find a small to medium-sized fund that spends less than 1 percent of their capital on overhead and administration. Then, set aside some money each week or month to be invested in the fund. Select a fund that concentrates on asset growth rather than income production. Don't shy away from front-load funds that require you to pay an up-front charge if the administration fee is low and the track record is good. Besides, we are in the fund for the long haul—at least five to ten years—not for short-term profit. Similarly, don't give in to temptation and pull the dividends out of your investment and use them to live on. Reinvest any income the fund produces, and rely solely on salary increases to improve your lifestyle, buy gifts, take vacations, etc. Your investment monies should be kept sacred.

With this savings and investment plan in place, the next step is to buy a better, more valuable home. The purchase of a home is not a onetime event. Savvy Americans will find themselves buying new homes on an ongoing basis throughout their lives, generally moving from a small starter home or apartment to a medium-sized home or apartment, then to a larger home or apartment, and perhaps finally—after their children have left the nest—back to a small home or apartment. As they move along this home-owning path, they will continue to put money into their mutual fund, increasing the amount of their investment whenever possible. In this way they will continue to build up their net worth.

At some point in their financial lives I may encourage them to buy a vacation home to enhance their lifestyle. Of course I caution them to continue their savings, and to realize that a vacation home should not be looked on as an investment, but as a luxury. Any profit that results from the eventual sale of this second home is a bonus. I might also counsel them to tap into their savings and real estate investments in order to start their own business. Investing in yourself is not a gamble if you have what it takes to be a successful entrepreneur, especially if it is done rationally and follows a well-thought-out business plan.

The overriding theme of this investment and savings plan is that our financial life is an ongoing one. Retirement is simply an option that an individual may or may not choose. Above all it should not be a goal. Instead, our financial lives should be led with an eye toward continuing to increase our net worth, and continuing to take advantage of our stream of income and abilities to leverage. The goal should be to get the maximum benefit from our money and to enjoy our lives to the fullest.

THE FIVE RULES OF INVESTING

In my years of financial advising I have developed a series of ironclad rules that I pass on to my clients. They are:

1. You get what you pay for.
2. There is no such thing as a free lunch.
3. Luxury cars, boats, collectibles, art, jewelry, gems, precious metals, and antiques are for pleasure, not investment purposes.
4. Insurance policies are never investments.
5. Never agree to an investment, regardless of who suggests it, without first getting some literature, studying it, and thinking about it overnight.

AVOIDING INVESTMENT FRAUDS

Everyone dreams of doubling their money in thirty days, or making a no-risk investment that yields an incredible return. Feeding our imagination are the stories we've heard of people who made millions buying a penny stock, or the poor fools who passed up a chance to make a small investment that turned a miraculous profit. Unfortunately, these dreams and folk tales often make us vulnerable to unscrupulous salespeople. And as more and more insider trading and banking scandals come to light, public confidence in traditional investment avenues shrinks, and the con artist's job gets easier. Here are some tips on spotting and avoiding investment frauds:

- Never purchase investments over the telephone. If the pitch sounds legitimate, set up an appointment to visit their office, or ask them to mail you information. Any salesperson who discourages you from visiting their place of business or says they have no promotional literature is probably a fraud.
- Throw away chain letters. These are nothing more than illegal pyramid schemes designed to make money for the originator of the letter. Simply following the instructions in the letter could make you a party to a federal lawsuit for violating postal laws.
- Don't let yourself be pushed into making an investment due to its being a limited-time offer. If the "window of opportunity" is too short to allow for serious thought and investigation of an investment, it is probably a scam.
- Beware of time-sharing. Since federal legislation cleaned up a great deal of phony land sales, con artists have moved into the time-sharing business. Before investing in any time-sharing facility, investigate it thoroughly.

- Never make investments through the mail. The rare coins you see advertised could turn out to be gold-painted lead when they arrive . . . if they arrive at all.
- Always get the opinion of an unbiased financial advisor—either an attorney, accountant, or a financial planner who charges by the hour—before making any substantial investment or signing any contract.
- Buy a financial instrument only from a salesperson who sells more than just that one type of instrument. When a salesperson promotes a variety of different instruments, he or she will be more apt to offer something that suits, or comes close to suiting, your individual needs.
- Remember, if something sounds too good to be true, it probably isn't.

JOB AND CAREER SHIFTS

Making Them Positive Steps

When an experienced individual must make a job change—whether by design or default—it's frightening to find that many doors are shut simply because of age. But a job change can be an opportunity, a chance to take an inventory of your life, put your abilities and skills in perspective, and to move forward with renewed vigor.

A seasoned person has probably never done his or her job as well as now. Experienced individuals have a greater capacity for learning and applying new ideas than the neophyte, who is still struggling to apply the lessons of academia to the real world. Years of actual practice in business have made you adaptable, colorful, and creative. I have found that far from being weathered, the veteran has a patina that radiates excellence.

In general, the suddenly liberated businessperson is faced with three alternatives: find another job in the same industry; find another job in a different industry; or become an entrepreneur, working for him or herself, perhaps as a consultant.

Finding another job in your own field may seem the safest and quickest path. But quite often interviewers distill our lives down to a job history—a curve that peaks and then tapers off. In their minds, an experienced person may have reached his or her peak and is now beginning a downslide. They don't realize that in life there can be multiple beginnings. It's your job to demonstrate and prove this to them. Don't make an orthodox presentation. Show the interviewer that you are not your résumé. Present him or her with an inventory of your personal and professional assets. Open up a real window on your professional life and let the interviewer see the discrete strengths you have to offer. Itemize your ideas and philosophies. Indicate your strengths and skills. If you recognize that you are more than your job history, so will the interviewer.

Be aggressive when dealing with the issue of age. Realize that your age and experience may be intimidating to the interviewer. Say that your age isn't a problem for you, so it shouldn't be for them, and reiterate all the advantages that a seasoned person would bring to their company, including experience, wisdom, patience, understanding, and tolerance. Internalize and project the idea that your age is certainly not a negative factor since you are an active, vital, vibrant human being.

Another alternative for the individual who must make a job shift is to change careers. This can also be difficult since people think all careers and industries are very different. They are wrong: all businesses are fundamentally the same. They require the same intelligence, the same abilities to communicate, the same interpersonal skills, and the same business creativity—the cerebral freedom and ability to accept and absorb new information even if there is no particular need for it at the moment. If you have been able to succeed as an executive in one business, you will be able to succeed in another. All that's different is the jargon—and that you can learn in a couple of days. If you can internalize this notion and know that you are fully capable of making the shift, you will signal that to others.

During your discussions with personnel people and interviewers they may stress how different their industry is. Agree with them verbally, but stress your past success, your current skills, and your ability to bring a new perspective and a knowledge of something else that may be of benefit to their organization.

If anyone asks why you are changing careers, tell them it is because you find their industry more exciting. If you are coming from an industry that is suffering layoffs, tell them that you have long wanted to leave that industry, and that the current economic slowdown was the factor that finally convinced you to make the shift.

To shift careers may actually be the best thing to do if you are in a troubled industry. If there are problems in your industry, you can bet that there are hundreds, if not thousands, of others like yourself who are out there looking for the now-scarce positions in the field. By moving into another career or industry you broaden your opportunities and increase your chances of finding another position rapidly.

These job hunts can be long, daunting processes. No less difficult, but potentially far more rewarding, in my opinion, is the third option: going into business for yourself.

At this point in your life you have that unique package of

skills that makes for a successful independent businessperson. You have learned how to set realistic goals. A seasoned person hits the entrepreneurial trail in full stride. You have already lived and learned about yourself, others, and business. There are no misconceptions that have to be shed. You've already weathered the tests of the business world and have come out on top. In addition, the new reverence for consultants, and the shift from in-house to outside advisors, opens up a host of opportunities for the entrepreneurial business executive.

I have made many career changes and finally went into business for myself at the age of forty-eight. It was scary, but there were no surprises. I had experience and seasoning and knew what to expect. I set my goals, knew how to reach them, and realized that it would take time. I have never felt so productive or been so alive. As long as you continue to move forward, you will find work exciting and rewarding. God readily gives us the chance to start another life on the foundation of our prior experience.

ADVANCE PLANNING FOR JOB SHIFTS

Employers, even large corporations, are no longer the paternal entities they once were. In the past few years we have seen widespread layoffs, forced early retirements, and attrition programs on the part of companies that used to take pride in taking care of their employees for life. Employees are now viewed as current assets that can be discarded whenever it suits the bottom line. The answer to this changing employer attitude is to become proactive: seek out new jobs; investigate new career options; prepare to spring into business on your own; sow the seeds for positive job and career shifts. And resow them each and every year by staying in touch with contacts and staying active in associations. Establish and expand your personal network of peers, advisors, clients, and associates. You must take charge of your own career because no one else will—especially not your employer.

FOR MORE INFORMATION . . .

You can learn more about job and career shifts from the following books:

- *Careering and Re-Careering for the 1900's* by Ronald L. Krannich
- *Do What You Love and the Money Will Follow* by Marsha Sinetar
- *Guerrilla Tactics in the New Job Market* by Tom Jackson
- *Playing Hardball with Soft Skills* by Steven J. Bennett
- *Rites of Passage at $100,000 +* by John Lucht
- *Wishcraft: How to Get What You Really Want* by Barbara Sher

JOB INTERVIEWS

Preparing and Presenting Yourself

No matter how extensive your experience, and regardless of how brilliantly you present your credentials in your résumé, the final judgment on whether or not you are the best person to fill a position will be made only after an interview. And even though you spent a considerable amount of time and effort in writing up your résumé, looking for job opportunities, and applying through the mail, it is nothing compared to what you will have to do in order to make the most of an interview.

It is vital that you never just wing an interview. Even if you aren't really interested in the position in question, preparing for and going through an interview can be an invaluable experience. Not only will it make you more comfortable with the entire process, it may also open up unforeseen opportunities. An interviewer can become an ally in seeking out other jobs or in helping tailor your presentation skills.

The most critical phase of the interview process actually takes place before you meet with the other party. As soon as you learn that you have made it onto the "short list" and will be interviewed, start preparing yourself for the confrontation. The better prepared you are, the better your chances of getting the job. Preparation will not only convince the other party of your professionalism and sincerity, but it will also boost your self-confidence. And that will come through loud and clear during the interview itself.

First, find out all you can about the position, the organization, the interviewer, and the industry. Speak to any contacts you have inside the organization, or to anyone you know in the same industry. Go to your local library and research the company. Find recent news articles dealing with the company and industry in newspapers, magazines, and trade journals. Get ahold of the last three annual reports. Find out what the company perceives its mission to be. Read the chief executive officer's letters to shareholders. Also, get copies of the company's recent 10K and 10Q statements so you can get an unbiased view of their finances.

Don't limit your research to objective data. If you can, find out about the style and personality of the company. Is it ultraconservative or innovative? Does it look for "loyal soldiers" or "intrapreneurs"? Learn as much as possible about the company's policies and practices.

Next, take the time to check your credit bureau report. More and more companies are using these files in order to make judgments on the character of job candidates, so it makes sense to clean up yours as much as possible.

Prepare answers to the most commonly asked interview questions. Practice your responses so that they are concise and reflect positively on your skills and abilities, highlighting your strengths and minimizing your weaknesses. Here are some typical questions you should prepare answers for:

- Why do you want to work here?
- Why are you interested in this particular position?
- Why do you think you are qualified for this job?
- Why did you leave your last job?—or
- Why do you want to leave your current job?
- What do you consider your strengths and your weaknesses?
- What are your career goals?
- Where do you see yourself in five years and in ten years?
- What did you like about previous jobs and what did you dislike?
- How would you characterize your work style and your management style?
- How do you make decisions?
- Have you ever had a difficult boss and how did you handle him or her?
- Have you ever had to discipline an employee or fire someone?
- What do you consider your greatest personal accomplishment and professional accomplishment?
- What are your hobbies?
- Are you willing to relocate?

Remember that the interview is your chance to sell yourself, and that you may only have a few minutes to do it. The more polished your answers the better you will come across.

Many interviewers admit that they often reach a preliminary decision about a candidate within the first five minutes—almost immediately eliminating some candidates, while reserving judgment on others. That's yet another reason why preparation, which makes you more comfortable and better focused, can be invaluable.

It is also why your appearance must be perfect. Whether we like it or not, first impressions are often based on what we look like. Obviously you should be appropriately dressed. The secret to making the best impression is in being as conservative in appearance as possible. For men that means a conservative suit and tie—no flashy European-cut suits or loud ties. For women that means a conservative suit or a skirt and blouse—no cleavage. Keep jewelry to a minimum: a wedding ring and watch for a man, a simple necklace, one tasteful bracelet, and stud earrings for a woman. Your clothes should be cleaned and pressed, and your shoes should be polished. Your grooming is just as important as your attire. Your hair should be neat and clean; hands and fingernails should be spotless. Make sure you get a good night's sleep before an interview—it shows if you didn't. And pop a subtle breath mint in your mouth thirty minutes before the meeting, making sure to spit it out before the actual interview.

Take the time to read the morning paper thoroughly prior to an interview. If the interviewer brings up a story in the news, or an article in the paper that relates to the company, you had better be aware of the article and able to discuss the topic intelligently.

Good manners are, of course, essential to making a positive impression. Greet the interviewer enthusiastically, giving a firm but not overpowering handshake, and make eye contact. Smile when you say hello—you would be amazed at what a great ice-breaker a smile is—and keep on smiling as much as you can. Use the interviewer's name as frequently as possible throughout the entire meeting. Don't sit down until the interviewer invites you to. If they offer you coffee or a snack, turn them down politely. Even if they smoke and tell you to feel free to light up, don't. Don't remove your suit jacket unless they invite you to.

Pay attention to your body language. Sit up straight, with your back firmly in the chair. When listening, lean forward slightly. Don't gesticulate wildly, point your finger, or sit with your legs or arms crossed. Make smooth, open, relaxed gestures. Eye contact is important, but don't get into a staring game. Always let the interviewer win any eye contact games. And never look at your watch—that indicates boredom.

If possible, initiate the conversation yourself. It can be a casual comment about something in the office that is interesting, or even an observation about the weather. If there was an item in the news recently about the company, mention it. Your intent should be to engage in a friendly conversation with the interviewer. You are not on trial and you are not a prisoner of war being interrogated by the enemy. Both you and the interviewer have a mutual goal—finding out if your needs and the needs of the company are complementary—so there is no need for the process to be antagonistic or confrontational.

Let the interviewer do most of the talking in the early stages of the interview. Find out as much as you can about the position and the type of person they are looking for. This will help you in presenting your experience and qualifications in the best possible light. Feel free to ask questions of the interviewer, sharing your knowledge of the company and the industry. Here are some good questions to ask:

- Can you describe the major areas of responsibility for this job?
- What do you see as the major challenges of the job?
- To whom, or to what position, will this person report?
- How would you characterize the work atmosphere here?
- What qualifications do you consider most critical to success in this job?
- What is the status of the person currently in the job?
- Where does this position fit in the organization's structure?
- Are there any changes taking place in the organization that could affect this position?
- What problems does the organization have that this person could solve?
- What do you consider to be the negative aspects of the job?
- How soon are you looking to fill this position?
- What long-term career opportunities might be available for this person?
- What are the main challenges facing the company?
- Where do you see the company growing over the next five or ten years?

In the early stages of the interview you should try to convey to the interviewer your enthusiasm, energy, and sense of urgency. Your questions will display your intelligence and insight. They should show you to be articulate and thoughtful. Don't ask questions for the sake of asking questions or to show off your knowledge of the company—do it in an honest attempt to learn all you possibly can about the position and the company. Your sincerity will be apparent. Throughout the interview, stress your professionalism and ambition, and try to convey your decisiveness, self-confidence, and poise.

Once the interviewer begins to ask you questions, draw on

what you have learned from your own questioning. Draw on your preparation, but tailor your responses based on your perceptions of the company's needs. Don't be afraid to take some time to think about a question. If you need clarification, ask for it. Interviewers aren't concerned with how fast you reply, and generally, there is no "right" answer. They are looking for how you arrive at your response, how you organize your thoughts, and how articulately you present your feelings.

If you are asked negative general questions—about your weaknesses, for example—pick an area that is not directly involved with your job, then indicate how you are taking steps to improve yourself. For example, explain how you aren't as handy around the house as you'd like to be, so you are taking a home improvement course at your local community college; or mention that you aren't proficient with computers (as long as your job won't involve them), so you have bought a PC and are taking a course in beginning computing. The key is to show that you are aware of personal shortcomings and are taking steps to remedy them.

Avoid raising the salary issue yourself. Be prepared to respond, however, if the interviewer brings up the topic. It is essential to make the interviewer be the first to mention a price. If you mention a number, the only direction the negotiation can go is down. If asked directly about what salary range you are looking for, turn the question around, saying that the interviewer probably has a good idea of the market value of someone with your skills and abilities, and ask them what the company normally pays people like you. Explain that you are interested in a total package that involves benefits and potential for advancement, as well as salary. Once they mention a figure, you can always negotiate it higher.

General, open-ended questions such as "Tell me all about yourself" are really lobs, tossed to you to see how far you can hit them out of the park. Use them to your advantage. Rather than giving a personal history, stress your interests, convictions, strengths, accomplishments, and ambitions, placing them all in the context of how much of a benefit you would be to this company. Start your response by saying, "While there are many things I could tell you about myself, I think the most important one is that I am the best-qualified person for this job."

Keep in mind that if you are being interviewed by a personnel person, you will probably have to go through another interview with the person who is immediately superior to the open position. If that is the case, save personal comments—such as "I love that picture on the wall" or "I can see you are a tennis fan"—for your potential boss. Similarly, don't let the personnel person's discussion of salary keep you from moving on to the next interview round. If you get the person with the actual decision-making power to fall in love with you, it is possible to boost the salary range beyond the stated amount.

Interviewers will generally indicate when the interview has ended by thanking you for coming and indicating that they will be getting back to you in the near future. Use the farewell to score even more points. Try to get a better fix on how long it will take them to reach a decision. Reiterate your interest in the position. Thank them sincerely, using their names.

Even though the interview itself is over, the interview process is not. On your trip home from the meeting, jot down as much as you can remember about the interview. Make notes of points that seemed to impress the interviewer, and note any points you failed to mention. As soon as you get home, write a letter to the interviewer, thanking them for their time, and once again, reiterating your interest in the job. Describe your strengths, your understanding of the company's needs, and explain once again how the two lists match up well. Leave yourself an opening to follow up again in a few weeks' time. Thank them for being so considerate and attentive.

If after three weeks you have still not heard from the company, follow up with a second letter, repeating the points made in your initial follow-up, and adding something, perhaps a point you left out of your initial discussion, or a clipping of something pertinent to the company.

Intensive preparation, effective presentation of your skills and abilities, and professional, prompt follow-ups will show interviewers that you are enthusiastic, confident, articulate, and above all, a valuable potential addition to their staffs.

ANSWERING THE THREE TOUGHEST QUESTIONS

Often, a savvy interviewer will pick up on a weakness in your armor and attack it. How you respond to such attacks can be the difference between receiving an offer and being rejected. Here are some of the tougher questions interviewers ask, and some appropriate, unattackable answers:

Q: "Why were you fired from your last position?"

A1: "I was asked to do something illegal/immoral/unethical and refused to do it."

A2: "I had extraordinary personality differences with my immediate supervisor. He/she became so dependent on me that they suddenly saw me as a threat to themselves."

A3: "My immediate supervisor propositioned me repeatedly, and the personnel department refused/was unable to do anything about it."

Q: "Why is there this gap of time on your résumé?"

A1: "My spouse became ill and I had to attend to him/her/our children. I did, however, keep up my contacts and in fact pursued some continuing education."

A2: "I had to sell/liquidate/revive the family business. The family did not want outside people to become involved."

Q: "I see you have no experience in . . ."

A: "I am aware of that. In fact, I have been looking for/have just signed up for/have just started a course on that very subject to make up for my deficiency."

Of course, it's important that your answers be true as well as reassuring *and* unassailable.

FOR MORE INFORMATION . . .

- You can learn more about job interviews from the following books:
- *Knock 'em Dead With Great Answers to Tough Interview Questions* by Martin Yate
- *Sweaty Palms: The Neglected Art of Being Interviewed* by H. Anthony Medley

LAND

Buying It for an Investment

Land has always been a popular investment, perhaps because the notion of owning property conjures up images of baronial estates and feudal manors. While feudalism died over five hundred years ago, and the baronial estates up for sale are few and far between, the purchase of land can be a sound investment as long as you know what you are getting into.

Land is a good investment for a variety of reasons:
- it offers a substantial return on investment;
- it allows you to take advantage of leverage;
- long term, its value will increase since there is a limited supply;
- it can serve as a hedge against inflation;
- it grows in value by itself, requiring no management; and
- it may produce income as well through rentals or leasing.

On the other hand there are some negatives you should be aware of. Land is really only a good investment if you are willing to hold on to it for a long period of time. Short-term buying and selling of land will not lead to profits. Also, property taxes are on the rise all across America, meaning that your costs of carrying a piece of land can grow each year. Finally, land is not an orderly type of market. There are no comparables out there for you to check since every piece of land is different. In addition, the value of land is based on its potential productivity—in other words: the future. That means you will be buying based on your own, not the market's, estimate of what the land is worth, and holding on to it for a long period of time, during which your costs may rise each and every year.

These positives and negatives have to be factored differently depending on the type of area in which you are buying. There are basically four types of areas in which land is for sale these days: suburban, exurban, recreation, and retirement.
- Suburban land will cost the most, but is the least risky—since development has already begun—and is the quickest to grow in value.
- Exurban land—that which is just beyond the developed suburbs—is more affordable, but requires more investigation

and grows in value more slowly. In order for it to be worthwhile there must be adequate transportation and utilities already present, and some commerce nearby.

- Recreation land is very affordable, but during periods of recession both the rental and selling markets will dry up. For it to be valuable, recreation land must both be within weekend driving distance from a major urban area and have some special property, such as being on water, near a ski slope, or on top of a beautiful mountain.

- Retirement land is also affordable, but will require the longest wait of all for it to be profitable since there is already a glut of housing in these areas. The next surge in development won't come until the baby boomers are ready to retire.

The best way to look for land to buy is by finding an area that interests you, then asking around. Speak to real estate brokers—both commercial and residential—and local bankers. In order to find good investment property you'll have to do some detective work. That's because you are probably best off avoiding land that is already being actively peddled.

The secret to buying well is in making the approach yourself. In other words, you should buy land, not have it sold to you. All of the gimmicks and hustles used to sell property actively just add to the price and insure that you won't get as good a deal. Don't believe rumors you hear about international airports or highways that are about to be built nearby. The rumors were probably spread by the current owners of the land. And even if they are true, by the time all the speculators buy up the property, whoever was going to do the building will probably discover that the land is now too expensive and will look elsewhere. It is also a sine qua non for the seller of the land to help the buyer by providing some form of financing for the purchase.

Once you come upon a potential purchase, study it carefully. Does it have access or is it landlocked? Make sure utility service is in place nearby so the land can be used right away, and check that there are no environmental impediments to arranging for waste disposal. Look at it during both day and night hours. Check up on it in all weather conditions, and if possible, during all four seasons. The best land to buy is high and dry and elevated from any nearby road surfaces.

Make sure to check any surrounding open land for signs of dumping or hazardous-waste disposal. And check with the local office of the Environmental Protection Agency for any limitations they may have placed on the development or use of the property. Assume that the worst possible use will be made of any open land surrounding the site you are looking at.

The single most important factor when buying land as an investment is to have a description and picture of your potential buyer in mind before buying it yourself. What do they want in a piece of land? If you plan on selling to commercial interests, remember that flat land with a large road frontage is what they are looking for. If you are planning to sell the land for residential purposes, rolling hills and scenic vistas are best. It is also possible to alter the land to fit your potential buyer, making it more attractive. For example, leveling the site and clearing trees might make it easier for a commercial builder to visualize his project. Planting trees and doing some minor landscape improvements can enhance the property's value to a residential developer.

Beware of empty lots in otherwise built-up areas. The natural forces of capitalism would have developed such a piece of property if it was healthy. An isolated empty lot is undoubtedly diseased in some way and should be avoided like the plague.

In any case, bear in mind that the profit you make from land comes through savvy, intelligent buying, not fancy marketing or salesmanship. Also, remember that land has its own timetable. You cannot predict where or when development will take place. That's why you have to be willing to wait for your investment to pay off. But don't make any investment that threatens to take longer than your lifetime to become profitable.

BUYING LAND TO BUILD A HOME ON

All of the normal rules for buying land as an investment hold true for buying land to build a home on, with one addition: beware of overbuilding. The general rule of thumb is that the value of the home should be no more than three times the value of the land. That means that if you buy a piece of land for $100,000, you should not spend more than $300,000 on the home you are building. If you do, you will have serious trouble recouping the value when it comes time to sell.

FOR MORE INFORMATION . . .

You can learn more about buying land from the following book:
- *Investing In Land—How to Be a Successful Developer* by Ralph R. Pisani and Robert L. Pisani

LAWSUITS

Responding to a Summons

We live in a litigious society in which people leap to sue each other over even the most minor disputes. Suing has become such an all-American practice since it can be an effective negotiating tool to scare the other side in a dispute. Ambulance-chasing personal-injury lawyers are fanning the flames of litigation mania by encouraging lawsuits in an effort to collect contingency fees.

Most people panic when they get sued. They wrongly believe that they are one step from jail or the poorhouse and begin to consider fleeing the state or selling all their property. They don't understand that it is easy to file a lawsuit and that anyone can sue anyone else for any reason or for any amount. Receiving a summons simply means that the other party has either found an attorney willing to pursue the matter or has stopped by their local stationery store, purchased a summons form, typed it out, and mailed it to you.

A summons is simply formal notification that a legal action has been filed against you and that you are required to appear in court on a given date. It may be handed to you personally or served through the mail. In either case, note the day you receive the summons. You will have a set number of days from this point in time to respond. Don't worry about the date typed on the summons—that simply indicates when it was prepared. All you need to be concerned with is when you actually received it.

Sometimes collection agencies send threatening letters designed to look like a summons. The way to tell the difference between a threat and an actual summons is to look for wording such as "you are hereby summoned to appear in court and file an answer . . ." If the letter does not clearly and specifically state that it is a summons to appear in court, then it is not a summons.

Don't be surprised if you are sued a long time after an accident or incident occurred. Most personal-injury lawsuits are filed two or three years after the incident—cases only move swiftly on television or in films. Also, don't confuse a summons with a subpoena. A subpoena is an order to appear in court and give testimony or submit documents, for someone else's case. It means you are being called as a witness, not that you are being sued.

If you receive a summons, remain calm and bear in mind that the worst thing that can happen to you is that you may have to pay some money—almost always substantially less than what you are being sued for. In most instances, lawsuits in this country involve personal injuries and accuse one party of either physically or financially harming the other.

Invariably these lawsuits ask for much more money than the amount actually in dispute. Let's say you are having a dispute with someone over $5,000. You may well get a summons suing you for $1 million—$5,000 plus $995,000 for punitive damages, emotional distress, and anything else they can come up with. This is simply a negotiating technique. The party suing hopes that the large sum will scare you into suddenly settling the dispute and paying the $5,000. They do not really expect to get $1 million from you; they just want to shake you up.

Regardless of how ridiculous a lawsuit may be, it is essential that you have your attorney look over the facts of the case. Gather all the information and documents you have pertaining to the situation—including such items as canceled checks and receipts—and bring them with you to the lawyer's office. In most cases your attorney will recommend that you settle, usually proposing, for example, that you offer the other party $1,000 of the disputed $5,000 to drop the case. A good attorney will go the extra mile in trying to settle a case out of court since a lawsuit will cost the client at least $6,000 just in legal fees. In addition, regardless of what happens in the case, you will incur other expenses as well and have to spend a great deal of time away from your work.

If your attorney advises you to settle, take the advice. Lawyers know more about how complex and costly the legal system is than you do. Recognize that in advising settlement your attorney is looking out for your best interests, not his or her financial interest. You may well be completely in the right in the lawsuit to recover the $5,000, but proving it in court will cost you at least $6,000 and a great deal of time and energy. In this environment of litigation mania, a small settlement is often better than a major victory.

TWO ALTERNATIVE RESPONSES TO LAWSUITS

If you have the resources to pay for the disputed matter, but have chosen to withhold payment for some reason, you can avoid calling in your attorney by taking one last shot at settling with the other party. Call them on the telephone and say, "I think I can save you some money in legal fees. Instead of giving your lawyer twenty-five to fifty percent, why don't you let me pay you what I think is fair." This may open the door to person-to-person negotiation and keep the matter from turning into a lawyer-to-lawyer dispute. If you don't have the resources to pay at this time, call the other party's attorney and say, "There is no question you can get a judgment on me, but I just don't have the assets to settle the matter right now. I need more time. What are you willing to do for me?"

LAWYERS

Finding and Selecting Your Legal Advisor

The single most important professional you will ever hire is your attorney. Not only will your lawyer help draft your will and the contracts to buy and sell your home, but he or she will be your main conduit to other professionals, opening up their Rolodex for your perusal. He or she is both your most expensive advisor and your most trusted ally, potentially involved in some of the most difficult and intimate decisions and actions in your life—marriage, divorce, adoption, civil or criminal trials, and estate planning, for example. That's why it is absolutely essential to find an attorney with whom you have a personal rapport and in whom you have complete confidence.

The only way that can be done is to develop a list of candidates through the personal recommendations of friends and relatives whose opinions and intelligence you respect. Pay careful attention to the advice of people whose lives parallel your own in income and in circumstances. Get more than a name and a general impression. Ask detailed questions about their relationship with their lawyer: Was he or she easy to reach on the telephone? Did the attorney return phone calls promptly? Did he or she keep your friend fully informed? Was service satisfactory? Were the fees bearable?

Keep in mind that you are looking for a generalist, not a specialist. Your personal attorney should be well versed in all areas, but must be willing and able to refer you to specialists should the need arise. For example, your personal attorney may handle your estate planning and real estate transactions, but refer you to a matrimonial attorney for divorce proceedings or to a litigator for personal-injury cases. That's one reason why when it comes to personal attorneys, I recommend you hire an experienced lawyer from a small firm. Large firms mean large fees and impersonal services. Young lawyers will not have the experience or contacts you need from a generalist, and they may not have yet developed the necessary humility to acknowledge they don't know everything. Beware of attorneys who act gruff and proudly proclaim that they are back-alley fighters—they will probably turn around and fight dirty with you as well. Don't be impressed with lawyers who claim to have judges in their pockets—they are probably lying, and if they aren't, they and the judges will probably end up in jail.

Since you and your attorney are going to have to have a close personal relationship, a personal interview is a must. In addition to gauging the personalities and the work habits of the attorneys, you should find out as much as you can about the ways they do business and treat their clients. Ask which matters they handle personally, and which they pass on to their staffs. If a great many things are left in the hands of associates and paralegals, ask about their backgrounds and experience. If you have a specific problem looming in the near future, ask the attorney how he or she would handle it. Find out if the attorney will be taking your place as a negotiator or will simply sit by your side, whispering advice in your ear.

Ask about fees and charges. Most attorneys charge by the hour. Fees vary dramatically from city to city and from lawyer to lawyer depending on experience, reputation, and location. On average, an experienced attorney in a small firm in a medium-sized city will charge between $100 and $150 per hour. While on the subject of fees, find out what the services of other members of the firm cost.

If you feel you cannot afford the attorneys' fees, tell them. In most cases fees are negotiable. While they may not be willing to lower their prices, they may be open to extended-payment plans. Ask for estimates of the total cost for some standard procedures, such as drawing up a will or helping in the purchase of a home. Yearly retainers only make sense if you will be using the attorney's services on a continuing basis for a variety of tasks. As with other professionals, the terms of your agreement with your lawyer should be spelled out in an engagement letter.

The single most important thing to remember when choosing an attorney is to go with your gut instincts. If there is something about the person you are meeting with that makes you uncomfortable, scratch him or her off the list. Your attorney must be your confidant as well as your legal advisor. You have to be as comfortable with them as you are with a baby-sitter.

LAWYERS WHO ADVERTISE

Once taboo, legal advertising has become increasingly common. I believe that there is nothing wrong with lawyers advertising. The

First Amendment gives everyone the right to freedom of speech and expression, and barring attorneys from soliciting business through the media, I believe, violates that right. The issue is not should lawyers advertise, but should consumers pay attention to their advertisements. The lawyer/client relationship is built on trust, sensitivity, caring, intimacy, and socioeconomic compatibility. It is impossible to judge a lawyer's character, ability, ethics, or empathy from an ad. All you can learn is their rate schedule and how successful they claim to be. Disregard all legal advertising. There is nothing wrong with considering using attorneys who advertise; just base your decision on your interviews with them, not their advertising.

LEVERAGE

Using Its Power Wisely

Leverage is perhaps the most powerful financial tool available. Simply put, leverage is the process of borrowing against a future stream of income in order to buy something in the present. The most obvious examples of leverage are mortgage loans, installment loans, and credit card purchases.

In order to see just how powerful leverage can be, let's look at how a mortgage loan works. By paying a $10,000 down payment on the purchase of a $100,000 house, and leveraging the rest (agreeing to pay a specific amount each month out of your future stream of income), you obtain ownership of a $100,000 asset by paying only $10,000; and that asset grows based on its $100,000 value, not on the cash you put into it.

But there is a flip side to leverage, making it just as potentially dangerous as it is potentially wonderful. Leverage has to be constantly supported by a stream of income large enough to support both interest and amortization payments. If your stream of income decreases or stops entirely, you will be faced with a financial crisis. A perfect example of misused leverage is our federal budget deficit. In fact, overleverage has become endemic in America, infecting people from all walks of life and in every economic group.

Our government has continually borrowed against its future stream of income in order to spend the money in the present. Unfortunately, the government's stream of income has not increased enough to keep up with its increasing amount of purchases. The government is now borrowing money just to pay off the interest on the money it has already borrowed, reaching years and years into the future against income that will be generated by our grandchildren's taxes.

Luckily, individuals can't go quite that far overboard. Banks in this country are only willing to loan money to individuals for a maximum of thirty years, so it is impossible for you to get your children as well as yourself into hock. However, that doesn't stop thousands and thousands of Americans from overleveraging themselves into personal bankruptcy each year.

Obviously, taking complete advantage of the leverage available to us, while not tying up too much of our stream of income, is a delicate balancing act. I have found few people who can actually manage it well. Most often, people err on one side of the equation or the other, treating leverage as a curse and losing out on all the things it can do for them, or becoming addicted to its power and getting in over their heads.

In order to maintain this delicate balancing act, you need to keep some principles and rules in mind. First, remember that leverage can never take the place of cash. If you increase your leveraging in order to pay off your old leveraging, you are just robbing Peter to pay Paul. A day of reckoning will come, and the further you get into debt the worse the eventual outcome will be. If you find yourself overleveraged, the only sound way to respond is to increase or reallocate your stream of income by selling an asset, getting a raise in salary, or taking the money you are spending on other things and using it to pay off your debt instead.

Always keep track of how much of your monthly income you have leveraged against. You should always leave yourself with enough room so that if your income shrinks or disappears completely for a short period of time, you will still be able to pay your monthly charges. This can be tough to do since as soon as you begin to take advantage of leverage (by taking out a loan or getting a credit card), all sorts of other lenders start to approach you, encouraging you to borrow from them.

Make sure that your use of leverage is a conscious, not reflexive, act. Only take out loans or use credit cards for things that you need. Use cash to pay for your wants. That's a principle that will work in both good and bad economic times. There is nothing wrong with borrowing to buy a home, to buy a sensible car, or to take a much needed, restful vacation. But it is a mistake to use leverage to buy a mink coat, to buy a luxury car, or to take a sight-seeing trip.

Finally, don't let your age be a deterrent to using leverage. I believe that borrowing money may actually extend your life. My parents took out a thirty-year mortgage on their current home when they were in their seventies. If banks don't have a problem with it, why should you?

WHEN ARE YOU OVERLEVERAGED?

The simple answer is when you find yourself struggling to pay your bills. However, it's possible to be overleveraged—at least in the eyes of other potential lenders—even if you're not struggling. According to most institutional lenders, you're overleveraged if more than 36 percent of your gross (before taxes) monthly income is going to pay debt. I think lenders are, understandably, a bit too conservative with this figure. I believe that you can get away with 40 percent of your gross monthly income being devoted toward your debt—especially if part of that debt load is a low-interest student loan. While that means you may need to work harder to borrow money and pay more attention to how you fill out loan applications, you should be able to handle the load.

WHAT TO DO IF YOU ARE OVERLEVERAGED

It is the height of stupidity to hold on to an asset if you have found that you cannot afford the cost of leveraging it. Rather than struggling until you actually own the asset, sell it and use the proceeds, and savings if necessary, to pay off the loan.

THE ONLY TIMES YOU SHOULD USE LEVERAGE

1. When starting a business.
2. When buying an asset that the seller will help finance.
3. When buying your first home.
4. When you need nonelective surgery, have to be hospitalized, or need to attend a detoxification program.
5. When you are paying for a college education.
6. When you need a medicinal vacation.
7. When buying a necessary big-ticket item.
8. When buying a prudent automobile.
9. When making renovations to your home that will add to its value.
10. When setting up a margin account for investment purposes.

LIFE AND HOMEOWNER'S INSURANCE

Calculating How Much Coverage You Actually Need

Most Americans underinsure their lives and overinsure their personal property. They tend to waste their money on "ego" insurance or by protecting items of personal property that have no tangible value whatsoever and could never be replaced in any event.

This morass of mistakes is directly attributable to insurance company propaganda. Hard-sell marketing and sales efforts have spread misinformation and fear. The image of the benevolent insurance company protecting you in your hour of need is a myth. Insurance companies get you coming and going: agents get rewards for selling policies that are worth lots of money, while adjusters are rewarded for settling claims for as little money as possible. They may rush to a disaster scene dressed in the garb of an emergency worker and offer to give you a check on the spot, but that's only because they've found that the sooner after a disaster or accident they settle with you, the less you are willing to accept.

Insurance companies are like any other for-profit organizations. Poorly managed insurance companies can, and do, go broke, while well-run companies rarely take risks. An insurance company doesn't reach into its own pockets to compensate you for a loss. Acting as a stakeholder, the company takes the money you and others pay as premiums and puts it into a pool. Since only one house is likely to burn down at a time, or one person in a class is likely to die at a time, the insurance company gets to invest the rest of the pool and keep the profits. It also charges all the members of the pool (policyholders) a fee to cover their overhead. If they are forced to pay out more than they expected, they simply raise their premiums.

It is in an insurance company's best interest for you to insure everything for as much as possible. Advertising, marketing, and sales pressure is geared toward convincing the consumer of the need for sizable, wide-ranging insurance coverage. Your actual insurance needs are often much lower than insurance companies claim.

Insure only personal property that has a real cash value, and that you would ordinarily replace if it was damaged or lost. No amount of money can compensate you for the loss of your grandmother's cameo. Rather than paying a high premium on it, just be careful.

Your homeowner's insurance should cover only the value of your residence and not the land the building sits on. Banks providing mortgages will often require you to cover 80 percent of the purchase price—even though this may be higher than the replacement value of the structure. While in the early years the value of your home may be 90 percent structure and 10 percent land, as time goes on the land increases in value faster than the structure.

Get an unbiased appraisal of the replacement value of the structure independent from the land and insure for that amount—land cannot burn down. Buy the leanest policy with the fewest extras you possibly can. And take as high a deductible as allowed. The secret is to insure for disaster, not routine damage. If you make a minor claim, your premium may go up more than the settlement you received. Avoid "blue ribbon" policies that insure the food in your freezer and provide for stays in luxury hotels—they are strictly ego enhancers.

Even more important than life insurance is disability coverage. Americans are four times more likely to be disabled between the ages of thirty-five and sixty-five than to die. The coverage provided by employers is skimpy and short term at best and should be supplemented by your own policy with a respectable waiting period.

Life insurance is needed only if you have dependents and a small estate. Take out just enough insurance to pay your bills, keep dependents on their feet for three years, and to send the kids to college. Don't view life insurance as an indication of your worth as a human being or as a legacy to your heirs. Its purpose is to replace you—temporarily—as an income producer and to take care of responsibilities (college educations) and outstanding short-term debts (credit cards). It is foolish to insure the lives of your children—can you buy a replacement for them? Likewise, forget about such nonsense as double indemnity—it's just a legalized form of gambling.

Always buy term life insurance—it is the least expensive and affords the best coverage. Term policies can be compared company to company, unlike other types. While it only lasts for up to five years, don't believe claims that it is only "temporary" coverage. While whole-life policies remain in force for your entire lifetime and do build up equity, their yields are pathetic. Their only virtue is as a form of forced savings. Term premiums may increase in later years when you buy another policy, but that is when you will need the least coverage. Although whole-life premiums appear lower overall, they are artificially high in the early years and artificially low later on. Once you reach retirement age most of your obligations will have been met, and your estate should be sizable enough to sustain you or your dependents.

In order to calculate how much life insurance coverage you actually need, total up taxes, funeral costs, three years of day-to-day living expenses, and children's education costs. Next, determine approximately how much income a working spouse, or a spouse who returns to work, will produce. Add to this second figure the value of investments that could be liquidated. Subtract this potential income from the likely expenses. The balance is the amount of insurance you need.

Select a term policy that is renewable until age sixty or sixty-five. When comparing policies, go by the "interest-adjusted net-cost index," not the premium. Buy only from a company rated highly by securities ratings firms such as A.M. Best, Moody's, Standard & Poor's, or Duff & Phelps. And pay the premium annually—it ends up costing much less.

Don't take out insurance that names your creditors as beneficiaries. Mortgage and credit card insurance policies are inevitably more expensive than term life insurance. Similarly, avoid policies that duplicate the coverage you already have. Most homeowner's policies and many credit cards provide travel coverage, for example.

Never buy insurance through the mail, from a vending machine, or from a company's agent. Use an insurance broker who represents more than one company. (Obviously, the more companies the broker represents the better off you are.)

Constantly check your insurance coverage. Every two years shop around for alternative policies. Companies and brokers never publicize new offerings that could offer savings. Once you are insured they forget all about you. Send copies of your policies to a handful of reputable brokers, including your present broker, and ask them to bid on your coverage, getting you more coverage for the same price, or the same coverage at a lower price. If you find you can do better, switch brokers and companies.

FOR MORE INFORMATION . . .

You can learn more about life and homeowner's insurance from the following books:
- *The Complete Book of Insurance* by William Kent Brunette
- *The Family Insurance Handbook* by Les Abromovitz
- *Winning the Insurance Game* by Ralph Nader and Wesley J. Smith

MEMBERSHIP APPLICATIONS

Measuring Up Financially and Socially

One of the most intimidating experiences you can ever have is applying to join a social club or a cooperative apartment building. Often these groups are intentionally discriminatory, looking to insure that only "their type" of people are accepted for membership. Even if the club or building isn't entirely snobbish, you can rest assured that the individuals who sit on the board or membership committee will be. They often act as self-appointed gatekeepers, limiting access to what they feel is their private domain.

Personally, I cannot understand putting up with such foolishness for strictly social purposes. If, on the other hand, social connections will serve to speed up or solidify your career success, or the apartment is just what you have been looking for, it may be necessary to swallow your principles and learn to play the game.

Generally, membership applications will ask for two types of information: financial and social. In most cases, in order to check on your financial status, an organization will request you to submit a net-worth statement. These statements are traditionally prepared by accountants, but when applying to a membership organization, it is better to do it yourself if possible. For example, many people forget to include their personal property on a net-worth statement. Possessions, such as artwork, antiques, and collectibles, can boost both your financial and social status in the committee members' eyes—just be careful that none of them are controversial or indicative of an extreme lifestyle. Remember to include any monies owed you and the dates when you will be receiving payment, and gifts and bonuses that you receive regularly. It goes without saying that this statement should be typed and professionally presented.

What makes applying for membership in these organizations even more daunting and frightening is that they do not stop at scrutinizing your finances, but choose to examine your social life as well. Since most families didn't come over on the *Mayflower* or belong to the social register, it is important to provide third-party assurance of your personal stability. The best way of doing this is to submit letters of reference from authority figures—clergymen, bankers, doctors, lawyers, accountants—that attest to your responsibility and good citizenship. When asking these professionals for a personal letter of reference, provide them with a sample you wrote yourself, stressing that you are offering it only as a form for them to follow. Nine times out of ten a busy professional will simply retype your letter and sign his or her name to it.

If you personally don't have the connections to get such testimonials, ask your parents to have their professionals vouch for you. Most social organizations believe that "the acorn doesn't fall far from the tree."

Quite often, membership applications include questions on what other organizations you belong to or support. Avoid mentioning any organizations whose political or ideological bent might offend someone. You should appear noncontroversial . . . and just like the other members of the club or co-op. Be sure to list professional organizations to which you belong. Membership in cultural organizations is a plus and is always noncontroversial. In many cases, a $25 or $50 donation is all that it takes to legitimately call yourself a member of a museum or arts organization. Support of nondenominational, noncontroversial charities is also looked on positively.

Be wary of questions asking you to describe yourself. Certain words will immediately frighten membership committees. Calling yourself ambitious, zealous, self-assured, colorful, eccentric, flamboyant, determined, or even creative will bring up negative connotations. Instead, stick with such descriptions as charitable, quiet, restrained, and God-fearing.

While I am all for taking prudent shortcuts—colorizing your qualifications and presenting your credentials in the best possible light—I do not advocate that you lie on your application. There is no organization important enough, or apartment wonderful enough, for you to violate your principles totally. It is all right to play the game, but don't deny who or what you are in the process.

PERSONAL LETTER OF REFERENCE

Dear . . .

The purpose of this letter is to recommend (applicant) to you. It is with great pleasure, and without qualification, that I provide such a recommendation.

(Applicant) has been a good and trusted friend of mine for the past (number) years. As a friend I find (applicant) to be warm, understanding, sensitive, fun, and intellectually stimulating. I admire (applicant) for having achieved professional success without compromising any of the human qualities that endear (him or her) to me. (Applicant) is a self-made, talented, successful person.

In the time I've know (applicant) (she or he) has been consistently reliable, responsible, and considerate of others. I believe that (she or he) will be an asset to (organization).

Should you have any questions, or wish to discuss this recommendation further, please feel free to call my office.

Sincerely . . .

BUSINESS LETTER OF REFERENCE

Dear . . .

I understand that (applicant) has applied for (description) for which I would like to highly recommend (him or her).

In my capacity as (title), I have worked with (applicant) for the past (number) years and find (applicant) to be a person of good character, great skill, and of strong moral fiber.

I am very proud to call (him or her) a colleague. (Include a brief description of the applicant's responsibilities.)

If I can be of further help, please feel free to contact me.

Sincerely . . .

ATTORNEY'S LETTER OF REFERENCE

Dear . . .

The purpose of this letter is to recommend (applicant) to (organization). It is with great pleasure that I do so.

I have known (applicant) for many years. During that time (she or he) has consistently impressed me as a sober, responsible person of considerable substance. (Applicant) has a keen sense of community participation and social value, which inevitably results in an improvement to any setting shortly after (she or he) arrives.

As (her or his) attorney, I have found (applicant's) business and financial judgment both sound and conservative. (She or he) has always sought the proper advice. (Her or his) career development results from skillful, adept career planing, which must be admired.

Given the foregoing, my recommendation remains unreserved. Should you have any questions or wish to discuss this recommendation further, please feel free to call me at (telephone number).

Sincerely . . .

ACCOUNTANT'S LETTER OF REFERENCE

Dear . . .

As the personal accountant and friend of (applicant), it is my pleasure to provide a letter of reference on (his or her) behalf.

I have handled (applicant's) taxes and personal financial management while (he or she) has been a resident of (state). (Applicant) is very conservative in (his or her) financial management and has always displayed a high degree of integrity in the conduct of (his or her) affairs. (He or she) has a financial plan that covers both growth and contingencies.

(The accountant can provide a specific history of the applicant's financial assets and income if required.)

I highly recommend (applicant) as (description).

Feel free to call me if you have any questions.

Sincerely . . .

BANKER'S LETTER OF REFERENCE

Dear . . .

This is a response to a request concerning the banking relationship of (applicant). It is my pleasure to inform you that (applicant) has been a valued client of our bank since (date). (His or her) relationship consists of (a description of the banking relationship including types of accounts, balances, and dates opened).

We can assure you that over the years (applicant) has consistently demonstrated a very conservative and responsible approach in the handling of all (his or her) financial affairs with us.

If you have any questions regarding (applicant), please call (telephone number).

Very truly . . .

MORTGAGES

Understanding, Selecting, and Shopping for the Consumer's Most Powerful Tool

There are three great misconceptions about mortgages. First, many people believe that a mortgage is a tool of last resort; that individuals should only borrow the money to buy a home if they cannot afford to pay cash. Second, most Americans look on a mortgage as a ball and chain; a thirty-year shackle whose removal is cause for celebration. And third, some people still feel that bankers and other mortgagees are simultaneously tightfisted and conniving lenders: difficult to borrow from and just waiting to foreclose, eager to get their hands on your home.

Actually, no one, regardless of financial resources of age, should pay cash when purchasing a home. Rather than being a time to celebrate, the cessation of a mortgage is a time to mourn—and then to take action and remortgage. And finally, far from being tightfisted skinflints, mortgagees are just about the easiest people in the world to borrow money from.

By paying cash for a home you let one of the most powerful tools capitalism offers—leverage—slip through your fingers. And while leverage can be a two-edged sword, carrying the potential for financial problems as well as life enhancement, the purchase of a home is the single best and safest time to use this financial weapon. (For more information on these factors, see the chapter on leverage.)

Suffice it to say that a home mortgage allows you to invest a relatively small amount of cash—generally 20 percent of the purchase price—and still enjoy almost total control over and use of a very expensive and beneficial asset—your own home. (For a discussion on both the financial and emotional advantages of home ownership, see the chapter "Buying vs. Renting a Home.") No less important is the fact that by taking out a mortgage you enable your 20 percent down payment to grow as if it were five times greater. The $40,000 you put down on a $200,000 home actually grows as if it were $200,000.

If you had the $200,000 in cash, and spent it on a home, that money would grow at the same rate as the value of the home—

historically, one percentage point above the inflation rate. By taking out a mortgage instead, you lock your 20 percent down payment into growing at this rate, while freeing up your remaining $180,000 to invest at higher rates. In effect, taking out a mortgage allows you to multiply your financial power dramatically and, I believe, lead a more enjoyable and productive life.

Of course there is a cost for using this tool: the interest charged on the loan. But the damage is mitigated since interest paid on mortgage loans is tax deductible. Home ownership truly is one of the few tax shelters available for the average American. And while rising interest rates do have an effect on how much you can afford—the higher the interest rate the higher the monthly payment and, therefore, the less you can afford to borrow—they need not force you to postpone or abandon buying a home. All it forces you to do is be more resourceful. Remember that while you can always buy a less expensive home when interest rates rise and your affordability decreases, a seller has no such option. He or she has only one product available. If an increase in interest rates dries up the demand for homes, sellers will be more willing to reduce their prices and/or help you finance your purchase themselves.

The advantages and benefits of having a home mortgage are so dramatic that, rather than burning the mortgage when it's finally paid off, you should go right back out and get another one . . . regardless of your age. There is no reason why older Americans shouldn't also avail themselves of the power of a mortgage. Even if you or your parents don't live long enough to pay off a mortgage, there's no problem. There is no shame in dying and leaving an unpaid mortgage. If you're worried that your estate or significant other won't be able to meet the entire monthly payment, don't pay cash instead or opt for mortgage insurance. Simply take out a life insurance policy with a benefit large enough to pay down the mortgage to an affordable level. Banks don't care about the age of borrowers, only their ability to meet the monthly payments. My parents just recently took out a thirty-year mortgage on a retirement home in Florida . . . and they are both over eighty.

What's incredible about home mortgages is that they are just as beneficial to lenders as they are to borrowers. There is no safer, more profitable loan than a home mortgage. That's why so many different types of lenders are now in the market. Not only are home mortgage loans available from mutual savings banks and savings and loan associations, but commercial banks, credit unions, finance companies, and even some insurance companies have now jumped into the business. All these lenders realize that borrowers will do almost anything to keep their homes—the last loan a borrower would ever default on is a home mortgage. And rather than being eager to foreclose, lenders are incredibly reticent to take back possession of a home. They are in the money-lending business, not the real estate business. While lenders have tightened their policies since the free-wheeling 1980s (see page 206 on the demise of future forecasting), they are still ready, willing, and able to make mortgage loans. Regardless of your age or financial situation, there is a mortgage out there for you.

Before I explain how you can go about finding one, let me explain what it is. While a mortgage is a complex arrangement consisting of many provisions and clauses, basically it is any financial instrument in which title to real estate is reserved as security for the payment of a debt. Mortgage loans consist of two basic parts. The first is a promissory note: a simple agreement on your part to repay the loan. The note will explain the details of your agreement—how much is being borrowed, what interest is being charged, when payments must be made, and what charges are assessed for paying late or early.

The second part of the mortgage loan differs depending on what state you live in. Most states practice what's called lien theory, and the second part of the mortgage is called . . . a mortgage. But fifteen states—Alabama, Arkansas, California, Colorado, Delaware, Illinois, Mississippi, Missouri, Nevada, New Mexico, Tennessee, Texas, Utah, Virginia, West Virginia—and the District of Columbia go by title theory, and the second part of the mortgage loan is called a deed of trust.

The major difference between the two theories is how the title to the home is held. In lien-theory states, the lender holds title to the property as collateral security for the promissory note. In title-theory states, the title to the home is held by a third party called an escrow agent. While most of the differences are basically legalistic and administrative, one is important to note. In lien states it takes much longer—anywhere from three to nine months—for a lender to foreclose. It takes less than ninety days for a lender to foreclose in a title-theory state. That generally means that lenders in lien-theory states are more reticent to foreclose.

Because of their safety and profitability and the increased competition, mortgage lenders go to great lengths to make their deals appear more attractive than the lender around the corner. The typical camouflage consists of charging more up front and less each month, or vice versa. In addition to charging for administrative chores—called origination fees—and appraisal, legal, and application fees, some lenders charge points, which are advance interest payments. When bankers say you will have to pay one point up front they are really saying you'll have to pay one percent of the principal at the time of the closing. You are still paying the same amount of money—and it's still tax deductible—but the timing of the payment is different. To make comparison shopping a little easier, the federal government now requires all mortgage lenders to advertise and openly state the average percentage rate (APR) of a loan. That's the effective percentage you'll be paying when interest, points, and other fees are all figured together.

But this federal regulation hasn't kept lenders from coming up with a host of innovative, often enticing, mortgage products. When your parents took out a mortgage all they had to do was choose either a twenty-five-year fixed-rate mortgage or a thirty-year fixed-rate mortgage. Today the waters are much cloudier. Lenders still offer the traditional 25- and 30-year fixed-rate mortgages, but they also offer fifteen-year fixed-rate mortgages and an incredible variety of variable-rate mortgages. Among these are: one-, three-, five-, and seven-year adjustable mortgages; adjustable-rate mortgages tied to different indices; renegotiable-rate mortgages; graduated-payment mortgages; shared-appreciation mortgages; and reverse-annuity mortgages. For most people, however, the choice really comes down to opting for either a fixed-rate mortgage or an adjustable-rate mortgage.

FIXED-RATE VS. ADJUSTABLE-RATE MORTGAGES

Fixed-rate mortgages are fairly straightforward. You pay a predetermined rate of interest, which is fixed for the entire term of the loan, so you have the same mortgage payment every month for as long as thirty years. This means that while your income continues to increase, your cost of shelter will remain constant, freeing up your money for other uses.

Another advantage to fixed-rate mortgages is that they allow you to develop equity within a relatively short period of time. Even though your payment remains constant, the portions of the payment that go toward interest and principal change over the years. Early on your payment will consist almost entirely of interest. Then after a period of time—generally twelve to fifteen years, you will have paid off all the interest and the payment will start to be applied to your principal. Developing equity in your home is important, not because it signals that you are on the way to paying off the mortgage, but because it provides you with an added source of collateral for further leverage. You can borrow against your equity to finance home renovations, to pay for a child's college education, or even to start your own business. (For more information see the chapter on home-equity loans.)

Having an interest rate locked in for thirty years can be both an advantage and a disadvantage to borrowers as well as lenders. If interest rates increase, borrowers who are locked in a lower rate benefit, while lenders suffer. When rates decline, fixed-rate borrowers suffer and lenders benefit. Lenders protect themselves from market fluctuations by charging more up-front points on fixed-rate loans than on adjustable-rate loans. Borrowers can protect themselves as well, by keeping an eye on whether or not it makes sense to refinance their mortgages. (For more information, see page 209 on mortgage refinancing.)

Some years ago, innovative bankers, looking for additional ways to protect themselves against detrimental interest-rate fluctuations, developed the adjustable-rate mortgage (ARM). By linking the rate of interest they charged home buyers to an economic index that reflected the state of the economy, they could keep from being hurt by locking up their money. To make these ARMs more attractive to borrowers, lenders offered lower up-front costs and the potential for monthly payments to decrease as well as increase. They offered caps on how high and how frequently interest could increase, and offered borrowers the opportunity to pay off the entire loan, without a penalty, within ninety days of an increase in interest. And because lenders felt more secure about the profitability of ARMs, they could be less strict in their underwriting. This innovation revolutionized the mortgage business.

ARMs offer some important advantages to borrowers. The lower up-front costs and less stringent underwriting have made it easier for people with less money in the bank and lower incomes to be able to buy homes. Rather than hoping increases in their income will eventually outpace increases in the interest rate and cost of living, enabling them to afford a fixed-rate mortgage, buyers can now get into a home earlier and make the usually sound bet that their income will at least keep pace with increasingly large monthly payments. The disadvantage of an ARM is that it takes longer to build up equity in a home.

The decision of whether to take out a fixed-rate or an adjustable-rate mortgage depends on your particular circumstance. I advise buyers who are planning to spend a long period of time in a particular home—more than ten years—to opt for a fixed-rate mortgage. That way they'll be able to build up their equity quicker. I advise buyers who don't intend to spend a long period of time in this home to opt for an adjustable-rate mortgage. That's because they'll spend less up front and won't have a chance to build up equity anyway. Individuals who, for one reason or another, are unsure whether their income will continue to increase, should select a fixed-rate mortgage, on which the monthly payment is completely predictable. Finally, if clients have a hard time meeting underwriting standards for any reason, I suggest they pursue ARMs, since the qualifications are less strict.

SHOPPING FOR A MORTGAGE

Whether you are shopping for a fixed-rate or an adjustable-rate mortgage, the process is the same. All mortgage lenders are looking for three things: that you're willing to pay back the loan; that you're able to pay back the loan; and that the value of the collateral offered to secure the loan—the house you are buying—is sufficient. If you meet these three qualifications you will get the mortgage. The value of your collateral is verified by an independent appraiser hired by the bank to estimate the value of the home you want to buy. Other than possibly debating an erroneous judgment, there is little you can do to affect this analysis. However, there is a great deal you can do to boost your chances to pass the other two analyses.

Mortgage lenders judge your willingness to pay back the loan not by the sincerity of your oaths but by your past performance and stability. Before they agree to a loan, lenders will run a thorough credit check on potential borrowers. In order to make sure you pass the test, beat the lenders to the punch and precheck your own credit-bureau files. Correct and cleanse them of anything that could make a lender balk. (For more information on how to do just that, see the chapter on credit-bureau reports.)

With your credit report sparkling and clean, you can begin to shop around for potential lenders. Compile a list of all the financial institutions in your area that offer mortgages. Don't limit yourself to just the local mutual savings banks and still solvent savings and loans; include commercial banks, responsible finance companies, credit unions, and anyone else you can find. Check the Yellow Pages to see if there is a mortgage compilation service in your area. These companies offer lists of mortgage lenders and the products they offer, speeding up your investigation immeasurably.

Call every lender on your list, introducing yourself as a potential customer, and ask to speak to a loan officer about either fixed-rate or adjustable-rate home mortgages. Don't worry about having to work your way up the ladder. These institutions are in the business of lending money and home mortgages are among their favorite products, so you should have no problem getting someone to spend time talking to you. And be prepared—you will be spending a great deal of time talking to each person. You need a tremendous amount of information about each loan product offered by the institution in order to have the basis for an accurate comparison. (For a list of all the information you need, see the mortgage-shopping worksheet at the end of this chapter.) If you're cordial, pleasant, and patient you'll be treated similarly by the loan officer.

After calling all the lenders in your area, compare the information you've compiled to find which offers the product which best suits your individual needs. Obviously this is a customized decision, but remember to take into account all the factors on the worksheet. Once you've selected a lender and a product, stop by and pick up an application.

Mortgage applications generally all look alike. They are primarily designed to determine your ability to pay, but also seek to reinforce the judgments on your willingness to pay that will be made upon examination of your credit file. The applications are complex questionnaires asking everything from your gross salary to your addresses for the past five years. There will be areas for you to compile a list of your assets, including bank accounts, and all your obligations and outstanding debts. These applications are so complex and complete because they take the place of a personal interview. Your answers will be assigned numeric values based on the lender's scoring system. That's why it's essential you customize the application by supplementing your responses, maximizing your strengths, and minimizing your weaknesses. (For more information on how to beat scoring systems, see the chapter "Establishing Credit.")

When you've completed your customized application, put on

your interview suit and head over to the lender's offices. Rather than just dropping your application, and your hopes and dreams of owning a home, into the lap of some clerk, you are going to enlist an ally, someone to help shepherd your application through the bank's bureaucracy.

Upon arriving at the lender's offices, ask to speak to a loan officer. In a warm and caring manner, humbly explain to the loan officer that yours is special application. Point out the supplements to your answers. If you've had to clean up your credit file, show proof of the cleansing. Stress how carefully you've prepared the application, and plaintively ask your shepherd to keep an eye on your package as it works its way through the process. If you can get a loan officer to attach a name, a face, and a warm personality to that application package, you'll have gone a long way toward ensuring you'll get the fairest possible treatment. Ask you shepherd if it's all right to call with any questions—the officer will immediately agree, but will appreciate your asking. If you've done everything correctly, you should have commitment papers in hand within five weeks.

If, however, something goes wrong, don't panic. An initial rejection isn't the end, it's the beginning of another process. Remember a rejection is simply a reaction to your application package, not a permanent judgment that you aren't qualified to own a home or receive a mortgage. Telephone your shepherd and ask why your application was denied. (By federal law anyone rejected for a mortgage loan must be given a reason.) Find out what the appeals process is, and if there is none, create your own. (For information on how, see the chapter "Rejections.") While you're appealing this initial rejection, go back to your mortgage shopping worksheets, find another potential lender, and start the process all over again. There is a mortgage out there for you—it's just a matter of finding it.

But don't worry about potential rejection now. Because of the care with which you'll clean up your credit report, compare mortgage lenders and products, fill out your application, and find a shepherd, you'll probably have no trouble getting a commitment.

When you do get the commitment papers, don't rush to sign them. Once you've signed commitment papers they become legally binding contracts that cannot be changed. Up until the signatures are on the bottom line the terms are still negotiable. Telephone your attorney, tell her you've received the commitment, and schedule a meeting to go over the papers. Photocopy the documents and send a copy to the attorney's office so she can review them prior to the meeting. Then call your shepherd and thank the officer for all the effort on your behalf.

Your meeting with your lawyer is to be sure the commitment matches what you were told over the telephone and put down on your worksheet. If there are any areas you aren't sure about or would like to change, contact the lender. When all the details are ironed out, sign the papers and return them to the lenders. It's probably a good idea to deliver them in person to your shepherd. It's always nice to have a personal contact at a lending institution, and now that you've formed one it makes sense to maintain it.

On your way home from the lender's offices pick up a bottle of champagne. It's time to celebrate. You're about to buy a home.

THE DEMISE OF FUTURE FORECASTING

For generations American lenders followed strict guidelines for underwriting home mortgages. They would lend only up to 75 percent of the appraised value of the property in question, and made sure that borrowers were spending no more than 28 to 30 percent of their gross monthly income on shelter (including mortgage principal and interest, taxes, and maintenance). But then came the real estate boom of the 1980s. Lenders, seeing real estate values skyrocket and eager to cash in on the market, became more daring. They began lending up to 90 percent of appraised value and started being more flexible with their judgements of income. They believed that real estate values would continue to rise dramatically, meaning that their 90 percent stake would be, in effect, only a 75 percent stake within five years. They started looking, not just at what a borrower was currently earning, but at their potential income. If a borrower received a sizable bonus, they would project that such a bonus—or an even larger one—would be forthcoming every year. They justified this uncharacteristic optimism by calling it future forecasting. Their bubble burst with the collapse of the real estate market in 1988 and the overall economic recession which followed. Lenders have once again returned to the traditionally strict guidelines for home mortgage lending. That doesn't mean they've stopped financing home purchases, only that mortgages are now smaller and harder to get than during the 1980s.

MORTGAGE SHOPPING WORKSHEET

Use the following worksheet when shopping for home mortgages. Fill out one worksheet for each bank you contact, and after you've checked with all your potential sources, compare the results.

Lending institution _____

Telephone number _____

Name of contact _____

Address _____

	Plan A	*Plan B*	*Plan C*
Adjustable Rate Loans			
Interest rate	_____	_____	_____
Adjustment period	_____	_____	_____
Index	_____	_____	_____
Adjustment period cap	_____	_____	_____
Lifetime cap	_____	_____	_____
Convertible	_____	_____	_____
If yes, when and	_____	_____	_____
What's the cost	_____	_____	_____
Loan term	_____	_____	_____
Points	_____	_____	_____
Origination fee	_____	_____	_____
Loan-to-value ratio (LTV)	_____	_____	_____
Average percentage rate	_____	_____	_____
Fixed Rate Loans			
Interest rate	_____	_____	_____
Points	_____	_____	_____
Origination fee	_____	_____	_____
Loan term	_____	_____	_____
Loan-to-value ratio	_____	_____	_____
Average percentage rate	_____	_____	_____
All Loans			
Non-income verification	_____	_____	_____
Nonstandard LTV	_____	_____	_____
Debt-to-income ratio	_____	_____	_____

Application fee   _____ _____ _____
Appraisal fee   _____ _____ _____
Credit check fee   _____ _____ _____
Credit bureau used   _____ _____ _____
Bank attorney fee   _____ _____ _____
Prepayment penalty   _____ _____ _____
   If yes, when and   _____ _____ _____
   What's the cost   _____ _____ _____
Response/processing   _____ _____ _____
   time
Length of commitment   _____ _____ _____
Commitment renewable   _____ _____ _____
   If yes, at same rate   _____ _____ _____
   new rate   _____ _____ _____
   procedure   _____ _____ _____
Rate lock-in   _____ _____ _____
   If yes, at application   _____ _____ _____
   At commitment   _____ _____ _____
   At closing   _____ _____ _____
   What's the cost   _____ _____ _____
Special programs   _____ _____ _____
Preferred customer bene-   _____ _____ _____
   fits

Documentation Required With Application

Fees   _____ _____ _____
Paystub   _____ _____ _____
Tax returns   _____ _____ _____
Profit-and-loss statement   _____ _____ _____
   (for self-employed)
Contract of sale   _____ _____ _____
Offering plan, proprietary   _____ _____ _____
   lease, and by-laws
   (for co-ops and con-
   dos)
Building financials   _____ _____ _____
   (for co-ops and
   2+ family dwellings)
Other   _____ _____ _____

REFINANCING YOUR MORTGAGE

The conventional wisdom has always been that if current mortgage interest rates are two points below what you're paying it makes sense to refinance. But like most rules of thumb, this formula doesn't take into account unique circumstances. For example: A one-point drop in interest may mean a substantial savings for someone carrying a $500,000 mortgage, while a two-point drop in interest may not be significant for someone carrying only a $30,000 mortgage. Rather than relying on conventional wisdom you should do your own calculations. Any time the mortgage interest drops one percentage point or more below what you are paying, use the following worksheet to determine whether it makes sense to refinance.

Current monthly payment	$_____
Minus new monthly payment	−_____
Equals potential monthly savings	$_____
Multiplied by 12 months	× 12
Equals potential yearly savings	$_____
Multiplied by term of loan (i.e., 30 years)	× 30
Equals total potential savings	$_____
Cost of up-front points	$_____
Plus bank's attorney's fees	+_____
Plus your attorney's fees	+_____
Plus bank's application and appraisal fees	+_____
Equals total cost of refinancing	$_____
Divided by potential monthly savings	÷_____
Equals number of months it takes to break even	_____

FOR MORE INFORMATION . . .

You can learn more about mortgages from the following books:
- *The Field Guide to Home Buying in America* by Stephen M. Pollan and Mark Levine
- *The New Real Estate Game* by Hollis Norton
- *Tips and Traps on Buying a Home* by Robert Irwin

MOVING

Insuring It's Your Possessions That Get Taken for a Ride

The average American makes six major and numerous other minor moves in his or her lifetime. Not only is this transaction expensive (a major move costs between $3,000 and $5,000) and traumatic, but it is also completely one-sided. You are putting your possessions in the hands of movers you have never met before, and who aren't relying on repeat business for their livelihood. Close to 50 percent of all moves result in some damage to possessions. In addition, the standard practices of the moving industry are so complex and confusing that it is easy for unaware consumers to be taken advantage of.

While your heart may be yearning for your new home, it is essential that your mind remain focused on the move itself rather than dreaming of the future. You should only begin celebrating and relaxing after your possessions are safely unloaded in your new home.

The first thing to do when you are planning a move is to solicit bids from a number of different moving companies. Rather than rely on moving-company whims, draw up your own specifications—a checklist stating what is to be moved, how far, how long it should take, and what other services are required—and have moving companies bid on it. This will let you make an accurate price comparison.

Make sure to check on each mover's reputation with the Better Business Bureau. Interstate movers are regulated by the Interstate Commerce Commission and are required to provide you with a copy of a government pamphlet detailing your rights when moving. They must also provide you with a copy of the company's performance record for the past year. Local movers, on the other hand, are subject to no specific regulations. Since it is an inexpensive business to enter—all you need is a strong back and a van—many less than savory characters have entered the local moving market, making it doubly important to check their reputations and ask for references. Avoid fly-by-night operators. If a moving company won't give you an exact pickup or delivery date, refuses to give you references, has a telephone that is only answered by a machine, and/or discourages you from watching them load and unload, you can bet they are ripping you off.

When soliciting price quotes from moving companies, beware of nonbinding bids. These estimates, often given by slick salesmen who have never moved anything in their life, are intentionally low in order to attract business. Instead, ask for a binding bid or combination estimate. A binding bid will probably be the highest estimate you receive, but it will indeed represent your actual cost. A combination bid binds the mover, not you. If, on the day of the move, your possessions weigh less than the estimate, you pay the lower amount. Needless to say this is the best option for consumers and the one that movers try to avoid.

Ask about add-on costs, extra fees, and surcharges. While the prices for interstate moves are standardized, moving companies pad their bills by charging additional fees for packing, unpacking, disconnecting appliances, and moving unusually heavy items. Carefully check all estimates to see if they have added fees for extra, unnecessary frills, or if they have left out the charges for needed services.

Steer clear of moving company insurance policies. Most moving companies limit their liability to sixty cents a pound—which means that if your one-pound Ming vase is broken, you will receive only sixty cents. In addition, payouts come directly out of the moving company's coffers, not from an insurance fund, so it is difficult to collect. Instead, check to see if your homeowner's insurance offers moving coverage, and if not, inquire about a rider to your policy. They are often quite inexpensive and can provide you with effective protection.

Investigate the company's tipping policy before the day of the move. Ask your salesperson or an office contact about the standard tipping policy and decide ahead of time how much you will tip. Consider tipping 50 percent in advance if you have particularly precious objects. Don't be intimidated into tipping more than you intended. A woman moving alone should have a male friend or relative on hand to discourage any attempts at intimidation.

Get the name of a contact at the moving company's headquarters or main office who will be available on the days your possessions are loaded and unloaded. If you have any problems with the movers themselves, or if a problem arises, don't hesitate to drop the name of your contact, or pick up the telephone and give them a call.

When your possessions are being loaded, check the driver's list of items—called a bill of lading—and make sure that the condition of each item is duly noted. It may sound like a hassle, but this list is the only way you will be able to verify that damage occurred during the move. Don't sign the bill of lading unless you have read it, agreed to its contents, and verified that the correct date of delivery is included.

Interstate movers charge based on their calculation of what your possessions weigh and how far they must be moved. That's why it is important for you to be present whenever your possessions are weighed. An unscrupulous mover can falsify the weight of your load, thus adding substantially to your bill. You have the right to witness the weighing and to even request a reweighing if you are suspicious.

Local movers often charge an hourly fee for each vehicle and person required to move your possessions. While having more movers may speed up the move, it may also result in a larger bill than necessary. Discuss the alternatives with your salesperson, and make sure that your crew isn't padded on the actual day of the move.

Keep an eye on the entire unloading process and make sure that the driver accurately notes the condition of items when they are unpacked. If you discover something damaged, leave it in the packaging and immediately contact the company to place a claim. Generally you have up to nine months to file a claim with the company.

To insure that your move goes smoothly you must take an active role, even if the movers imply that you are intruding. After all, these are your prized possessions and you have a right to see that they are cared for properly.

NEGOTIATING PRICES

Striking the Best Deal When Making Purchases

You don't have to be a born haggler to negotiate prices effectively. And it is actually possible to negotiate the selling price of almost every object you buy, regardless of its size, ticketed or asking price, or where it's being sold. The only thing that should keep you from trying to negotiate the price of a purchase is if you estimate that it will take you more time than it's actually worth—bargaining for an hour over $5 for example. Otherwise, you should feel free to negotiate the price of every product or service you buy, whether it's a home, your accountant's bill, or a new television set.

The first key to being an effective price negotiator is knowledge. You must know as much as possible about the item you are buying and the person selling it.

If it's a consumer product, or personal property that you are buying, you should know who makes it (the actual manufacturer may not be the brand-name one); how reliable it is; how it stacks up against its direct competitors in terms of price and features; the list price; the normal selling price; and the bottom price or dealer's cost. Since the rules of markup are hazy today, with different retail channels claiming to offer discount prices, it is essential to come up with an accurate appraisal of what is actually the lowest price available.

When buying real property—a home, land, or a business—a savvy buyer will try to learn why it is being sold and what is its market value. There is a big difference between market value and bottom price. All real property has a market value, which is generally represented by a range. A home, for example, that you may initially say is worth $200,000 actually has a market value of anywhere from $185,000 up to $215,000, depending on its unique qualities.

All of this preliminary research will pay off when it comes to the actual negotiations. If you are aware of the motivations of the other party, you may be able to take advantage of them. If, let's say, the sellers of a home you are interested in buying have already bought another home and are concerned with selling their old home right away, they may be willing to accept an assurance of speed—having a preapproved mortgage or cash—in exchange for a sizable price concession. Learn all you can about the other party by observing appearances and attitudes, then try to do a little undercover work by asking around. Even if you never use this information, it will make you more comfortable during the negotiations. Similarly, knowing the true bottom price can save you sizable amounts of dollars and make you more powerful. One of the secrets of professional negotiators is to work up from cost or bottom price, ignoring list or asking price, since the seller has already added on a profit or markup to come up with the original figure.

But before you begin discussing price, you must first make sure that the person you are dealing with actually has the power to negotiate. All too often we waste valuable time and energy trying to bargain with people who don't really have the power to make a decision. That's why one of the first things you should say to a salesman is, "I have already done a great deal of research and am interested in discussing price, but before we begin, I'd like to make sure that you have the power to negotiate price." In many instances the person with the power to make a price concession is insulated from buyers. Whether it is the owner of a home being shielded by a real estate broker, or the manager of a car dealership being protected by a floor salesman, you must try to get through to the person with the decision-making powers and deal directly with them.

One of the problems with negotiations is that they are set up from the beginning as adversarial relationships in which one party is the winner and the other is the loser. In many cases people hold on to positions simply to save face. Actually, an effective negotiation is one in which both parties come out winning—perhaps not by as much as they would have liked, but they can still walk away from the table happy. That's why in most instances it is better to negotiate purchases in person. Telephones often make people braver than they actually are—it is easier to be tough with a disembodied voice than with someone sitting across the table from you. Being with the other party, face-to-face, lets you create a positive environment.

Creating a positive environment is really easy. Be friendly, warm, and caring. Smile. Dress and act in a completely neutral manner. Don't use confrontational body language such as crossing your arms over your chest, furrowing your brow, or scowling. Instead, make a conscious effort to relax, and use open, soft gestures. Let them do most of the talking. However, don't nod or unconsciously mutter yes to their comments or questions. Your agreement to their arguments is valuable and should not be thrown around lightly.

In most instances the seller is going to have the first offer already on the table—a price tag on personal property or an advertised asking price for real property. That means it's up to you to break the ice and respond. Never discuss price immediately. Begin instead with a compliment. Say that the item in question is wonderful and beautiful. Explain that you have done a lot of research and a lot of looking, and clearly this item is the best you have seen. Next, explain that you are a serious buyer, are willing to make a deal, and are open to negotiations. Then it's time to talk dollars and cents.

There are a great many different theories about negotiating, and new books on the subject come out every year. But in the final analysis all price negotiating is just salami slicing. The seller starts with a high price and the buyer starts with a low price, and they move, bit by bit, slice by slice, to a compromise position where both can be happy. If they can reach an agreement there is a sale. If they can't, the buyer withdraws and the seller waits for someone else to come along.

When you are buying personal property, say to the seller that you understand they want to get their list price, and that you agree they are entitled to a reasonable markup, but that your research has revealed that the product is available for . . . and then quote the bottom price you have uncovered. Ask them if that is a price they can match, or if not, what is their best price?

Coming up with an offer is bit more difficult when buying real property since there is no one correct price, but rather a range of prices. Since your goal is to pay a price in the lower end of the range, you should begin with an offer that gives you some room to move up into that range. That allows the other party to see you make concessions and gives them a reason to make concessions as well.

The entire process of give-and-take, offer and counteroffer, is called incremental negotiations and has a logic all its own. The first offer from a buyer generally signals what he or she is willing to pay—the midpoint between the asking price and the offer. The seller's response to the buyer's first offer generally signals what he or she is willing to accept—the midpoint between the offer and his or her response. Understanding this will let you maneuver the compromise point toward your end of the price range. And that really is all you can ask for. In order to be a successful negotiator you have to be wiling to pay within the market value range, otherwise you will never be able to make deals.

Let's say that you are interested in buying a home that has an asking price of $215,000. In the course of your investigations you discover that the market value of the home is between $185,000 and $215,000. If you make an initial offer of $185,000, you are signaling that you would be willing to pay $200,000 for the home. If the seller responds by lowering their price to $210,000, it probably indicates that they too would be willing to compromise on $200,000. If instead they drop their price only slightly, to $214,000, they are looking for you to come up with an offer of over $200,000. You, on the other hand, should respond similarly by jumping to only $186,000. A desperate seller may foolishly drop their price dramatically in response to your initial offer, making a counteroffer of perhaps $190,000. Instead of grabbing it, offer $187,000, which is probably the price they are willing to accept.

It is important to provide reasons for each price offer you make. This shows that you are acting logically, not capriciously. If you are buying personal property, your first offer should be accompanied by a reason such as, "I believe that other similar objects have sold for that price recently." If you are buying real property, you should provide a reason for your offer's being less than the asking price—the need to replace the roof, for example. For each concession you make you should also provide a reason— that you won't have to do any additional landscaping, perhaps. If you are negotiating over personal property, say that you are willing to come up from your bottom price since this was from a mail order company that doesn't provide repair service.

Never bid against yourself. If the seller makes no response, tell them that you are willing to negotiate if they are, and repeat your original offer. Anyone who increases or decreases his or her price without a corresponding concession from the other side is asking for trouble. You have broadcast your desperation. All the other side has to do is sit and wait for you to come up or down.

The other important technique that buyers can use to their advantage is to take up as much of the seller's time as possible. All sellers want to close their deals quickly. Sellers of personal property want to go on to other customers and make more sales, and sellers of real property want to have the money in the bank earning interest, or have the money available to buy replacement property. The more time you can get the seller to invest in you, the more likely you are to get them to come down to your offer. Setting up negotiations for the end of the day, or the end of the week, puts added pressure on sellers and creates deadlines in their minds. In addition, try to increase your offer by the smallest increments you possibly can—thousands instead of tens of thousands of dollars, or ten dollars instead of hundreds of dollars.

Effective negotiating requires patience and time. Unless you are willing to do your research and take your time in reaching a compromise, you won't be able to come out a winner.

FOR MORE INFORMATION . . .

You can learn more about negotiating prices from the following book:

- *You Can Negotiate Anything* by Herb Cohen

NEIGHBOR DISPUTES
Getting Along With the People Next Door

While your home is your castle, you still have to deal with the people in the castle next door regardless of whether you live in a mansion on twenty acres, a split level on one-quarter of an acre, or a studio apartment in a high-rise building. Theoretically, and often legally, you have the right to do almost anything to your home or property as long as it is okay with local zoning laws and building organizations. But legal theory and real-life practice are two different things.

Whether we like it or not, our neighbors do impact on our lives. The way they care, or don't care, for their home reflects positively or negatively on the value of our own home. Neighbors can also be a part of our support systems. When you are younger and are new to a community, you often reach out to your neighbors for friendship and camaraderie, especially if you are all in approximately the same age group. Then, gradually, as you become more and more settled, you and your neighbors drift apart, since often the only thing you have in common is proximity to each other. But eventually things come full circle. In a retirement community, neighbor ties become important once again as older people come to depend on each other for help in the day-to-day tasks that are becoming increasingly difficult for them to do alone.

If a neighbor's tree blocks the sunlight from your deck, you are within your right to trim that portion of the tree that extends onto your side of the property line. You own not only the land your house sits on, but the air rights above it as well. In practice, however, it makes sense to discuss the situation with the neighbor beforehand.

Similarly, you are allowed to build any type of fence you want, as long as it is on your property. However, fences that are put up for malicious reasons may be illegal, depending on where you live. In some states, the motivations for constructing a fence have nothing to do with its legality, while in others—such as Michigan, North Carolina, and Georgia—you can successfully sue over "spite" fences.

When you are having a problem with a neighbor—a roaming dog or loud parties—the best thing to do is to try to negotiate one-on-one. See if you can work something out between you. After all, you have to live with these people.

If nothing comes from your personal negotiations, you are within your rights to contact the local police department. Most municipalities have ordinances about keeping dogs restrained and keeping noise down during early-morning and late-evening hours. A friendly visit and warning from the local cop may help end problems before they become chronic.

Occasionally even these warnings may not be enough, and you may be tempted to bring the matter to court. Wait. Mediation may be a better way to handle the problem. According to the American Bar Association, there are mediation panels for just these types of disputes set up in each of the fifty states, and there are more than 22,000 trained mediators ready, willing, and able to help resolve minor neighborhood disputes. If mediation doesn't help, you can also turn to small-claims court for justice.

As long as you are not doing anything hazardous to your neighbors, you can legally do almost anything you want to your property. But in practice that can lead to trouble. Even if you don't socialize with your neighbors, your children might socialize with their children, so be aware that conflicts may affect them rather than you.

During the early 1960s my family and I lived in a neatly manicured, middle-class suburban neighborhood. One of the major concerns of my neighbors was lawn care. I, on the other hand, a city boy through and through, couldn't care the least about my lawn. Subtle comments from neighbors just made me more determined to cultivate "the natural look." Finally, when the comments became less subtle, I went outside and mowed my initials into the lawn as my way of thumbing my nose at their conformity. I was feeling very proud of myself until my youngest daughter came home in tears. It seems that all the other kids in the neighborhood were told not to play with her since her father was "a nut." As soon as I realized that my stubborn adherence to principle was making her life miserable, I hired a local boy to mow the lawn regularly. However, I also put the house up for sale and moved within the year.

NET WORTH

Calculating and Demonstrating Your Financial Worth

Personal net worth statements have become increasingly important. Most membership applications—whether for country clubs, co-ops, or condominiums—are now asking for this type of self-analysis. Rightly or wrongly, people are making enormously important judgments of you based on this statement. They erroneously believe that as net worth increases, so does stability, predictability, and good character.

In order to meet the needs and expectations of membership committees, it is important to prepare a Technicolor net worth statement that defines important nuances and highlights areas of particular merit. Unfortunately, few accountants know how to draw up anything other than a textbook black-and-white net worth statement.

The simple definition of net worth is the difference between your assets and liabilities—at least that's what your accountant will say. But that basic formula is outdated and limiting. To project your net worth accurately you have to take into account reasonable expectations, the real market value of your assets, as well as the realistic—as opposed to legal—nature of all your liabilities.

The first place where a parochial net worth statement can be colorized is the section listing all of your personal property and how much it is worth.

All your personal property has increased in value since it was purchased. The item that you purchased fifteen years ago costs 250 percent more today, if you calculate inflation at 7 percent a year. Use that multiple when listing values.

Antiques have a remarkable cachet today. Place any item more than fifty years old in a separate antique section on your statement, and make sure to reflect its current market value. Scour the attic, cellar, and garage for items of value.

Even if you aren't the original owner of the Mercedes or BMW in your driveway, it still represents a hefty asset. Call it a pre-owned automobile and itemize its value appropriately.

Another way to enhance your net worth statement is to include monies owed you—even by parents and/or children—and recurring gifts as assets. List any debts owed you, and simply note the probability and rate of payback. If you receive a periodic gift of $1,000 from your parents, include that on your list of assets as well. Add a note describing its current value and the likelihood of its being a recurring event.

Many applications will request that you note the original cost of any real estate you own. That doesn't preclude you from also calculating and listing its current market value.

If you have any contingent liabilities that may have to be listed—for example a loan you cosigned for a relative or child—include a statement that shows how highly unlikely it is for it to fall to you due to the net worth and income of the primary borrower.

All of these techniques are entirely ethical, valid, and justified. In fact, they are essential if you are going to present a net worth statement that accurately reflects your true financial status. As long as membership organizations see fit to judge your character by the size of your wallet, you have every right to present yourself in the best possible light.

SAMPLE NET WORTH STATEMENT

Assets
Cash in banks   _____
Savings and loan shares   _____
Investments (stocks and bonds)   _____
Investment in own business   _____
Real estate owned   _____
Automobiles   _____
Personal property and furniture   _____
Life insurance cash surrender value   _____
Other assets
    Total Assets $_____

Liabilities
Notes payable
    To banks   _____
    To relatives   _____
    To others   _____

Installment accounts payable
   Auto   _____
   Other
Mortgages payable on real estate   _____
Unpaid real estate taxes   _____
Unpaid income taxes   _____
Loans on life insurance policies   _____
Other debts
   Total Liabilities $_____

Net Worth (Total Assets − Total Liabilities) $_____

NURSING HOME CARE

Minimizing Its Economic Impact

The sad truth about nursing home care in America is that the consumer has no choices. We are in the midst of a nursing home crisis: the demand for beds far outstrips the supply. Unless current efforts to build more homes are increased dramatically, this crisis will turn into a national disaster as the baby boom generation reaches maturity. In this environment, any discussion about how to select a nursing home would be laughable if it weren't such a traumatic situation.

As if the lack of space weren't enough of a problem, the cost of nursing home care when it is obtained is astronomical. The average cost for one year of nursing home care in America is $22,000—of course the fees are much higher in the major metropolitan areas. Medicare will pay for only one hundred days of care in a nursing home, and only under certain conditions. And aside from specific long-term-care insurance policies, health insurance plans do not cover extended nursing home stays. That means that the sizable cost of care must be covered by the patient and his or her family.

Medicaid can come to the rescue and pick up the tab for a stay in a nursing home, but to qualify for this program, an individual must have almost no assets. All retirement income and pensions must also be turned over to medicaid. And if your parent does qualify for medicaid, it will be even more difficult to find a bed for them, since nursing homes—whether for-profit or not-for-profit— give priority to those people on their waiting lists who can pay for care themselves.

The solution to this nightmare situation is to plan and prepare carefully for the possibility of having to enter a nursing home. This preparation means disposing of an elderly person's assets so that they are not completely exhausted by the cost of care, while retaining enough assets so that they can pay for three to five months of care on their own.

Once a person reaches the age of sixty he or she should carefully begin placing all his or her assets under joint ownership, either with a spouse or a child. Then, as soon as it begins to be clear that nursing home care may be necessary, they should begin signing over the assets to the spouse or child. When medicaid calculates a person's assets, they will consider only 50 percent of a joint asset as belonging to the individual in question. The catch, however, is that any transfers or changes in ownership that take place less than thirty months prior to the application for medicaid are considered to be simply attempts at shielding assets and are therefore ignored.

If you are placed in the position of having to arrange nursing home care for an elderly parent or a spouse, you must take action as soon as possible. Convince the elderly person to make the financial transfers necessary, bringing in outside experts if need be. Social workers and attorneys from local legal aid societies can be of tremendous assistance in explaining to your parent or spouse that this is a necessary and legitimate process. Keep enough money in the person's name so that they can "buy" their way into a nursing home, but then qualify for medicaid within four or five months.

Until the current nursing home crisis is addressed, this is the only way you can guarantee both that your loved one will get into a home, and that there will be some assets left to be distributed to his or her family as had been intended.

FOR MORE INFORMATION . . .

You can learn more about nursing home care from the following books:
- *How to Choose a Nursing Home* by Joanne Meshinsky
- *When Love Gets Tough—The Nursing Home Decision* by Doug Manning

PERSONAL FEES

How Much to Charge for Part-time Consulting

Consulting has become widespread throughout the business world. Many executives now realize that they can cut costs by bringing outside experts into their company for a short period of time to do a specific job, rather than paying the salary and providing benefits for a full-time staffer. Full-time consultants are able to set their fees through the traditional method—calculating their overhead, expenses, and adding a profit margin—but for the person doing part-time consulting, setting and communicating fees is a vexing problem. And most often it's the consultant's own ego that's to blame.

The secret to setting and sticking to a fee is to realize that a consulting fee is not a measure of your worth as an individual. You are not charging for yourself, but for a product: your services. Quite often, consultants will ask the prospective client, "How does a thousand dollars a day sound?" as if they were looking for approval. You'll never hear a grocer ask a customer how two dollars for a can of tuna sounds.

Separate your ego from the process. You aren't measuring your own value, you are simply putting a price on a commodity. Even though it is a cerebral product, your services should be treated like any other item that has a market value.

If the client attempts to negotiate your fee, deflect him or her by simply stating that "that is the price." If the client can't afford your services, so be it. Any movement off the stated fee will indicate that you don't value the product. If that's the case, why should the client value it?

The fee itself should be whatever the market will bear, just as it is with any other commodity. Check what others in your area are charging for similar services and price your own services accordingly. While it is easiest to determine fees on an hourly basis, these types of figures often frighten clients who have no concept of how long a task or project will take. If possible, set a fee for a full day's work or a half-day's work, basing your charge on a full day's comprising twelve working hours. One guideline to consider is that the federal government is currently paying $1,500 a day to its consultants. Don't feel guilty about the size of your fee. Remember that in hiring you the client is avoiding the added expense of a full-time employee.

Once you separate your ego from your fee you'll find that the whole process of negotiating for consulting work becomes very simple. The client can choose to pay for your services or not. In either case the integrity of your fee is untarnished.

CHARGING FOR TRAVEL TIME

I believe that it is perfectly justifiable to charge for the time you spend traveling to or from a consulting job if it involves time spent thinking and preparing. On a one-day job, for example, it is acceptable to charge for your time traveling to the site in the morning, but not for your time spent going home at night.

WORKSHEET FOR DETERMINING CONSULTING FEES

Overhead (your monthly fixed expenses)

Rent	_____
Utilities	_____
Telephone	_____
Continuing education	_____
Office expense	_____
Supplies	_____
Postage	_____
Insurance	_____
Other	_____
Total monthly overhead	_____
Divided by 30	÷ 30
Equals daily overhead	_____
Divided by 8	÷ 8
Equals hourly overhead	_____

Salary

Appropriate monthly salary	_____
Divided by 30	÷ 30
Equals daily salary	_____

Divided by 8   ÷ 8

Equals hourly salary   _____

Hourly overhead + hourly salary
  equals hourly fee   _____

Multiplied by number of hours de-   x hours
  voted to project

Equals fee   _____

Billable expenditures (your variable expenses)

Travel (to consultation)   _____

Entertainment   _____

Photocopying   _____

Other   _____

Total billable expenditures   _____

Total billable expenditures plus total fee equals total   _____
  bill

PRECIOUS METALS AND GEMS
Buying Into a Refugee Mentality

Whenever there are economic or political tremors in the world, sales of precious metals and gems increase. For some reason people feel that in unstable times they are best off investing in the most basic of substances. They evidently subscribe to the old refugee mentality that you should convert your assets into objects you can carry or hide on your person. Unscrupulous sellers prey on these fears and tout the benefits and stability of gold and diamonds. Regardless of the political or economic climate, I have never heard a good argument for investing in precious metals or gems. Despite the claims of salespeople, gold prices, for example, remained stagnant throughout the Persian Gulf crisis. By all means buy these magnificent baubles for adornment, but never buy them for an investment.

PRENUPTIAL AGREEMENTS

Drawing the Battle Lines . . . Just in Case

In this age of money obsession and widespread divorce, prenuptial agreements have increasingly become a popular financial planning device. These contracts, signed by a couple before they marry, stipulate how much of the other spouse's assets a partner can claim if they divorce or if one of them dies. While these agreements make a lot of sense financially, especially if one partner comes to the marriage with substantially more assets than the other, I believe they are being misused.

Second marriages, in which one or both parties have children from prior marriages, should definitely be preceded by a prenuptial agreement.

While the various permutations of such agreements are limitless, the standard features might include:

- schedules outlining 100 percent of the premarriage assets of both parties;
- acknowledgments that each party is aware of and agrees with these schedules;
- provisions for the disposition of these premarriage assets upon potential termination of the marriage;
- provisions for the disposition of marital assets upon potential termination of the marriage; and
- a statement that whatever state guidelines or laws that exist for the distribution of assets upon termination of a marriage are waived and replaced by the prenuptial agreement.

It's vital that each party to a prenuptial agreement be independently represented by an attorney. If both partners use the same attorney, it's very likely the agreement would be set aside by the courts if there was a dispute. Although prenuptial agreements make sense for second marriages, I believe first marriages should avoid these documents like the plague. Legally dividing up assets and designating shares makes a great deal of sense when it is used to protect children and dependents. But simply drawing the battle lines for a divorce with the only intent being to shield your assets from the other party is a mistake. It is subliminally setting the stage for marital troubles by assuming problems.

If one or both parties to a first marriage feel the need to protect their individual assets, they should simply keep their bank accounts and assets separate even after getting married. Then at some point when they feel comfortable, they may convert them to joint assets; or they may continue to keep some of their assets separate. While this may be an indication of some reticence at getting married, it is better than printing up the blueprint for a divorce before you even tie the knot.

PRIVACY RIGHTS

Keeping Yours Intact

As we go about our daily lives, shopping, making telephone calls, applying for jobs, credit cards, loans, and insurance policies, and visiting physicians, an incredible amount of personal information about us is collected by those we come in contact with. In the 1990s, this information is becoming much easier to collect, store, manipulate into lists or profiles, and transfer to others, thanks to rapidly improving communications and information technologies. While some of this personal information is legitimately needed by businesses, a great deal of it is not. And with each year that passes, our control over personal information and who has access to it weakens. In order to keep your privacy intact in the 1990s, take charge of the situation and implement this ten-step program:

1. Obtain a copy of your credit report and check it for mistakes. (For more information see the chapter "Credit Bureau Reports.") Instead of waiting for a credit rejection, take the initiative and examine the reports the major credit bureaus (Trans Union, TRW, Equifax) have on you now, before they interfere with your attempts to get a job or a loan. You can obtain a copy of your credit file by providing the credit union with your name, social security number, and your addresses for the past five years. There is usually a small fee involved, but if you have been turned down for credit recently, you may be able to obtain a copy for free.

2. Get a copy of your personal file from the Medical Information Bureau. This data bank is maintained and shared by insurance companies and contains both medical and nonmedical information. You can get a copy of the nonmedical information simply by writing the bureau (P.O. Box 105, Esses Station, Boston, MA 02112). The medical portion of the file will be released only upon a doctor's request, so have your personal physician ask for a copy and then pass it along to you.

3. Sit down with your doctor and review your medical file, making sure it is accurate and complete. Inaccurate information

could lead to problems in emergencies or in obtaining insurance or employment.

4. When filling out warranty, rebate, and incentive questionnaires, omit information that clearly is irrelevant. Many companies and organizations use these programs to collect marketing information and often sell it to others.

5. Protect your telephone privacy. Investigate and consider using the soon-to-be-available caller ID technology, which displays the telephone number of the person calling, allowing you to screen which calls you will answer. Another way to screen calls is to use an answering machine, which lets you monitor the call before picking up. Finally, do not hold confidential conversations on cellular or cordless telephones—calls can easily be monitored, either intentionally or unintentionally.

6. When calling 800 or 900 numbers, request that you not be included in subsequent marketing programs. Often, these telephone exchanges use their own caller ID systems to automatically match your name and telephone number to your address, creating a list for direct mail and telemarketing programs.

7. Subscribe to the Telephone Preference Service, sponsored by the Direct Marketing Association (11 West 42nd Street, New York, NY 10017), which provides telemarketers with a list of people who do not wish to be contacted. This saves them money and your annoyance.

8. Subscribe to the Mail Preference Service, also sponsored by the Direct Marketing Association, which takes your name off mailing lists.

9. Don't reveal too much information over the telephone. If a telemarketer requests more information than seems necessary, refuse to provide it. Never give your credit card number over the phone unless you initiated the call or are conducting a transaction with a well-known vendor. Similarly, never give credit card numbers or your social security number to someone who requests it for "identification" reasons.

10. Write letters to organizations and companies that send you unsolicited mailings, solicitations, and catalogs, and ask that your name be removed from their mailing lists.

RAISES

Tips and Techniques for Moving in the Right Direction

Getting a raise has never been easy, but today, with employers cutting costs and thinning out staff, negotiating a pay increase is even more difficult. But with the right research, attitude, and presentation it is possible to get a fair increase from even the most frugal of employers.

There are few more frightening situations than asking for a raise. The first step in the process is to eliminate fear by realizing that an employer's decision is only a judgment on the amount you are paid for the services you provide. In no way is it a reflection of your value as a human being. Employers bring their own fears to the raise negotiations: Are you going to leave the company if you don't receive an adequate raise? Is the company's pay structure fair? As you'll see, savvy raise negotiating involves eliminating your fears and playing to employers' fears.

Many employees don't even attempt to negotiate raises since they are told the company has "a system" for pay increases. In most cases this is simply a smoke screen. Managers generally have at least 20 percent latitude in setting salaries and are often given a total budget for staff that they are allowed to allocate as they see fit. And even if there is a system, it can always be amended for special circumstances, such as an increased contribution to the company or a change in job description.

Since there is no monolithic system that dictates raises, it is up to you to take the matter into your own hands. Start by doing research on your company. What is the salary structure of the organization? Are there standard raise guidelines? How strictly are they enforced? Are there any precedents for circumventing the rules? What are your peers earning? And who has the power to grant your raise request? Go back and consult the research you gathered when you applied for your job and update it, paying careful attention to how the financial health of your company has changed since you were originally hired.

Next, calculate your value on the job market. Check the Bureau of Labor Statistics, competing companies, trade associations, trade-magazine surveys, help-wanted advertisements, employment agencies, and headhunters for an accurate appraisal of what your salary should be. It may even be worthwhile to start looking for another job as a way to determine your value.

Take inventory of your job performance. Are you making a greater contribution to the company? Has your job profile changed? Document your personal inventory in a written memo. This can be presented to a supervisor unfamiliar with your performance or used as an outline for discussions with your immediate boss.

There are good and bad times to ask for a raise. If during your most recent salary negotiation a review date was agreed to, stick to it. If no mention was made of a review, wait one year. Of course, there are exceptions to this rule: if your previous increase was an interim raise; if your job description has changed dramatically; or if your research indicates that a delay might improve your chances of success. It is always better to ask for a raise before annual budgets are drawn up, prior to inventory, and at the start of a new selling season. Then again, delaying could result in your being offered a token increase. Remember, the key to any successful negotiation is to take control of the situation. It's better to jump the gun and be in charge than to be forced to negotiate up a token offer.

Once the general time frame for your raise negotiation is established, try to schedule it for a Tuesday, Wednesday, or Thursday, in the late morning or early afternoon.

Before you actually enter into negotiations, have a specific target number in mind. Without a number, the discussion will center on whether or not you deserve a raise. With a number, the issue becomes how much of a raise you deserve. Base this salary figure first on your research and an appraisal of your needs. Don't inflate it for negotiation's sake, and preface all discussions by saying, "I don't care to play negotiating games; the figure I've arrived at is a sincere and reasonable one and reflects my market value."

One reason so much fear is attached to the raise negotiation is that there have never been rules of etiquette for the situation. At uncomfortable times Americans like to fall back on traditional rules of behavior. With that in mind, here is a brief course in raise conduct:
- Project warmth and caring, but veer away from friendship.
- Listen more than you speak, letting the employer fill conversational gaps if they arise.

- Maintain direct eye contact.
- Refer to the company, not your boss, as your employer.
- Act as you would in any other significant business transaction.
- If the other party seems in any way preoccupied, adjourn the meeting.
- Don't go in as an adversary.
- Don't threaten or make demands, but don't be tentative either.
- Don't personalize the discussion, keep it businesslike.
- Don't nod in agreement with what the employer says; you may imply concessions you don't want to make.
- Don't project guilt about asking for a raise.
- Don't use words such as "sir"; simply call the other party "Mr., Ms., or Mrs. Jones."
- Don't be humble about your accomplishments.
- Don't be sidetracked by employer resentment or anger.

Muster all your evidence and persuasiveness to back up one single argument: your compensation no longer matches your contribution either because of your accomplishments or a change in your job description. This is the most powerful tack an employee can take in any salary discussion.

Of equal importance to a successful raise negotiation are your responses to the counterarguments of your employer. A strong response based on merit will refute just about any objection. For example:

- If your employer says, "You haven't been here long enough to get a raise," respond with, "I don't think you can fairly measure my value to the company by the length of time I have been here. Let's look at what I've accomplished since I've started."
- If your employer says, "We have a policy of . . .," or asks, "How can I pay you so much more than Jones?" respond by asking, "Am I to understand that no matter how hard I work or how successful I am here I won't be rewarded for it? I have always operated under the assumption that excellence would be rewarded here."

Perhaps your employer will try to plead poverty, saying that there just isn't the money available right now for a salary increase. In that case, ask if they agree that you deserve a raise. Just having turned you down, they are unlikely to do so again. At this point you can get a commitment to negotiate at a specific date in the future with an understanding that the raise will be retroactive. If the mood is right, you can even negotiate the raise at this meeting. A third response to the poor-timing counterargument is to expand your request to include things other than money—I call this "the raise mosaic."

Throughout your negotiation you should keep in mind that compensation includes more than the numbers on your paycheck. You can turn your raise request into a mosaic by asking for more vacation times, a more desirable schedule, a better title, an improved health or pension plan, equity in the company, tuition reimbursement, a better office, a secretary or assistant, use of a company car, or an expense account. By bringing additional issues to the bargaining table you will invariably do better than if salary is the only item under discussion.

Some employers will try to regain the control you have wrested away by making a compromise offer. Don't accept or reject it right away. In fact, ask to have the meeting adjourned and make another appointment. This will catch the employer by surprise and give you time to think the offer over, giving you back control over the negotiation. While thinking, reformulate your original request, adding arguments you overlooked or left out, and introducing new issues other than money. This allows you to set the agenda for the next discussion. Patience is power in raise negotiations. The longer you can keep the matter under discussion the better you will do.

Rarely will your request for an increase be met with a flat no. Rejection usually takes the form of a token increase. If this happens to you, keep discussing the matter and try to win a commitment to renegotiate in the near future. Schedule a subsequent meeting and mount an appeal—it's tough to turn someone down twice. Treat this apparent rejection not as a decision but as an interpretation of the facts you presented. Bolster your argument with new facts and ask for a reinterpretation based on this new information.

Carefully analyze the reasons for a rejection. Use the raise negotiation as a reexamination of your job situation. This insight, while not as valuable as increased compensation, is important and telling. If the company doesn't have enough money to pay you what you're worth, can you afford to stay there much longer? If your accomplishments are undervalued, aren't you hurting your career by remaining? Perhaps your contributions aren't that significant. In that case this probably isn't the job for you. Consider this: the biggest raises in compensation usually come through job changes.

FRINGE BENEFITS AND PERQUISITES

There are basically two types of fringe benefits or perquisites: monetary and psychic. The secret to savvy raise negotiating is being able to tell the difference. For example, medical and dental coverage for you or your family members has a definite monetary value, as do life insurance policies and retirement plans. A company car can be very valuable if gas, repair, and insurance bills are paid by your employer. Similarly, a clothing allowance can be of benefit. Expense accounts, drivers, corner offices, the key to the executive washroom, and occasional seats in the company box at the baseball stadium, on the other hand, are strictly psychic in value and should not be part of your raise mosaic.

BREAKING THE ICE

The first thing that you should say to the other side during a raise negotiation is, "I love my job, but I have a problem, and I need your help with it."

DEALING WITH A FLAT NO

While it is unlikely, occasionally bosses do respond to raise requests with a flat no. In that case, the best thing you can do is start looking for another job.

A GUARANTEED WAY TO GET A RAISE

The best way to guarantee that you get a raise in salary is to find a higher-paying position at another company. After you've lined up another job and are sure you're prepared to accept it, approach your current employer and say, "I must tell you that I have been approached by another company, which has offered me a substantial salary raise. While I would prefer to stay here, I really must give priority to my/my family's financial health." If your boss matches, or improves on the other company's offer, you have gotten yourself a raise. If your boss doesn't match the other offer, accept it, and you will also have gotten yourself a raise.

RAISING CASH

Dealing With Immediate Cash Flow Crises

Regardless of his or her income, almost everyone, at one time or another, is faced with a financial emergency where the overwhelming priority is raising cash as quickly and as painlessly as possible. No matter how astute or savvy your financial planning, a debt may come due prematurely, an income source may dry up overnight, or sudden medical expenses—not covered by insurance—may arise. Too many people view cash flow emergencies as signs of failure, admissions of poor planning, or as reasons to feel guilty.

Nothing could be further from the truth. Any stigmas you attach to the process are self-imposed. You need not be a supplicant. There are people willing to help and resources available that you can tap. Once you eliminate these inhibitions and put aside foolish notions of pride, you'll find that raising cash need not be embarrassing—it's just hard work.

One warning: do not use the following methods to raise money for foolish things. These are effective techniques that should be reserved for true emergencies only. In almost every case they can be used only one time, so make sure your need is great.

The first thing to do when strapped for cash is to close out any IRA or Keogh accounts that you have established. Don't hesitate or feel guilty about this raid on your retirement money. It is utter nonsense to preoccupy yourself with age sixty-five if you have a problem at age thirty-five or forty-five. Any penalties you incur will be outweighed by being able to solve your immediate cash problems.

The other two best methods of raising cash are selling assets and borrowing. Which technique you use depends on how great your need is. In general, asset replacement yields less money, is slower, and is more of a personal burden, yet is the less public method. Borrowing will, in most cases, provide more money in a shorter period of time, and be less of a hardship, but will require a public appeal.

There are some assets that are relatively painless to part with. A thorough search of your home—including your closets, jewelry boxes, attic, cellar, and garage—and your safe deposit boxes and vaults may yield up assets that were dormant or even unknown. It's often extraordinary what you'll find gathering dust.

Old is in today. Yard sales of antiques and collectibles are all the rage, and in fact "preowned" objects are considered chic. Furniture, luggage, appliances, clothing, jewelry, china, tableware, toys, and even baseball cards are all being bought by both collectors and average people today. Old savings bonds that have sat in the vault since your graduation or wedding can be cashed in. Presents that you never use, such as crystal and silver serving pieces, can all be sold. Your affection for the person who gave you the object shouldn't get in the way of your converting it to cash in an emergency. And there's no reason that the yard sale concept can't be adapted to urban living—all it takes is a classified ad and some signs in the neighborhood.

Borrowing need not be begging. Frame the transaction as a business deal with a payback plan and interest payments clearly explained. Tailor each arrangement to fit the needs of the individual lender and present it as a short-term loan. Remember, the nest stays open long after emancipation in today's world, so if your parents are financially able to help, don't hesitate to ask them. Approach other family members and friends as well.

If you have elderly relations who have set money aside for you in their estates, ask for the money now. Explain to them that not only are you in desperate need, but that this way they will be able to see the benefits of their bequests and receive your thanks.

Above all, remember that you are not a failure or stupid because you need to raise cash. There's no need to go about with your hat in your hand. Rather than feeling sorry for yourself, get to work and take control of the situation.

YARD SALES

The secret to successfully raising cash through a yard sale is to remember that you are not a retail store. You must be flexible in your pricing and be willing to accept any reasonable offer. Begin the day by placing a price tag on every item. Every thirty minutes cross off the numbers on your price tags and lower them 10 percent. Continue in this vein until everything is sold. Don't bother to make temporary repairs to broken items, just clean and dust all your wares and note that everything is sold "as is."

READING

How Much Is Enough?

It has been said that we live in the information age. Advertisements constantly buffet us saying that unless we read this or that publication we aren't being totally informed. Yet none of us has the time necessary to read everything that's touted as valuable and essential.

The way to begin prioritizing your reading is to realize that you are not missing anything by not reading every publication on the newsstand. In fact, by trying to read everything you are wasting valuable time and probably missing out on some information that could really be valuable.

With that attitude in place, begin dividing all your reading into four categories. In order of their relative importance they are news, vocational information, literature, and gossip/entertainment. Once you have successfully categorized all your publications, place the appropriate emphasis on each publication.

Next, begin to analyze the publications in each category. The single best source of news is a major daily newspaper. I firmly believe that every thinking American should read the daily newspaper each and every day. (If your local paper isn't up to snuff, subscribe to *The New York Times*.) That doesn't mean you have to read every single word in the paper. Newspapers are excellent prioritizers of information. They place the most important stories—the news you need to know—on the front page. In addition, newspapers' stories are written in what is called an inverted-pyramid style. That means that the most important facts are packed into the early paragraphs. The further you get into the story, the less important or vital the information.

Each morning, over breakfast, read the first few paragraphs of every story on the front page of each section, then skim the rest of the paper. Dog-ear the pages with stories, columns, or reviews you are interested in and set the newspaper aside until later in the day. When you get back to the paper, go directly to the dog-eared pages. Subscribe to one local weekly newspaper, even if only for the advertisements, but keep it in the bathroom for casual browsing.

The weekly newsmagazines, while excellent publications, are basically recaps of what you could have read on the front pages of your newspaper during the previous week. Don't subscribe to a newsweekly. That will invariably result in a pile of unread magazines and a feeling of guilt. Instead, pick them up if you see something interesting on the cover, or if you have been out of touch for a week and need to catch up quickly.

Vocational reading should be limited to one trade or professional magazine. Select the bible of your industry—often the one with the most advertising—subscribe to it, and keep the most recent issue on your bedside table. For example, if you're in the clothing business, *Women's Wear Daily* should be on your nightstand. Pick it up before bedtime and skim it, reading only those stories you find interesting or that directly pertain to you and your career. Forget about newsletters and bulletins: they are simply condensed versions of information you will be getting elsewhere.

To be a well-rounded person, conversant on a variety of topics, it's necessary to read some literature, both factual and fictional. That doesn't mean you have to work your way through Tolstoy's complete works, however. Instead, go to the library and a good magazine stand once a month and browse for interesting titles. If you find a general-interest magazine that you like, avoid pressure to subscribe. Pick up another issue only after you have finished reading the one you already have in hand. When at the library, take out only one book at a time. Once you finish it, or decide to abandon it, return it to the library and select another. Make a conscious effort to devote some time each month to reading literature. Try doing your literature reading while traveling on business trips or while commuting back and forth from work.

The only time you should pick up and read a gossip or entertainment publication is when you have finished reading everything else. These magazines and newspapers are just sources of vicarious thrills—you don't need to read them to be a thinking, informed American.

SORTING YOUR MAIL

The best way to save time when going through your mail is to throw out anything that isn't sent with first- or second-class postage. The sender has made a value judgment by choosing how much to spend on postage. Any mail sent with third-class postage contains third-class information. If the sender isn't willing to spend twenty-nine cents to send it to you, you shouldn't even spend twenty-nine seconds opening it.

STEPHEN POLLAN'S READING LIST

I read *The New York Times* every morning. Rather than try to digest everything in the newspaper, I read the first paragraph of the stories on the front page of each section. If a story intrigues me, I read it completely. Once I've finished with *The Times*, I pick up *The Wall Street Journal*, and again, limit my reading to the first paragraph of stories unless they are particularly interesting. I subscribe to the local bar association journal to keep up with the latest developments in the law. The magazine sits on my bedside table for late-night skimming. I have a backlog of issues of *The New Yorker*, which I bring with me for in-flight reading. And, of course, I immediately read anything written by my wife or children in its entirety.

RECORDS AND PAPERS

What to Keep and What to Throw Away

M ost of us, unsure of what papers and records are really important, needlessly clutter our homes and offices with receipts and checks and bills and carbon copies, in the mistaken belief that it's better to err on the side of caution and save everything. What all this hoarding really does is make it more difficult to find records that really matter and more time-consuming to prepare our tax records.

In order to dig yourself out from under the avalanche of paper surrounding you, begin by getting your priorities straight and clearing your current files of all unnecessary papers.

If you don't need a record for tax purposes, or if it can be easily and inexpensively replaced, throw it away. Similarly, don't save more than one record of any single transaction. You don't need both a receipt and a canceled check for the same tax-related item—save the check and throw away the receipt. The only exception to this rule are receipts from drugstores that show that you purchased prescription medication as opposed to cosmetics.

Hold on to your monthly credit card statement only until you receive your canceled check paying the bill, then throw both statement and check away. There is no reason to hold on to your canceled checks or credit card receipts unless they will be needed to prove personal or business tax deductions. And if they are for amounts under $25, you can toss them anyway, since the IRS does not require receipts for any deductions under $25.

Monthly bank account or investment statements should be kept until you receive your year-end summary. However, if the statement contains confirmation of a trade or dividend reinvestment, keep it in your files. Keep your regular pay stubs in a file until you receive your year-end 1099 form reporting your total salary and tax payments.

Since sales tax is no longer deductible, there is no reason to save every receipt. The only ones you need to hold on to are those for expensive items that may be covered by insurance.

Checks and receipts for maintenance work on your home need

not be saved since the expenses are not tax deductible. But if you plan on selling your home in the near future, hold on to them as proof that the property has been kept up well. It is important though to keep records and receipts of permanent additions to your home since they will help defray any taxes you may have to pay upon selling the home.

Go through your insurance files carefully and throw away any policies that have lapsed or are no longer in effect. Insurance companies often send a new policy every time you renew, and these files can turn into nightmares unless they are kept up-to-date. Look for old medical insurance policies and ID cards that are no longer in effect.

In all this cleaning out of your files let common sense be your guide: if you are having trouble with a particular creditor or investment, hold on to all your records just in case you become entangled in a dispute.

Once you've succeeded in weeding out unnecessary papers from your files, it's time to determine how long you need to hold on to the remaining records. The rule of thumb is that most records should be retained for at least six years and then discarded, since that is how far back the IRS can request documentation for a claim. (Generally they will only ask for three years' worth of records, but if they suspect you have underreported income, they can go back a full six years. If they suspect you of fraud, they can go back to the dawn of time if they choose.) If something tells you to hold on to that old accident report for more than six years, by all means do so.

Here is a list of some common records and papers and an explanation of how long they should be kept:
- 1099 forms—six years
- accident reports—six years
- alimony agreements—as long as they are valid
- alimony payment records—six years
- birth certificates—for life
- brokerage fund transaction reports—six years
- certificates of deposit—as long as they are valid
- charitable-contribution receipts—six years
- custody agreements—until the child is emancipated
- death certificates—for life
- divorce decrees—for life
- evidence of unpaid debts—until they are paid
- home improvement receipts—as long as you own the home

- house deeds—as long as you own the home
- insurance policies—as long as they are valid
- Keogh statements—six years
- loan records—six years
- medical bills—six years
- military papers—for life
- naturalization papers—for life
- negotiable instruments—as long as they are valid
- nondeductible IRA records—six years
- partnership agreements—as long as they are in force
- partnership returns—six years
- powers of attorney—as long as they are in force
- prenuptial agreements—as long as they valid
- property tax records—six years
- receipts for major purchases—as long as you own the item
- stock option agreements—as long as you own the stock
- tax returns—six years
- title insurance policy—as long as you own your home
- trust agreements—for life
- vaccination records—for life
- wills—for life
- X-ray films—for life

After culling your files of unnecessary papers and then determining how long you should hold on to your remaining records, the next step in organizing your documents is to create three important records of your own:

1. a list of your financial assets;
2. an inventory—on videotape or with photographs—of valuables, including appraisals of very valuable items; and
3. a medical history of you and each of your family members, compiled by contacting physicians and asking for copies of their files.

The final step in organizing your records and papers is to determine where they should be stored. The best approach is to separate your papers into three categories: those you may need on short notice; those you will need only rarely; and those you need to separate from your home to prevent their being lost in flood or fire.

Papers falling into the first category—which would include most of your financial records, birth and death certificates, and insurance and funeral information—should be stored in your home in a filing cabinet.

Documents that will rarely be needed—such as certificates of deposit, partnership statements, marriage and divorce records, and military and citizenship papers—should be stored in a fireproof box in your home.

Information you wish to safeguard from potential loss in a fire or flood—your household inventory, certificates of deposit, stock certificates, and bearer bonds—should be stored in a safe deposit box.

Essential legal documents—such as wills, prenuptial agreements, and adoption papers—should be kept on file at your attorney's office, and a duplicate original should also be kept in your possession.

IMPORTANT WARNING

Some states seal safe deposit boxes, even those held jointly, after one party dies, so either have two separate safe deposit boxes for you and your spouse, have the information available elsewhere, or be prepared to rush to the bank ahead of the state. It is also a good idea if a third party, such as your eldest child, can gain access to a safe deposit box used by you and your spouse.

Rejections

Overcoming the Word No

Hearing the word *no* and realizing that you have been rejected can be a depressing experience. So often we pin our hopes and dreams on the decisions of others, giving them tremendous power over our emotions and our lives. But things need not be this way. By placing rejection in its proper perspective and dealing with it rationally, we can improve both our chances at future acceptance and our emotional well-being.

A rejection is rarely a decision. Most often it is a reaction based on a given amount of information. It has absolutely nothing to do with your worth as a person or your skills and abilities. Interestingly, it takes a greater effort to say no than to say yes. Positive responses also come more naturally. When we respond positively to an idea, an offer, or a suggestion, we automatically receive something in return. When we respond negatively, we receive nothing.

There are two different types of rejection/reactions. One is an unthinking, official reflex action, usually made by a lower-level operative of some type who has neither the ability nor the freedom to make anything but the most superficial objective analysis of a situation. This is the type of rejection we deal with most often. A bank teller, for example, may refuse to cash a check drawn on an account in his or her bank simply because you don't have an account with them. The second type of rejection is a more reasoned reaction, made by a person who has the power to weigh various factors and make a subjective analysis. A corporate vice president, after weighing your proposal to take on their public relations business, may decide that you are not experienced enough to handle the job.

In the first instance, a reaction was made based on a set of precise rules and regulations. The way to respond to this type of reflexive rejection is to push the up button and get to a person who has the power to make a reasoned decision. Politely accept the decision of the first individual, but state that you believe your circumstances are unique, and request to speak to a supervisor.

Nothing is ever written in concrete, and there are actually few firm and fast rules in life. Continue to proceed up the ladder until you reach someone with the power and authority to make a subjective analysis of your situation.

If you receive a reasoned rejection, don't accept it as the final word on the matter. Explain to the decision maker that you have a problem and you need their help with it. Never attack a rejection and say that it is a mistake, and never question the other person's ability or judgment. Ask them to reconsider their decision based on new information. If you have additional ammunition, bring it into play. If you don't, come up with some by digging deeper into your resources or by restructuring your argument. It is twice as hard to reject someone two times.

Pick your battles carefully, however. Appeals to higher authority and requests for reconsideration are powerful tools that should not be used lightly. Never appeal a rejection unless it is vital for you to be accepted. In many cases, a rejection is an indication that the time or situation just isn't right. It could be a message to you to rethink your position. Whenever a door closes, another opens, and each rejection is the prelude to an acceptance somewhere else. But if it is necessary for you to fight for acceptance, remember that the secret to overcoming rejection is to be resourceful and determined. A no is merely a pit stop on the way to a yes. The only rejection that is truly final is death.

DIALOGUE FOR OVERCOMING A REFLEXIVE REJECTION

It's important to be both grateful and determined when going over the head of a reflexive decision maker. Say, "I know you've done the best you can, and I truly appreciate everything you've done and all the time you've spent." This shows you are a caring person while acknowledging that your interaction with this person is at an end. That's important because you don't want to give them an opportunity to grab the reins again. Ask them why you've been rejected and listen carefully to their answer. With a plaintive look go on to say, "I have one more favor to ask of you. Can you tell me who I can speak with about special circumstances?" No one will deny such a reasonable request. Once they offer up a name thank them profusely and ask if they would mind introducing you to the person. Such an introduction signals to the next decision maker, however subtly, that your appeal has the approval of the first person. If you're able to maneuver yourself into a personal introduction, thank the first person once again in the presence of their superior.

DIALOGUE FOR OVERCOMING A REASONED REJECTION

If you're unable to get a personal introduction to a reasoning decision maker, begin your dialogue by saying you're there on the recommendation of the reflexive decision maker. While not as effective as a personal introduction, this also implies that your appeal has approval. Explain your "special circumstances," using those exact words. Make as powerful a case as possible specifically addressing the reason for rejection given by the first individual. If they turn you down as well, once again ask for a reason. At this level, the reason given will generally be that it's "against policy." Thank the reasoned decision maker for the time and effort. Ask if you can "speak again if your circumstances change." This lays the groundwork for being able to approach the reasoned decision maker directly later for a reconsideration based on new facts. Add, however, that you would "like to speak to someone responsible for setting policy." Once again ask for a personal introduction. Engage the policy maker in an intellectual discussion of how your special circumstances should allow for a change in policy. If that doesn't work, withdraw graciously, return home, and compile the new facts for your reconsideration. When your material is ready, bypass the reflexive decision maker and make your appeal directly to the reasoned decision maker.

RELOCATING

Placing More of a Priority on Your Environment

The traditional notion of relocating is that it is forced upon you either by career choices, mistakes, or by old age and ill health. We decide to pursue a chosen profession and then seek out a place where there are employment opportunities. We find ourselves in trouble and mistakenly believe that a fresh start somewhere else will help us get our lives together. We leave the job market and feel we must seek out a community inhabited solely by other retirees.

But relocating should not be solely a reactive decision. The environment we live in has a great deal to do with both our physical and mental health. There are actually cities that breed sickness and depression through their physical and psychological atmospheres. Alternatively, there are magical places that radiate health, vitality, and happiness. I believe that we should place a higher priority on where we live and actually take positive steps toward finding a "home" of our own.

As early as you can in life, find a place you love and try to relocate there. Don't treat the location as a spot solely for vacations or retirement. To the extent you possibly can, try to make that place a permanent part of your life. One of your goals, along with personal fulfillment and career success, should be environmental happiness. I don't mean to discount roots. I have found, however, that roots don't dig down into the ground in a specific place, but reach outward to those we love. They are able to remain strong and alive even when they stretch great distances. I also don't want to minimize the constraints careers often place on our freedom. But I believe that there are ways around most of these constraints, and that there is nothing wrong with sacrificing some income for happiness.

There are actually many opportunities for us to relocate to a place we would love to live. When most of us graduate from college, we immediately return to our parents' environment and begin our lives there. It would be just as feasible to find some other place that perhaps offers us more of what we personally are looking for, and to begin our lives there. A job or career change is another opportunity to relocate. In fact, being willing to relocate opens up all sorts of new possibilities and avenues. One excellent option is to try to match up your entrepreneurial dream—if you have one—with your dream location. If you are going to launch your own business, why not do it in a place you love? (For some suggested locations, consult the annual "most livable cities" ratings, which are covered in the major newsweeklies.)

Remember, however, that relocating won't let you escape your past problems or mistakes. In addition to packing our clothing, our possessions, and our furniture, we also bring our emotional baggage with us when we move. A new place won't make you sane if you are insane, won't make you well if you are sick, and won't make you secure if you are insecure, but it can be the final piece in the puzzle of our lives.

RELOCATING TO RETIRE

Too many people immediately assume that as soon as they leave the job market they must head south. There is much to be said for warm weather, but there is also something to be said for culture and intellectual stimulation—two things sorely lacking in most retirement areas. Don't let yourself be forced into moving away from your current home or the area you live simply by societal pressure. Remember that mortgages are not balls and chains, but are in fact life extenders—there is no reason you can't refinance your current home, or take out a mortgage to buy a new home, even if you are seventy or eighty years of age. And while it is nice to be with people in similar situations to yours, it is even better to be part of a vibrant community that has people of all ages. My advice to retirees is to select a place where they will be happy—whether it's north, south, east, or west of where they currently live, or even if it is where they currently live—and spend the rest of their lives there.

FOR MORE INFORMATION . . .

You can learn more about relocating from the following book:
- *Finding Your Best Place to Live in America* by Dr. Thomas F. Bowman, Dr. George A. Giuliani, and Dr. M. Ronald Mingé

RENOVATIONS

Investing in Your Present Home

Approximately $95 billion is spent on home renovation and fix up each year. An astonishing portion of this money is poured down the drain through overpayment, shoddy work, or a lack of knowledge as to what adds to the value of a home when it is finally sold.

Renovations are extremely expensive—running on average from $100 to $200 per square foot—and can be twice as expensive as new construction, since the work may well require demolition or removal and subsequently reconstruction and reinstallation.

It is time to spend big bucks and renovate only when you have decided not to buy a new home, yet still need more space (for a child, home business, or any other valid reason); more bathrooms; or a larger, more efficient kitchen. Merely wanting a better environment is never a good enough reason to renovate. The key word is *need*. Any renovation that solves a real need will add more to the value of your home than one that satisfies a want. That really is an important consideration in home renovation—making it a prudent investment in your real estate.

The highest return on improvements come from bringing your home up to par with others in the neighborhood. However, regardless of how luxurious you make a dwelling, its value will be limited by its location. Overimprovements, which make your home far more valuable than those surrounding it, will be sunk investments, never to be recouped in the sale of the property.

The four projects that add the most to value are the creation of more aboveground (not basement) living space; the expansion or renovation of a kitchen; the addition of another bedroom; and the addition of another bathroom.

Once you have decided on a renovation project, begin by having an architect or designer draw up a set of plans and specifications. Make sure that the plans meet local building department regulations, municipal codes, and co-op or condo rules. Plans and specifications are vital since you will want all potential contractors to work and bid from the same basic design. Otherwise you will be comparing apples and oranges.

In addition, it is important that renovations fit the existing character of your home. An addition out of character with your home becomes an unsightly appendage, detracting from, not adding to, its value. For that reason, prepackaged plans and specifications should be used only as a last resort.

Forget about doing the work yourself. Home buyers today are sophisticated enough to distinguish between professional construction and weekend handyman projects. Any renovations that are less than professional could end up detracting from, rather than adding to, the value of your home, since buyers may have to pay for demolition.

Interview reputable, professional contractors. This isn't the time to give your nephew a break. Ask how long each firm has been in business. Make sure they have all the licenses needed to do the job. Get from each a list of their six most recent jobs. Telephone the homeowners and ask if the work was done professionally, on time, and reasonably close to the budget—there is no such thing as coming in under budget. Ask for, and speak with a financial reference—such as their banker—and call the Better Business Bureau for the company's track record.

Once you have a list of three acceptable contractors, send each the plans and ask for a binding bid. While this will be higher than an estimate, it will give you a ceiling figure to work with. Select the lowest bidder. If all the bids come in over what you can afford to pay, go back and rethink your plans.

If two of your contractors come within 5 percent of each other, and the third submits a bid dramatically lower (10 to 15 percent), you should question the validity of the third bid. Just for your information, the standard bid is made up of about 40 percent labor, 37 percent materials, and 23 percent overhead and profit.

Once you have selected your contractor, run one final check by getting their social security number and asking your banker if he or she can get ahold of the contractor's TRW or Trans Union credit file. The worst thing that can happen is that they'll refuse. It's worth the attempt since if your contractor goes broke in the middle of the project, you'll be stuck. If your contractor refuses to provide a social security number, find someone else—they are hiding something.

Regardless of how reputable the contractor is, you need a

written contract. Any promises that don't appear in print will never come to fruition.

The contract should contain a one-year unconditional guarantee that is backed, personally, by the contractor (as opposed to a corporate guarantee). Payment plans should be stipulated. Arrange so that payments occur at stages in the project. The contract must allow you to retain 10 percent of each of these payments to insure that the contractor has a stake in continuing to work. Pay by check, never cash. When the job is completed, you'll have a 10 percent cushion to use as leverage to convince the contractor to come back for last-minute details. Clauses should also specify that the contractor obtain the necessary permits and insurance; release you from all liens upon final payment; and provide for cleanup after completion. And never sign any contract that doesn't have a specific completion date. Insert language that calls for discounts if the contractor fails to meet the deadline.

HOME IMPROVEMENTS' RETURN ON INVESTMENT

Here's a brief list of renovation projects and how much of their cost is recoverable through increasing the value of your home:

Improvement	Return on Investment
Adding a fireplace	85–125%
Sprucing up	80%
Adding a second full bath	110%
Expanding or modernizing a kitchen	85%
Adding a deck	80–110%
Adding a skylight	75%
Adding a new room (with a window)	75%
Replacing windows and doors	72%
Improving insulation	83%
Adding new roofing	80%
Adding a swimming pool	30–45%
Finishing a basement	15–20%

BUYING YOUR OWN MATERIALS

One of the little-known secrets of the home renovation field is that contractors often make a sizable profit on the purchase of materials. You might be able to save yourself a sizable chunk of money by purchasing materials yourself. When I was having renovations done on a home I own in Connecticut, I had a contractor friend in Maine purchase the materials up there and send them down to me by truck. My Connecticut general contractor wasn't too happy with me, but I saved a considerable amount of money.

HOME IMPROVEMENT SCAMS

Phony home improvement contractors are sprouting up all over America since, as the real estate market slows down, more people are deciding to invest money in fixing up their present homes. Estimates are that over $1 billion was lost on home improvement frauds last year alone. And in addition to the dollars lost in the original "improvement," the repair bills and legal fees that result can make the situation even more devastating. Be a savvy consumer by following these key points:

- Beware of model-home scams in which you are offered "free" home improvements if you tell your friends and neighbors about the product or service. Most often the fine print in these contracts requires you to pay for the work completely and says you get rebates for any referrals that result in sales.
- Watch out for phony inspectors who report that some aspect of your home is unsafe and needs to be replaced. They generally are front men for con artist contractors who follow up the "inspection" with a sales call.
- Avoid any workman who says that the material he uses is "maintenance free" or will "last forever." No substance affordable to the average homeowner is either maintenance free or indestructible.
- Beware of a contractor who drops the names of brands you have heard of and implies he has a special relationship with the manufacturers. Anyone can purchase any brand of material, and the quality of material used does not reflect on the quality of the workmanship.

USING CONSTRUCTION MANAGERS

If your renovation is going to have a budget of $100,000 or more, it makes sense to hire a construction manager to oversee the work. Architects will, for a fee, keep an eye on your contractors, but they are really looking out only for the integrity of their plans, not the integrity of your wallet. General contractors are concerned with maximizing their profit, not minimizing your costs. Construction managers, on the other hand, receive a flat fee—generally 2 percent of the budget—and are solely concerned with keeping the project as close to the budget and the completion date as possible.

Résumés

Turning Them Into a Window on Your Life

Résumés and curricula vitae are necessary evils. People, particularly potential employers, want to see a capsule summary of your life and experiences before they see you. That makes a great deal of sense if you are the person who has to wade through two hundred job applicants. Unfortunately, if you are the applicant, this understandable desire for impersonal brevity forces you to sum up your entire life and experience, your goals and aspirations, your accomplishments and successes, all in two pages or less.

You should approach writing your résumé as an exercise in self-analysis. The purpose of a résumé is not to get you a job, but to get you an interview. (For more information, see the chapter "Job Interviews.") It must pop out from the pile of papers on an executive's desk and say "I am special." That doesn't mean it should be handwritten, printed on pastel paper or card stock, or be done on an audiotape or videotape. All of those devices say "I am not traditional," not "I am special." Your specialness must come through in your description of your goals and experiences, not in your choice of typefaces or paper.

The best way to make your résumé stand out from the pack is to make sure that it is customized for the particular company or industry you are approaching. Your customizing should be subtle, somehow linking you and the company either through past experience or similar needs and interests. Mentioning the company itself in your résumé is a mistake—that makes your customizing all too apparent. Let the link between you and the company be inferred by the reader, who is looking for such things.

For example: a young magazine editor is looking for a new job. She decides to send her résumé to a publishing company that she hears is looking to increase staff productivity and boost ad revenues without increasing production costs. In order to subtly link her achievements and skills to the company's goals and objectives, she decides to stress how she was able to maintain quality and efficiency at her current job, even while having her staff cut by 25 percent; increase productivity at a prior job by 60 percent by instituting flexible scheduling; and cut production time in half at her first job by formatting the magazine herself.

This linkage should be accomplished in the first section of your résumé, which should be a brief summary of your experiences, starting with your present job and working backward in time. Find a thread that runs through all of your jobs, or a goal that you have been working toward, and highlight that as being what makes you a special person. Obviously, that thread or goal can be described differently to appeal to different companies or industries. This approach turns a black-and-white document into a window on your life, separating you from all the other applicants for the position.

Later on in the résumé, when you are describing each previous job individually, take special care to describe accomplishments as well as responsibilities. Each of these accomplishments should, once again, be chosen with the company or industry you are approaching in mind. The reader of the résumé may or may not have picked up your link to their company in your career summary, but if you reinforce that linkage through your accomplishments, they will definitely take the bait.

While I see nothing wrong with putting yourself and your accomplishments in the best possible light, I am opposed to lying on a résumé. Not only are outright falsehoods unethical, but they never work. Even if you get the interview and get the job, you will spend so much time covering up your lie that you won't have the enegy to become successful. And if you do become successful, it can all come crashing down if your lie is exposed.

By linking yourself to the recipient of the résumé you can dramatically improve your chances of being called for an interview. At that point your résumé can be put away. It has accomplished its job—for both employer and applicant—and from here on in you can speak for yourself.

DEALING WITH "NO EXPERIENCE"

Most people looking for a job for the first time bemoan the fact that they have no experience. They are absolutely wrong. They have been confusing experience with job experience. Rather than listing jobs you have held, you must show life experiences that are somehow related to the job you are seeking. If you majored in the subject or took classes on the area, that constitutes experience. If you volunteered or interned in the same or a similar industry, that is experience as well. Do whatever you can, including calling yourself "a student of the industry," in order to provide some type of experience.

DEALING WITH "JOB HOPPING"

Some executives are hesitant to hire individuals who have a history of moving from job to job after only short stays. The way to get around this hesitation is to explain, in your opening summary of experiences and description of accomplishments, how each new job has both increased your income and brought you closer to your goal—which obviously is the job you are applying for now.

DEALING WITH "DEEP ROOTS"

If your work experience involves one or two jobs that you have held for a long time, some executives might infer lack of ambition rather than stability. The way to avoid that is to show that your job description has changed and grown while you were on the job. Any changes in title or salary increases should be noted. In your opening summary of experiences, note that you were happy to remain at your longtime employer as long as you were moving toward your eventual goal, but now, in order to achieve your goal—the job you are applying for—you must leave.

DEALING WITH "TIME GAPS"

Any gap on your résumé rings an alarm bell in the reader's mind. That's why you should make every effort possible to fill in all your gaps. Some legitimate, and in fact positive, reasons for gaps are education, sabbaticals, and taking time off to write a book. If your gap was caused by a personal problem, don't attempt to explain it in writing. A reader will think the worst if they see vague phrases such as "medical problems" or "family difficulties." Instead, be prepared to explain these personal gaps during an interview.

FOR MORE INFORMATION . . .

You can learn more about preparing a résumé from the following books:
- *The Damn Good Résumé Guide* by Yana Parker
- *The Perfect Résumé* by Tom Jackson

RETIREMENT

The Great American Myth

I have made a discovery—the American notion of retirement is a man-made myth. For years now, Americans have been indoctrinated with a specious fact—that the culminating event in our business lives is a future point in time known as the retirement—and that we are financial failures if we don't prepare for it.

We are bombarded with a wondrous array of insurance schemes and financial gimmicks that purport to tackle this problem. This exercise in mindless and expensive squirreling away of resources is absurd. Retirement, you see, is not a reality. It is, in fact, a manufactured illusion perpetuated by the politicians, who fear that the weak, disabled, and dying elderly will be too great a burden for society. They want older Americans to conserve their money so that they'll all be self-supporting.

Preparation for retirement or work cessation is actually a negative project leading to stagnation, which could in turn hasten one's demise. Ironically, it is presented to us as an earned reward for a tough life.

Instead of a twilight, this time of life for most of us could be a time of renewal, a launching into the most productive time of our business and creative lives.

How should we plan our future financial careers? There are two simple rules—"keep your planning in the now" and "corporatize." Keeping your planning in "the now" means focusing on *your* life and the present, not the future and your heirs' lives. Rather than worrying about your eventual estate, concentrate on your own current and future needs. "Corporatizing" means operating your life like a business—as if you had to plan for perpetual existence. The goal of most corporations is sure, certain, continuous growth in predictable units of time or fiscal periods. Progress can be measured, and our financial moves kept in rhythm with economic and business changes.

Liquidation—or retirement—is never the corporate aim. Instead, the aim is an ongoing improvement of stockholders' interests, which are twofold—one, growing fiscal health; and two, the ability to cash in your resources at a future time determined by yourself and not society.

If, along the way, you are involuntarily forced to retire because the law or your company says so, you still have a choice. There is an inordinate demand today for experienced and seasoned veterans, and you can readily redeploy your assembled assets to work in new ventures and fresh enterprises.

Your long-term goal is not termination, but continuous, measurable growth. You and only you should decide your destiny.

RISK EVALUATION

How Daring Should Your Investments Be

The ability to measure risk and know how much you can handle is a sine qua non for making investments. Yet American ideals run counter to effective risk evaluation. Those who gamble and win are hailed as heroes. We never hear about those who gamble and lose.

For most of us, risk evaluation—the judgment of how much we should gamble on our investments—becomes an emotional process. We often wrongly equate risk with courage. Evaluating risk should be a pragmatic, reasoned process undertaken before *each* individual decision. It should not be an overall characterization that is applied to all situations.

Don't look upon risk as a win-or-lose situation—this brings your psyche into the process. Rather, regard risks as actions taken that worked, or didn't. Involving your ego in the process guarantees failure . . . and ulcers. If you can't keep your self-image and your investments separate and distinct, avoid any risk-taking.

There are certain basic rules about risk. The younger you are the more risk you can usually assume, simply because there is more time to recoup from a loss financially and emotionally. A thirty-year-old can make and lose a fortune three times. A sixty-five-year-old can rarely recoup from a devastating loss. If you fall somewhere in the middle, you have to begin making some judgments, both about the investment and yourself.

Before even considering risky investments, place four to six months' worth of normal living expenses in an accessible, risk-free investment—a certificate of deposit or an insured money market fund. This nest egg can keep you liquid if your more risky investments remain tied up or cannot be borrowed against. Until you have put this survival money aside, you're really not in a position to take major risks.

Next, rather than relying on preconceived notions, ask yourself these questions:

- Do you have obligations that aren't taken care of yet, such as paying for your children's college educations?

- What opportunities will you have to recoup a loss?

Don't permit your mortality to affect your risk evaluation. Creditors cannot reach beyond the grave. By all means protect your lifestyle, but don't worry about the hereafter.

One of the wonders of the capitalist system is that it has done a great job of helping you measure risk. The greater the potential reward or yield from an investment, the greater the risk involved. In the stock market, for example, shares of companies that have a lengthy history of success sell for a lower multiple of earnings than shares of companies that are relatively new. When evaluating real estate ventures, savvy investors base their yield projections on the quality of the tenant. For example, major corporate tenants are equated with lower, but more certain, returns. Divorce yourself from the mythological figure of the gambling investor. If an investment has integrity and falls within your bounds of acceptable risk, its lack of flamboyance should not deter you.

SAFE DEPOSIT BOXES

The Storage Places of Last Resort

Safe deposit boxes radiate a sense of security. Surrounded by steel bars, located in subterranean vaults, with double locks, full-time attendants, and elaborate entry procedures, these little strongboxes give the appearance of being the safest and most secure place to store valuables. And while to a great extent safe deposit boxes are extremely secure, they are not the panacea we perceive them to be.

A safe deposit box is the most expensive real estate you will ever rent—its per-square-foot rental is greater than apartments on New York's Park Avenue or homes on the French Riviera. In addition, whatever you place in the safe deposit box is not insured, as the fine-print disclaimer on your rental agreement with the bank will state.

The only things that should be placed in a safe deposit box are items you do not want to insure since they are irreplaceable—for example, jewelry with sentimental value—and papers that should be kept outside your home to protect them from loss in a fire, such as bearer bonds and inventories of the contents of your home. Other important papers should be kept in fireproof boxes or filing cabinets in your home.

The state sometimes seals safe deposit boxes upon the death of the tenant so they can examine the contents and determine if they are taxable. That's why you should always have at least one other person who has access to your vault so that if anything happens to you, someone else will be able to retrieve important documents before the box is sealed.

Finally, buy as small a safe deposit box as you can, or try to get around the need for one by storing your irreplaceable objects and documents somewhere else.

SAVVY SHOPPING

Buying Big-ticket Items Wisely

Some of the most successful snow jobs perpetrated on American consumers come from the manufacturers of expensive, luxury items. For their own survival these companies preach that you can't get along without the highest quality or the latest technology. Consumers have bought into this nonsense and continue to buy products they don't really need in an effort to keep up with the Joneses. They don't realize that manufacturers created these Joneses out of thin air.

Backing up the efforts of manufacturers are retailers, who have become the ultimate persuaders. Tools such as bait and switch, repackaging, floor models, and designer labeling add to the buying noise that consumers must deal with.

The simple solution to this sales pressure is to buy expensive items only when you truly need them. If the product in question is new on the market, before buying it, make sure you really need it. Don't be an innovator or "early adopter." The first person to buy a new product always pays more and risks purchasing a lemon from the first production runs. If you already have the product and are contemplating buying a replacement, check first to see if the item you already own can be repaired.

Similarly, analyze the timing of your purchase. Storewide clearance sales take place after Easter, around the Fourth of July, and just after Christmas. Each industry has its own model season. With a little investigation you can find out when new models are set to debut and save money by buying an old model that will be marked down for clearance. If at all possible, try to buy off season—air conditioners in the fall or winter, furs in the spring or summer.

The secret to savvy shopping is to become an expert in the product you are searching for. Visit a list-price retailer—either a department store or a specialty store—and pick the brains of a salesperson. What features should you look for? Which manufacturer makes the most reliable products? What can you reasonably expect to pay for the product? With this firsthand research stored away, head to the library and read product test reports. Call a repair service and ask them which brand is the most reliable. Throughout your investigation, keep track of specific model numbers, features, and list prices.

Bear in mind that brand names are only labels, not an indication of who is actually manufacturing the product. For example, there are almost no televisions manufactured in the United States, even though many carry American brand names. Consider store, local, and regional brands. These often cost less than national brands since their prices don't have to cover expensive advertising campaigns.

Now that you are an expert, venture out into the retail jungle. Comparison shop at least three different retailers, asking for their best prices on the specific model you are looking for. Don't let them throw you off the scent by suggesting alternatives—stay on the trail. If you are shopping for a product with few moving parts—speakers, computers, amplifiers, toaster ovens—don't hesitate to deal with reputable mail order companies. Items with moving parts are more prone to break down, so stick with local stores that have repair facilities. Avoid floor models and add-on sales such as service contracts and extended warranties.

Regardless of what big-ticket item you are buying, take control of the transaction: never rely on advertising claims; do your own independent research; and purchase only what you want to buy, not what the retailer wants to sell.

AUDIO EQUIPMENT

When shopping for a stereo system, spend the lion's share of your budget on the speakers—they make the most difference in sound quality. Don't buy a more powerful receiver or amplifier than you actually need. Beyond a point, higher power is just an ego trip and has little effect on sound. As long as you have enough power to drive your speakers at an acceptable volume level, you're fine. CD players are remarkably simple devices; expensive units have more features, not better sound. If you must buy a turntable, look for a reliable one with few features—spend your money on the cartridge instead.

VIDEO EQUIPMENT

Video products probably change more frequently than any others. In an effort to keep the VCR boom going, manufacturers bring out entirely new lines with only minor modifications. Try to keep features to a minimum, and look for units that are simple to use—it's surprising how many people don't know how to program their VCR. Televisions are undergoing rapid change as well. Despite the ego appeal of large screens, picture quality is still more important than size. Remember that your television and VCR are a matched pair—if one is cable ready or stereo, the other needn't be.

PHOTOGRAPHIC EQUIPMENT

Unfortunately, most people buy cameras with their egos, not their heads. Before you plunk down a fortune for a full-featured, single-lens reflex camera and a set of lenses and accessories, consider how often you have taken pictures in the past. A new camera will not make you take more pictures, regardless of what the photo industry claims. Snap-shooters should look for the simplest, smallest, and lightest camera they can find. A 35 mm, auto focus/auto exposure, lens-shutter model is fine for most people.

AIR CONDITIONERS

Air conditioners operate most efficiently when they are running at full power. Retailers have charts that can help you calculate how powerful a unit you need. Make sure to consider windows and solar exposure as well as room size. Since you will want your unit to operate at maximum efficiency, buy one that is slightly undersized. In addition, look for units with high energy-efficiency ratings (9.0 EER or more) and with thermostats.

HOME APPLIANCES

Professional-level home appliances have become chic in recent years, but don't fall prey to the trend. You only need a $1,000 mixer or restaurant-style range if you are operating a restaurant.

Built-in refrigerators and freezers are unnecessary indulgences, which don't add to a home's value.

TAG SALES

Quite often, tag sales are organized affairs run by selling agents hired by the homeowner. In addition to receiving a flat fee for organizing and running the tag sale, these agents get a commission on all merchandise sold. You can use this fact to your advantage by calling a sales agent aside and asking if you can leave "a bid" on an expensive item you fancy. Leave your name and telephone number and ask the agent to call you if no higher offer is received by the end of the sale. It's in the sales agent's best interest to follow up on your bid and urge the owner to accept your offer.

SEED MONEY FOR BUSINESS

Calculating How Much You Need and Then Raising It

The single biggest obstacle to starting a business, for most Americans, is raising the money. Few of us have such substantial savings or family wealth that we can simply leave our jobs, take money out of the bank, and set ourselves up in business. Instead, we must beg and borrow for funds to turn our entrepreneurial dream into reality.

But before you begin passing the hat, you have to make some accurate calculations as to how much money you will need. First, using a business plan, you will have to figure out how much money you will have to spend to get to the point where you can open up the door. This will include all your costs of preparing your space, buying equipment and inventory, preliminary advertising and marketing, deposits, professional fees, and licenses.

Next, again using your business plan's projections, calculate how much money you will need to cover operating expenses until the business reaches the break-even point.

Finally, estimate all the personal and family expenses you will have while the business is in its infancy. Even though your business plan may contain provisions for you to draw a salary, I guarantee that when push comes to shove, the first cost-saving device you will use is to forgo your own salary.

The total of these three calculations of expenses is how much seed money you will need in order to start your business.

Despite all claims to the contrary, banks will never provide seed money. Later on, when your business has a track record and a history of success, and you need more money to expand or modernize, you'll be able to turn to these institutional lenders. Until then, you'll have to look to your own pockets, and those of family and friends.

No one, not even a parent, will confidently provide you with seed money unless they see that you yourself are putting your savings on the line. That means you will have to invest all your available funds in the venture. Tap into your savings accounts and certificates of deposit. Close out your IRAs and cash in your treasury bills. Look in your safe deposit box for bonds that can be cashed in. Scour the house for jewelry or collectibles that can be converted to cash. Have a tag sale. Use every device possible to come up with cash.

After you have emptied the cash cupboards, consider taking out a second mortgage on your home, or a secured personal loan. Banks will be willing to provide seed capital as long as they hold something of greater value, such as your home, as collateral. While this is a serious step, it is one of the single best ways to obtain seed money and as such, is one of the major benefits of home ownership.

If, after all your personal fund-raising efforts, you still find yourself coming up short, it's time to turn to family and friends. Show them your business plan and explain exactly how much you need, and how much you are providing out of your own pocket. Tailor the deal you offer to the needs of each person you approach, and present it as a business opportunity, not a charitable contribution. For example, offer a monthly payback at a moderate interest rate to your maiden aunt, who is a nervous investor, while offering your risk-taking friend a much higher rate of return, but with payments deferred a few years. Put all agreements in writing, preferably in contracts drawn up by your attorney.

Approach everyone you know with the opportunity to invest. Leave no stone unturned. Contact your professionals and ask them if they have other clients who might be interested. If they are providing business advice, don't ask them personally for money. An accountant or attorney who has invested in a business will—consciously or unconsciously—offer biased advice designed either to maximize or to preserve his or her own investment. If you still don't have enough money, you might even consider taking on a partner.

Prospective entrepreneurs who, after totaling all their own available money and approaching all their family and friends, still come up short of the necessary amount have four alternatives.

First, they can decide to buy a franchise. It is much easier to obtain financing for the purchase and establishment of a franchise than for an independent business. Not only does the franchise have a track record that a bank can look at and judge, but the franchiser may have its own financing programs. The disadvantage is that rather than being a general, in command of his or her own fate, the entrepreneur will be a sergeant, following other peoples' orders.

Second, entrepreneurs can buy an existing business. Seller-assisted financing is commonplace in the purchase of an existing business, so entrepreneurs may find it easier than starting from scratch. Of course, in this case they will be modifying and operating someone else's business, not starting their own.

Third, they can go back to the drawing board and rework their business plan—possibly scaling things down in size or scope—in order to cut down on the money needed to launch the business. This can be a viable option as long as the integrity of the business plan and idea don't suffer in the streamlining process.

Fourth, they can decide to enter business undercapitalized. This is the most common choice, leading to an incredible number of failures. The number one reason cited for a small business failing in this country is undercapitalization. On the other hand, almost to a one, every successful entrepreneur I have ever met, interviewed, advised, or counseled says they entered business undercapitalized. The decision to enter business without a safety net is, perhaps, what makes them true entrepreneurs.

BRINGING IN A PARTNER

One of the best ways to obtain seed financing for a new business is to bring in a partner—this automatically doubles your sources of potential capital. But partnerships are delicate things. The best partnerships are those in which one partner remains silent, happy to reap the profits without meddling in the operation, or when the two partners bring different skills and abilities to the business that when combined, equal the total entrepreneurial package.

SELLING YOUR HOME

Getting a Top Price Speedily

During the 1980s sellers of real estate didn't really need much advice. Buyers were in such a feeding frenzy that all a seller had to do was put his or her home up for sale and pick and choose among all the bites. But now the real estate market has turned around. Demand is down and prices are dropping, and while the collapse of the market may soon level off, the days of easy sales are probably gone forever. That doesn't mean, however, that it is impossible to sell a home for a good price. It simply means that it requires a lot more work on the seller's part.

The place to start is by being a serious seller. Don't put your home up for sale if you are unsure about selling. Only by being willing to accept the market value of your home, no more and no less, can you guarantee that you will make the sale at a fair price. Keeping a home on the market at an exorbitant price will make it a stale listing. Soon, no one will come to look at the property since buyers and brokers alike will categorize you as "a problem seller." Similarly, you shouldn't leave your home on the block while progressively lowering your price. That's a sign of desperation. Buyers and brokers will keep waiting for you to make yet another price concession before giving your home serious consideration.

A serious seller puts his or her home up for sale at a price that accurately reflects its current market value. Despite what many people think, the real estate market is actually very logical. The value of your home is dictated not by the perceptions of you or potential buyers, but by what comparable properties have sold for recently. A comparable property is a home of similar size in the same location.

There are a number of ways to find out these recent selling prices. The sales of condominiums and private homes must be registered with either a city or county clerk or the registrar of deeds and are open for public inspection. Sales of cooperative apartments, on the other hand, need not be recorded. In order to find out these prices you'll have to check with a co-op board or a broker familiar with the area. You can also get a good idea of prices by consulting local newspapers and finding classified ads for homes comparable to yours. The best way to find out what comparables have sold for, and therefore, what your home should sell for, is by getting in touch with your area's experts: local real estate brokers.

Contact three real estate brokerage firms that regularly do business in your area, and explain that you are interested in putting your home up for sale and would like them to stop by and give you a price estimate. There will be no fee for this service unless you request a formal written appraisal. You can make a judgment on the validity of the brokers' estimates by gauging how much they link their opinions to concrete facts. The more specific a broker is in quoting comparables, the more accurate his or her estimate.

Beware of brokers who quote dramatically high prices for your home. They are playing to your ego to get you to sign an exclusive listing agreement with them. Once they get you to sign on the dotted line, they will then help buyers pressure you into lowering your price to a more realistic level. In any event, at this time you are not concerned with selecting a broker. Before you are actually ready to put your home up for sale, you have to do a great deal of preparation.

As you will discover after speaking to brokers, real estate prices are actually price ranges. In general, the value of a particular home falls within a range that can vary by 20 percent. For example, homes aren't worth $100,000—they are actually worth between $90,000 and $110,000. What separates the $90,000 home from the $110,000 home is its condition, its specific location, and the extent to which the buyer "falls in love with it."

The best way to insure that your home will sell for a price in the top end of its price range is to make it as unobjectionable as possible. Your home should have nothing wrong with it. That goes for its style as well as its actual physical condition. You may think that your authentic Victorian decor is the height of good taste, but a buyer who loves Eurostyle will be turned off by it. The answer then is to make your home plain vanilla—as acceptable to as broad a range of potential buyers as possible. Start by scrubbing everything in sight—especially the windows. Take an objective look at your home, keeping your eye out for any problems, such as stains, cracks, or mildew. Make sure everything mechanical actually works, including doorknobs, locks, light switches, toilets, cabinet doors, faucets, and toilets. Watch out for frayed or worn carpets. Keep a list of all your findings, then give serious thought to what preparatory projects you should undertake. The key words are *repair* and *restore*, not *replace*. (For more information, see the chapter "Renovations.") In most cases, money spent fixing existing features of the home will be recouped by getting a higher price. Money spent replacing existing features, on the other hand, will probably not be recouped. Here is a list of simple home projects categorized by whether they are musts, good ideas, or not worth the time and money before you try to sell your home:

Project	A Must	A Good Idea	Not Worth It
1. A thorough cleaning	√		
2. Repairing water damage	√		
3. Repainting	√		
4. Hanging new wallpaper			√
5. Repairing existing wallpaper		√	
6. Laying new flooring			√
7. Repairing existing flooring		√	
8. Regrouting wall tiles		√	
9. Cleaning floor-tile grouting		√	
10. Replacing appliances			√
11. Repairing appliances		√	
12. Restoring bathroom fixtures		√	
13. Replacing shower curtain	√		
14. Replacing kitchen cabinets			√
15. Renovating kitchen cabinets		√	
16. Replacing countertops			√
17. Increasing light bulb wattage	√		
18. Installing new ventilation systems			√
19. Eliminating odors	√		
20. Thorough extermination	√		
21. Adding strategic mirrors		√	
22. Thin out closets	√		
23. Thin out furnishings		√	
24. Replace broken windows	√		
25. Install new doorbell			√

While you are working on your preparation projects, take some time out to recruit and/or prepare your attorney. One of the secrets of getting the most out of the sale of your home is for everything to be done as quickly as possible. Every day that goes by between finding a buyer and getting the deal finalized and the money in your bank account adds up to lost interest for you. And with each day that passes from the handshake to the contract, the buyer gets more and more jittery, increasing the chances that they will lose their nerve and retract their offer. That's why you will want to have an attorney who will be prepared to write a contract and negotiate it within twenty-four hours of your shaking hands with the buyer. With your lawyer raring to go, call your accountant and have him or her begin to analyze what effect the sale of your home will have on your taxes. A good accountant can work hand in hand with your attorney in order to minimize your tax liability.

Once your home is prepared and your professionals are ready, it is time to get back in touch with the three real estate brokerage firms you contacted earlier when you were determining the value of your home. While it is possible to sell your home without the assistance of a real estate broker, I don't advise it. Dealing with buyers is a full-time job and is best done by someone who doesn't have an emotional stake in the sale of the home. And while doing without a broker will save you the 6 percent commission they receive from a sale, savvy buyers will immediately lower their offers by 6 percent if they know you aren't using a broker. It makes more sense to find a good real estate broker and let them do the selling for you.

Ask every broker you speak with for the names of their three most recent clients. Call these clients on the telephone and ask them about their experiences with the broker. The selection of a broker is actually a negotiating process, since every broker will ask you to sign a legal document called either a listing or brokerage agreement.

The two most common forms of agreements are exclusives and multiple listings. An exclusive listing grants one broker the exclusive right to sell the property for a limited period of time. The advantage of an exclusive listing is that it provides the broker with an incentive to promote your home. In exchange for this exclusive listing you should be able to negotiate an agreement in which the broker pays for a certain amount of advertising. The disadvantage of the exclusive listing is that other brokers may not be willing to show your home to prospective buyers since they will have to share any commission with the exclusive broker.

A multiple listing agreement places your home on the lists of many brokers. You are required to pay the commission to whichever broker brings in the actual buyer. The advantage to the multiple listing is that all of the brokers will actively promote your home since they each have an equal chance at getting the full commission. The disadvantage is that the brokers won't do any advertising for you since it isn't guaranteed that they will reap the benefits of such advertisements.

Whichever type of listing agreement you opt for, make sure you negotiate the terms of the agreement. The selling price you agree to in your contract with the broker should be at the upper end of the value range, without being unreasonable. This will provide you with some room to negotiate with buyers. Make these agreements for as short a period of time as possible—think 60 days rather than 90 or 120. You will want to be able to get rid of an ineffective broker as quickly as possible. Insert language in the contract that specifically states the services you expect the broker to provide: four open houses and fourteen advertisements, for example. While the standard commission on the sale of a home is 6 percent, it is sometimes possible to negotiate this figure down to five percent during the drafting of the listing agreement. In addition, most brokerage agreements contain language stating that the commission is due as soon as the broker produces a buyer. Change this so that the commission is only due if, as, and when title changes hands. Finally, your agreement should also include a list of all those things in the house that are not for sale, such as your washing machine and drier. It is better to use these as deal sweeteners later in the process.

After selecting a broker, your next step should be to provide them with an added weapon: the seller's book. Since most home buyers today see a tremendous number of very similar homes in a short period of time, and their tours are often cursory, it is important to give them something that will help them remember your home. This should be a simple handout of a few pages that itemizes and describes all the positive attributes of the home and provides descriptions of the house itself, and each individual room. Floor plans are helpful, as is such information as offering price, square footage, and monthly maintenance and utility costs. Make note of special features such as fireplaces, skylights, and recent improvements. If possible, include some photographs as well.

With your seller's book completed, place a pile of them by the front door, hand a copy of the key over to your broker, and leave the selling to them. Your presence can only hurt your chances to sell. You've carefully selected your broker and prepared your attorney and accountant, so place your home in their hands. Just remember that speed is vital. Every day that goes by lowers your chances of selling for a good price. Don't let the negotiating process become a win-lose situation. Bear in mind that while you may not be able to get exactly the price you would like for your home in today's buyers' market, in most cases you will be turning around and becoming a buyer yourself. The same forces that lowered the selling price for your home will also lower prices as you turn around and become a buyer.

SMALL-CLAIMS COURT

Fighting for Your Rights . . . And Winning

S uing in small-claims court is one of the most powerful weapons available to the average consumer. These "people's courts" offer aggrieved individuals a chance to take on even the largest of corporations on a level playing field. Unfortunately, few consumers know enough about the process to add it to their arsenal.

Small-claims court proceedings involve informal hearings at which any person or individually owned business can present a complaint against another person, partnership, corporation, or agency of government without using the services of an attorney. In general, claims must be $1,000 or less—though amounts vary according to individual state laws and can be as high as $5,000— and filing fees are $10 or less.

The big advantage to small-claims court is that it simultaneously makes the legal process easy for an individual consumer and difficult for a large corporation. These informal courts allow you to present your case yourself, thus saving legal fees and making it economically feasible to sue for small amounts. On the other hand, in many states, a corporation sued in small-claims court must be represented by an attorney. Most small-claims courts have evening sessions, and attorneys generally charge double for working at night. That means a corporation will have to pay legal fees that may be larger than the amount of the suit. Usually, corporations sued in small-claims court settle prior to the actual suit, or simply do not show up for the hearing. In the latter case the judge will award you a default judgment. The fact of the matter is, the bigger and more impersonal the defendant, the more likely you will win in small-claims court.

The secret to wielding this powerful tool is to understand how the system operates. Luckily, there is help available in the person of the clerk of the small-claims court, whose job is to help consumers press their claims. After you have decided to sue, speak to the clerk of the nearest small-claims court. He or she will be able to tell you in which jurisdiction your case must be heard. The location of the hearing may be determined by where you live, where the defendant is located, or where the problem occurred. The clerk will also be able to give you an outline of the procedures you must follow to bring suit. Many courts even have brochures and pamphlets describing the process.

The first step is to file a plaintiff's statement with the clerk and to arrange to have the defendant notified either in person or by registered or certified mail. If you are suing a business or corporation, you must be able to provide the court with the name of the owner. You can get this information by calling either the local tax or licensing agency, the secretary of state's office, the state's corporation commission, or the county clerk's office.

Once you have filed your suit, gather all the physical evidence you can to document your claim. Bring along before and after photos, copies of all correspondence, receipts, itemized bills, and warranties, for example. If you intend to present evidence from other parties, such as witnesses or independent experts, ask the clerk if written statements are acceptable.

Prior to your presentation, attend a session to familiarize yourself with the court. The more comfortable you are with the entire process the better your chances of winning. Remember that while these are informal hearings, not legal debates, you should still present your information in a logical manner. Don't read from a prepared text, however; rely instead on notes. Be brief, simple, and direct. Bring all your evidence with you and be prepared to provide it to the judge. Answer all questions honestly and directly. Try to remain cool, calm, and collected. If you have done your homework and have a just claim, the odds are on your side.

FOR MORE INFORMATION . . .

You can learn more about small-claims court from the following book:

- *Small Claims Court—Making Your Way Through the System* by Theresa Meehanrudy

Social Climbing

Making It Into the Social Register

There is absolutely no rational reason for wanting to become part of the social set. I don't believe that it helps either your financial or emotional life. With that said, here is a foolproof method for making it into high society: know where the social elite gather, get invited there, and mingle.

American high society has always seen its mission as being a patron of the arts and of culture. Rather than dedicating themselves to medical or humanitarian charities, the socially prominent gather around such institutions as ballets, symphony orchestras, arts councils, museums, and libraries. Your first step in the climb up the ladder is to pick up the newspaper and check for dinners or events promoting or raising funds for these artistic institutions.

Scan the social calendar for a fund-raising dinner for a cultural organization. Steer clear of performance-oriented events since there is no social interaction, and therefore, no chance to mingle. Try to select an institution that you have some interest in—that way you will have some common ground for conversation—and call them on the telephone. Explain that you would like to help them in their efforts and would like to attend the dinner/opening/ etc., but have not received an invitation. In most cases, these invitations are sent out not according to who is in the social register, but according to who has contributed money in the past. All you need do to get on a mailing list is to ask for an invitation and make a donation.

Once you receive your invitation, make sure you have appropriate attire. If that means renting a tuxedo, gown, or jewels, so be it. Arrive fashionably late and be as nonchalant as possible. Above all, do not act impressed or embarrassed. While you may not be seated at a prominent table, that doesn't mean you can't mingle freely. Small talk works best with strangers—just try to make sure that you aren't chatting with other social climbers. Remember that the most obvious common ground is the institution in question.

If money isn't an issue, you can rocket into social prominence by making a substantial donation and becoming a sponsor of an organization or event. Your name will be printed in the program or brochure, and you will suddenly find yourself at the top of mailing lists for other cultural events.

If you repeat this process often enough, you will find that people will begin not only to notice you, but to talk to you as well. Little by little, and donation by donation, you will climb, or buy, your way into the social elite.

SUMMER RENTALS

Shedding Some Light on a Blind Transaction

Renting a home for a week, a month, or the whole summer can be an affordable and rewarding vacation, particularly if you have children. A well-equipped, well-located rental home can be simultaneously less expensive and more convenient than even the swankiest resort hotel.

The problem with summer rentals is that invariably they are blind transactions. The only knowledge the renter has about the property comes from a classified ad, the owner, or a renting agent—all highly biased sources. An ocean view touted in an ad can turn out to be visible only from the roof. The fully equipped kitchen the owner boasted of may well contain only one pot—without a lid—three forks, and two coffee mugs. Telephone service, promised by the renting agent, might actually be a jack with no telephone and no service. A five-minute walk to a sandy beach may actually be a five-thousand-foot hike to a cliff overlooking a beach. Worse yet, you could arrive to find the house infested with fleas, or to find another family already ensconced in your rental unit.

The secret to making sure that your summer rental isn't a house of horrors is to make sure it isn't a blind transaction. Don't make judgments and decisions based only on what you read or are told. It is well worth it to make a separate trip to check out the home in question. If you can't do it, find someone you trust who can inspect the house for you. A good real estate broker can be of immeasurable help in checking out summer rentals. Just make sure that the broker has a good reputation and that you are comfortable with him or her and trust his or her judgment. If you find a broker you trust, stick with him or her for your summer rental each year. The best *time* to find summer rentals is the year before you will actually be renting.

Regardless of whether it is you, a trusted friend, or your broker, someone must inspect the house prior to your signing a lease. Make sure that all the utilities—gas, electric, septic system—are in working order. Count the number of beds and see

how comfortable each is. Examine the furniture, inside and outside, and check to see that the kitchen is fully equipped. Find out
if there are hospitals or doctors nearby. Determine exactly how
long it takes to walk to the beach or lake, and make sure that you
can obtain a pass if need be. If you have a particular interest—
such as boating or tennis—make sure that there are facilities
nearby and that these are open to renters.

It is vital that you read your lease carefully and be prepared to
negotiate changes. The lease should discuss repair obligations,
whether utilities are extra or included, trash removal obligations,
cleanliness of the house, furnishings, towels and bedding, kitchen
supplies, and laundry facilities. It should also specify a local care-
taker or agent you can contact if you need to have repairs made.
Try to insure that your only obligation as a tenant is to leave the
house the way you found it. Remember that verbal promises are
meaningless. No matter how many times the landlord swears that
there is a barbecue, don't believe it unless it is in writing.

Many summer leases require all, or half, of the total rent paid
up front. To protect yourself, you want to pay as little as possible
up front—particularly if you haven't personally inspected the
home beforehand—and wait until you arrive to pay your rent. In
some summer leases rent is due regardless of the condition of the
house. Change this to make the rent payment contingent on receiving the services specified in the lease. Finally, insist that your
security deposit be held by a third party. This will prevent the
landlord from holding on to your money unreasonably and will
make it tougher for him or her to claim and deduct "damages"
from your deposit.

TAX-FREE INVESTMENTS

Understanding Their True Advantage

A common misconception among average consumers is that tax-free investments are somehow safer than taxable investments. This mistaken notion probably stems from the fact that most tax-free investments are connected in some way to the local, state, or federal government, and that means they are as solid as the government itself. While that may be true in some cases, tax-free investments may also involve subsovereignties such as hospital authorities, transportation agencies, and job development agencies, which may or may not be stable.

People also assume that they are somehow making more money by investing in tax-free instruments. They feel that in addition to getting whatever interest the investment generates, they are also saving since they won't have to pay local, state, or federal income tax on the interest. While that is true, it does not necessarily make a tax-free instrument a better investment than a taxable instrument. Interest rates on tax-free instruments are automatically calculated so they are equivalent to, not better than, the rates on comparable taxable investments. For example, a normal money fund yield might pay 8 percent interest and be subject to taxes that reduce the figure to 5.5 percent. The equivalent (in terms of risk) tax-free money fund would generally pay a 5.5 percent interest yield. The income generated by the investment is, in the final analysis, the same.

The real advantage of tax-free investments is that they are based on the tax rate in place at the time you purchase them. While the taxable money fund may continue to pay 8 percent interest, as time goes on the tax on that income may increase, cutting the yield from 5.5 percent to maybe 4.5, then perhaps even 3.5. All the while, the tax-free investment will still be producing its 5.5 percent tax-free income.

Tax-free instruments are therefore excellent long-term investments. You are betting that, over the course of time, taxes will be increased . . . and that's a pretty safe bet.

TAX RETURNS

The Most Common Mistakes People Make

All the financial acumen and savvy in the world won't be enough if you make mistakes when preparing your tax return. And surprisingly, many otherwise astute individuals make foolish mistakes in April.

The biggest mistake any taxpayer can make is failure to have a certified public accountant fill out their return. Only a CPA is accountable. Forget about accountants who are busy only at tax time. And any professional that advertises has some need or reason to advertise.

Don't underestimate the risk in claiming questionable deductions. All the manpower that the IRS devoted to auditing the abusive tax shelters of the early 1980s has now been redirected in order to examine individual and small-business returns.

The technical assistance hotline provided by the IRS was a wonderful idea. Unfortunately, independent audits have found that at least one-third of the answers given are wrong. Don't rely on advice from this service. If you have a question, ask a qualified CPA.

Many individuals mistakenly believe that extensions give them more time to pay their taxes. Actually, they merely give you more time to file your return. If you owe a substantial amount in taxes and don't pay it by April 15, your extension will be ruled invalid.

It is also a mistake to submit returns with unusual deductions—such as sizable casualty claims—without also sending along materials, such as police reports, to verify your claims.

An incredible percentage of returns contain mathematical errors. Check your numbers three or four times before filing. Don't forget that only 80 percent of your entertainment expenses are deductible. Pay careful attention to deductions on home mortgage interest—the law has changed three times in the past three years. Remember that every person claimed as a deduction has to have their own social security number. And make sure you and your accountant both sign and date the return.

Regardless of how carefully you manage your financial life during the year, you have to be doubly careful in filing your return. Don't become complacent. Stay on top of the tax law and its ramifications. We haven't seen the last of tax reform.

DEDUCTIBILITY OBSESSION

Many of us have become obsessed with avoiding taxes. This mania has even progressed to the point where otherwise intelligent individuals will go miles out of their way to save a couple of dollars in sales tax—never calculating that added time and travel expenses make any savings moot. Worse yet, some people are now justifying purchases by saying that they are tax deductible. They are forgetting that while they may well be deductible, you still have to spend the money. Never use deductibility as a rationalization for making a purchase—it only clouds the buying process and makes spending money seem less painful than it really is.

THE ELEVEN MOST FREQUENT MISTAKES MADE ON TAX RETURNS

- Failing to sign the return and/or the check, or failing to have a spouse or CPA sign the return.
- Failing to include social security numbers for every person claimed as a deduction—particularly children.
- Simple mathematical errors.
- Relying on the advice of the IRS technical assistance hotline or a friend or relative, rather than a CPA.
- Failing to realize that business entertainment and meals are only 80 percent deductible.
- Claiming an IRA deduction even if it's not allowed under the law.
- Thinking that an extension gives more time to pay taxes, rather than just more time to file a return.
- Failing to show a profit for at least three out of five years on a Schedule C—otherwise the activity may be considered a hobby and not deductible.
- Miscalculating passive loss deductions.
- Incorrectly calculating the home mortgage interest deduction if the mortgage has been refinanced. The rules have changed so

often in the past four years that even some CPAs aren't sure of how it's done.
- Failing to consider other methods of computing taxation, such as the alternative minimum tax or income averaging.

FOR MORE INFORMATION . . .

You can learn more about preparing tax returns from the following books, both of which are updated annually:
- *Ernst & Young's Arthur Young Tax Guide*
- *J. K. Lasser's Your Income Tax*

TERMINATION

Dealing With Getting Fired

The anger, shock, and fear that strikes most people who are fired from their jobs can be paralyzing. While these feelings are understandable, they are completely off base. Getting terminated is not an indication that you are worthless as a person. You may well have been fired for economic reasons that have nothing at all to do with your skills, personality, or abilities. Or you may have been fired capriciously, at the whim of someone who is temperamental or who simply doesn't like you. Above all else it is important to remember that you are not defined by your job.

Even though your blood pressure is rising, and your resentment is surfacing, try to remain calm when you are being told that "your services are no longer required." Don't launch into a tirade or try to talk them out of their decision. Both tactics are counterproductive. A tirade will diminish your chances to get a large severance package, and you don't really want to get your job back anyway. If you are being fired, that indicates that you have no future in this job, and even if you manage to hold on to it through pleading and begging, you will still have no future. When the ax falls, it is time to look forward, not backward.

Negotiate as strong a severance package as you possibly can. Actually, you are in the best possible position to negotiate with your former employer: you have absolutely nothing to lose and they are probably experiencing fear and substantial guilt. Firing someone is painful and frightening for an employer. They may even leave themselves open to claims of discrimination. Fan those guilt feelings and fears. Talk about how much you enjoyed working there and how difficult it will be for you to find another job. Even if you don't really feel that way, act as if you do. You aren't going to be judged on your acting ability. Mention your nasty landlord, widowed parent, and starving children, if need be.

Ask for a reference letter to be written right then, and make sure that it's a positive one. If you find that isn't possible, enlist the aid of someone else, perhaps a sympathetic supervisor from another department, to provide a positive reference.

Ask for outplacement counseling, and if none is available, use that as a wedge to get more severance pay. Request use of your office and secretary for a specific period of time in order to help in your job search. Again, if you are turned down, use that as a reason to ask for more severance pay. While the norm is to receive two weeks' severance for every year you worked for the company, you are only limited by your hesitancy to ask for more.

Make sure you also ask for accrued vacation pay, sick-day pay, personal-day pay, as well as refunds of your contributions to company pension plans. Find out how to go about continuing your health, life, and disability insurance coverage.

Don't worry about tying up loose ends or helping to train your replacement. Once you have been fired, you have no responsibilities to do anything to help the company or the person who fired you. Remember, your main priorities are you and your family, not your former employer.

Of course, don't go out of the way to sabotage projects or operations out of spite. You want to leave on good terms with your coworkers, who may be excellent sources of job leads.

Do not leave your office without checks for the total severance package you have agreed to. Never let the employer talk you into coming back on Monday to pick up the checks. Your presence reinforces their guilt feelings, which may subside over the weekend, leading them to reconsider your package. Whatever their reassurances and guarantees, stay there until you have checks and all the proper paperwork in your hands.

There is no reason to hide the news from family and friends. They may be good sources of both support and job leads. Almost everyone gets fired at one time or another, and remember, it is not an indication of your value as a person. There is no need to feel ashamed. You are *not* a failure in life if you are fired.

As soon as you get home, sit down and calculate your financial situation. Go on an austerity budget, using your savings and severance as a cushion. Apply for unemployment benefits as soon as you can since it usually takes at least one week for the checks to start coming in. Determine how long you can last on your reduced stream of income.

Once you finish all your financial calculations, begin your job search in earnest. Don't let your current situation, or your recent termination, lead you to take the first job offer that comes along.

Establish clear-cut goals and pursue them. Develop a good résumé and be selective in sending it out, only answering ads and pursuing leads that meet your goals. Being underemployed or misemployed can be just as bad as being unemployed and can lead to getting fired once again.

Above all else, remain positive. You are in control of your destiny. Look on getting fired as a wonderful opportunity. Every time a door closes, another opens. You now have a chance to improve your career by getting a better job. Keep in mind that the biggest salary increases come from getting new jobs, not from getting raises.

HOW TO QUIT

The secret to quitting well is to follow the old adage "Never burn the bridges behind you." Even though you may be dying to tell your soon-to-be-former boss off, and even though he or she may deserve it, don't do it. You never know when you may work with, or for, the same company or individual again. Be apologetic. Tell them that this is an event beyond your control. Say that this was the best job and that they were the best boss you have ever had. And leave it at that. If the company has a history of honoring two weeks' notice, then by all means give it. An honorable employer will then pay the two weeks' salary, even if he or she requests that you leave right away. If, on the other hand, past experience leads you to believe that the company will fire you on the spot, then don't give any notice.

Vacation Homes

What to Look For in a Weekend or Summer Home

Ownership of a vacation home, which you can visit on week-ends or for the entire summer, is one of the great pleasures of life. My summer home on Martha's Vineyard probably gives me more joy than anything else in my life, aside, of course, from my wife and children. Owning a vacation home not only gives you the opportunity for frequent, inexpensive minivacations, but it may also be a good long-term investment.

While I believe that you should buy a vacation home as early in your life as you possibly can, purchasing one too early can dilute your ability to buy a new full-time home. That's why I think you should wait until after you have bought your second full-time home and have lived in it for three or four years before you consider buying a vacation home.

The key to being a savvy vacation-home buyer is to remember that your goals and priorities are different from when you buy a full-time home.

While location is important in the purchase of any real estate, it is even more important in the purchase of a vacation home. Remember, this is a home for rest, relaxation, and enjoyment, so the environment must match those needs. Similarly, look for a vacation home within a three-hour drive of your permanent home. If it is any farther away, your weekend visits will be rushed and tiring. Look to buy in a vacation-home community, rather than a full-time-home community. The last thing you need is for your vacation-home neighbors to be pressuring you to keep up with their efforts at neighborhood beautification.

Since you will be outside a great deal of the time you are going to spend at this home, place a higher priority on outdoor space than inside space. Buy a utilitarian home. This isn't a house for entertaining or impressing others or for everyday living. It should have just enough amenities and space for you to get by. Try to have your vacation home be as simple and comfortable as possible—it should represent an escape from your normal life. If you are a do-it-yourselfer, feel free to express yourself in your vacation home.

It is foolish to buy a vacation home with its investment value in mind. Worry about fun, not finances. Your purchase of a vacation home will end up being a good investment by default: if you buy something you love, you will hold on to it so long that it will naturally grow in value.

FINANCING VACATION HOMES

Traditional big-city banks often have a great deal of trouble with second home mortgages. They feel that you are somehow less serious about your purchase, or that you are jeopardizing your ability to pay back your regular mortgage. The way to get around this bureaucratic blind spot is to finance your vacation home through a local bank in the community where the home is located. These smaller community banks are happy to write second home mortgages and will often go out of their way to make things easy for you.

VACATIONS

What Kinds to Take and How to Pay for Them

Many Americans look on their vacations as an opportunity to travel to interesting places, see historic sights, and experience the excitement of a new setting. They eagerly anticipate their all-too-short vacations and try to pack every day full of activities and adventures. By the time they return home, they are in need of *another* vacation to recuperate from all their sight-seeing. They come back to their jobs tired, not rejuvenated.

Rather than viewing vacations as an opportunity to take in history and local color, look on them as a period of enforced rest. If, while going through the day-to-day business of living, you stick to the strategies and tactics offered in this book, you will have earned and will probably need a period of rest. A restful vacation is a medicinal expense. It is as necessary for your continued health as vitamins.

You cannot get the rest you need if you plan on seeing all of France in seven days, or if you plan on meeting a mate over a long weekend. Rest and relaxation are the keys to maximizing the benefits of time off from work. Go to a location that is slow paced and quiet. Bring along books, magazines, a swimsuit, and some sunscreen—whatever you need to relax.

Plan on taking a therapeutic vacation every six months. Take your therapeutic vacations anywhere you find restful. If your idea of relaxing is to sit by a crackling fire in a log cabin in the woods, don't fall prey to peer pressures and head to a tropical island.

Since it benefits both your mental and physical health, there is absolutely nothing wrong with paying for your two therapeutic vacations by credit card. Sight-seeing or adventure vacations, on the other hand, are once-in-a-lifetime luxuries—not therapies—and should be paid for only with cash.

Double your work efforts prior to your going on vacation to make sure that no loose ends are left hanging when you leave. A vacation is not a good way to escape problems. Any difficulties you have at home or at your job will find their way into your baggage no matter how far you travel or for how long.

TRAVEL AGENTS

All too often, travel agents are part-timers rather than true professionals. They have entered the business in an effort to make some spare change and travel cheaply. While they do have access to the lowest fares and rates, often you can bypass travel agents and still get the lowest rates by planning and booking reservations far in advance. Simply ask the ticketing agent or reservation clerk for the lowest possible rate, explaining that you are booking far in advance, without a travel agent, in order to get the best possible deal. While travel agents may have experience and expertise about places where you have never been, when planning far in advance it is just as easy, and cheaper, to invest in a good guidebook or to consult travel magazines. It is generally advantageous to use a travel agent when arranging foreign rentals, however, since you will need some unbiased opinions on the available accommodations. If you must use a travel agent, either because you are booking at the last minute or are renting overseas, ask other business people for recommendations. Select an agent who has a great many corporate clients—if nothing else this indicates that they are an experienced professional rather than a part-time dabbler.

ELIMINATING TRAVEL STRESS

It's common to feel anxious prior to leaving on a vacation. Perhaps you're worried about forgetting to pack something or are unhappy about leaving the office or your home unattended. Or maybe tight deadlines and rigid schedules just aren't your cup of tea. In order to overcome these jitters and make sure your vacation is truly relaxing and refreshing, follow these rules:
- Make checklists and pack a few days prior to departure.
- Try not to overwork the last few days in the office—it will leave you tense.
- Arrive at least one hour prior to air, sea, bus, or rail departures.
- Don't rush to be the first on board or off mass transportation.
- When driving opt for less heavily traveled routes.
- If a regular physical activity—i.e., a morning jog—is an important part of your daily life continue it while on vacation.
- Don't expect your tastes to change while on vacation—if you hate museums at home you won't like them while on vacation.

- Leave all business equipment and papers at home and limit yourself to no more than one call to the office per day.
- Make sure your vacation is long enough for you to relax, but not so long you start getting antsy.

SAVING TIME WHEN FLYING

One of the best ways to save time when traveling by air is to get around the airlines' rules and book "illegal" connecting flights. Most airlines won't book a passenger on a connecting flight that is scheduled to leave less than 45 minutes after the initial flight arrives. Generally, connections that are this close together don't even show up on the computer when the trip is being routed. Ask your travel agent to issue you two separate tickets: one for your initial flight and a second for the connecting flight. In most cases, this will cost no more than a single ticket. If your plane arrives on time you won't have to wait around the airport for the connection. If your plane is late you simply turn in the ticket for the flight you've missed for another ticket on the next flight to your destination. There's one catch: Make sure you carry on all your luggage.

SAVING MONEY WHEN FLYING

You can also save money by bending airline rules a bit. Let's say you're flying from New York to Denver. Thanks to the way airlines determine fares, the cost of a ticket on a flight that goes from New York to Los Angeles, with a stop in Denver, is often less than the cost of a ticket on a direct New York to Denver flight. Have your travel agent book you on the cheaper New York to Los Angeles flight, and when it arrives in Denver, simply exit the plane. Once again, make sure you carry on all your luggage. Don't advertise your brilliance, however. Airlines don't take kindly to such rule bending and, if they discover your maneuver, may try to charge you the higher fare.

It pays to be savvy when investigating supersaver fares. Sometimes the cut-rate fares are low enough that, even if there are restrictions, it costs less to purchase two round-trip tickets than one regular ticket. For example: an airline may offer a supersaver fare of $150 for a round-trip flight from Chicago to Minneapolis then back to Chicago, with the stipulation that you stay for seven days. You, however, can only stay four days. Upon investigation you find that a regular round-trip ticket with a four-day stay costs $400. Instead of buying the higher-priced regular fare, buy two of the round-trip supersaver tickets, one that leaves Chicago on the day you want to leave and another that leaves Minneapolis on the day you want to return. Buying the two round-trip supersaver tickets will save you $100.

When flying overseas ask your travel agent to get price quotes on what two one-way tickets, one to your destination bought here with American dollars and another to return purchased overseas with local currency, will cost as compared to a normal round-trip ticket. If the two one-way tickets turn out to be cheaper—as is often the case—buy a one-way ticket domestically and as soon as you arrive at your destination, convert your dollars to the local currency and purchase your one-way return ticket.

WEDDINGS

Insuring They're Celebrations, Not Shows

A wedding should be a celebration of the love between two people, shared by their families and friends. But all too often it turns into a demonstration of wealth, taste, and lifestyle that leads to bitter arguments and disputes between the bride and the groom or the two sets of parents. That's because when emotions and large sums of money get tangled together, logic often flies out the window.

And the sums involved are definitely large. While the bottom line will obviously depend on the type of wedding planned and the number of guests, a traditional wedding reception for 150 guests, held in a metropolitan area, can run from $15,000 up to $35,000. It is not unheard of for an elaborate wedding to cost upward of $70,000. The purchase of a wedding is one of the three or four largest expenses a person ever faces, along with buying a home, car, and funeral. Add to this the fact that the planning itself can take three to six months and must be done at least twelve months in advance, and you have a potentially chaotic scenario.

It isn't only the couple and their families who help create the turmoil surrounding weddings. The vendors involved do not rely on repeat business. They don't have to please you since, in all likelihood, you will never be using their goods or services again. And in an effort to squeeze every last dollar out of the situation, they play on emotions and guilt, continually repeating that this is "a once-in-a-lifetime event." It would be tough enough just dealing with one such vendor, but in the case of a formal wedding you will have to deal with bridal shops, tuxedo rental stores, florists, catering halls, caterers, clergy, printers, bands, photographers, jewelers, bakers, and limousine drivers.

Wedding planning doesn't have to become a contentious process. It can remain the joyful, celebratory pastime it was always intended to be, as long as all involved keep their wits about them and are honest about their wishes and feelings.

The best way to insure that this happens is to begin the planning by holding a family meeting. Everyone involved, from both families, must get together and openly and honestly address the difficult questions that lie just below the surface. Guest lists should be compiled as soon as possible, and the financial contributions of each side should be clearly understood. Don't stand on ceremony or let delays and subtle hints take the place of honest discussion—that can lead only to confusion and misunderstandings later.

The best place to begin, if you want to insure that this remains the celebration it is supposed to be, is with a guest list. Rather than determining a budget and then trying to stretch your money or eliminate guests, start with a clear picture of how many people you want to share in the event. Then come up with an idea of how much money you can spend on the affair. Plan your affair with the idea that you want to have the best party possible, with the people you want there, for the amount of money you can afford. If that means a cocktail-party reception or a brunch, or even a potluck dinner, so be it. The point of the celebration is sharing this wonderful moment with those you love, not impressing the neighbors or your future in-laws.

Once you have a budget in place, you must begin lining up the various vendors. When dealing with each, you must be prepared to be a savvy consumer and steer clear of the traps they set for unsuspecting buyers.

The sample food you taste, when shopping for a caterer, may not be cooked by the same person who will prepare the food for your wedding. Caterers may also try to talk you into having more food, more serving people, and more expensive dishes, silverware, and tablecloths than you really need. They may also try to pad your liquor bill by using top-shelf brands to prepare mixed drinks, or by opening more bottles than are actually necessary.

Photographers may show you sample albums taken by someone other than the person who will be shooting your wedding. In addition, they will try to retain ownership of the proofs and negatives, forcing you to come back to them to get additional prints. It's also possible that the charming salesperson you dealt with when signing your contract may be replaced by an obnoxious bore who annoys you and your guests with his or her gruff manner.

When buying flowers, you may well be paying a surcharge to cover the overhead of the florist shop if you deal with someone who has a prime retail location. It's even possible that you will end up with wilting, rather than blooming, blossoms.

A band, which often makes or breaks a party, might take breaks all at once, leaving your party without any music. Or worse, they could be completely out of touch with their audience—playing raucous rock to an older crowd or boogie-woogie to baby boomers.

All of this might lead you to believe that arranging an affordable, mistake-free wedding is impossible. It really isn't, it's just difficult and time-consuming. Rather than trying to be your own general contractor and do all of the negotiating and coordinating yourself, I would suggest that you use one of these three short-cuts:

- Hire "name" vendors. By using the very best, or at least the best-known, vendors in your area, you almost guarantee that they will do a good job. Their reputations are what their business is based on, and they cannot afford to do a bad job. Of course, their fees are higher than everyone else's, but if you can afford them, consider the added cost a form of "wedding insurance."
- Have the affair at a hotel. Most hotels have banquet managers who can arrange every type of affair, from small, simple parties to large, elaborate extravaganzas. They will also have "house" bands and florists, making your shopping a great deal easier.
- Hire a party planner. These wedding consultants are the general contractors of the industry. Often all you need to do is explain what you want, and how much you have to spend, and let them do the rest. Be careful, however, only to hire someone who works for a flat fee, not a percentage of the total cost.

The only alternatives to these approaches are to plan, prepare, negotiate, and cajole all the vendors yourself . . . or to elope.

FOR MORE INFORMATION . . .

You can learn more about planning a wedding from the following books:

- *Secrets to Throwing a Fantastic Wedding on a Realistic Budget* by Denise and Alan Fields
- *Your Complete Wedding Planner* by Marjabelle Young Stewart

About the Authors

Stephen Pollan, a nationally known financial consultant, is a personal finance commentator for CNBC/FNN, and has been seen on "Good Morning America" and "Today." He is also the coauthor, with Mark Levine, of *The Field Guide to Starting a Business*, *The Field Guide to Home Buying in America*, and *Your Recession Handbook*. Stephen Pollan lives in New York City and Mark Levine lives in Long Beach, New York.